More Than Words

More Than Words

400 *Pray Now* Daily Devotions

SAINT ANDREW PRESS
Edinburgh

First published in 2008 by
SAINT ANDREW PRESS
121 George Street, Edinburgh EH2 4YN

ISBN 978 0 7152 0847 2

British Library Cataloguing in Publication Data
A catalogue record for this book is available from the British Library

Typeset by Waverley Typesetters, Fakenham
Printed and bound by Bell & Bain Limited, Glasgow

Contents

Praise and Thanksgiving

Faith and Devotion

Our Life and Work

Hope, Comfort and Guidance

Justice and Peace and Forgiveness

Miscellaneous

Introduction

All the prayers in this volume draw on the Scriptures and they aim to focus our worship on contemporary life. The collection will help you whether you wish to build a prayerful life in the privacy of your own home or whether you are the worship leader of a congregation or a member of a study group. We hope that you will find the prayers inspiring, fresh, challenging and relevant.

This is not a time-based collection, and nor is it a programme. Instead, it offers the reader flexibility of use. One way is to start at the beginning and work through to the end. Another is just to dip into it, and another is to use the contents pages or indexes to find a specific prayer for a particular occasion, subject or mood. It is entirely up to you.

The prayers are arranged first of all in broad themes, as outlined in the table of contents. So if you would like a prayer of, say, praise and thanksgiving, you can browse that section to find something appropriate to your needs. For further help, there is a General Index and an Index of Bible Characters at the back, showing other topics and items of interest. Among the topics explored are: the journey of life, the Church, Christmas, Bible characters, places in the Bible, fear, greed, self-esteem, enlightenment, nature and conservation, and much more besides.

There is considerable diversity of style in this collection. Sometimes there is more than one prayer on a particular topic, each with its own perspective (for example, a prayer for oneself and another prayer for others). Sometimes there are Scripture Readings, which can be incorporated into your worship as you see fit, and there are Prayer Activities, in which a particular theme can be explored with the help of everyday objects or by allowing the reader to use his or her imagination.

For a structured programme of daily devotion, Saint Andrew Press publishes an annual volume, *Pray Now*, which is available from November.

Saint Andrew Press would like to thank John Bell, Alastair Cherry, Derek Browning, Gayle Taylor, Douglas Galbraith, Nigel Robb and all the contributors for their creativity and generosity of time.

God's World and Work

Creation (1)

The heavens are yours, the earth yours also; you founded the world and all that is in it.

~ Psalm 89:11 ~

Prayer for Reflection

Before my mind stirs
or my voice sounds,
You, Lord of Creation,
are being praised.

The song of the bird,
the lap of the wave,
the sap in the growing things,
the chase of the clouds across the sky
are all part of the pattern of a world you made
to reflect your glory
and to praise you.

Where I ignore the song of creation,
unstop my ears;
where I refuse to join it,
unloose my tongue
and let me be a partner in earth's praise.

Prayer on Today's Theme

Almighty God,
in the beginning,
you looked on creation
and declared that it was good.

Prosper and encourage those whose work and vocation it is to preserve and
    conserve the earth's goodness.

Let their words about acid rain,
    the ozone layer
    senseless deforestation,
    and global pollution,
move from being fashionable in conversation
to being fruitful in action.

And trouble the minds of all who live carelessly
as if this were not the only earth,
yet theirs the only generation.

Creation (2)

Prayer for Ourselves

How wonderful is your world, Lord.
Land, sea and air all are yours,
so too are the vast galaxies of space.
All creation rests in the palm of your hand.
Nothing is beyond your reach, no one is beneath your notice.
Lovingly, you provide for each of us.
You meet my every need,
    steady me when I stumble,
    lift me up when I fall.
May I never take for granted all that you have provided for me.

Prayer for Others

We are thankful, Lord,
that you have made each of us unique, created us full of potential,
placed in us something that is ours alone.
Remember, we pray,
those who feel they have so much more to give
    but no one seems to want to know;
those whose talents have not been recognised,
    whose career has not brought them fulfilment;
those who have never had the opportunities
    or the encouragement they deserve
and who have to live with frustration and disappointment.
Show them that in their very striving
    to develop their talents and qualities,
    although unseen and unsung,
they are true children of the Creator.

Eden

God saw everything that he had made, and indeed it was very good.

~ Genesis 1:31 ~

This is how you meant it to be, Lord:
Adam and Eve, living together in the garden of your delight,
caring for the earth and its creatures, talking and walking with you
among the trees in the cool of the day.

It's not a religious image, but a natural one:
all things enfolded in your peace, all things working together without
    tension or strain.

Lord, this is not where we are now: our world shakes and totters,
everything is out of balance, we scream at one another in the cool of the
    day,
and the earth and her creatures fear the sound of our footsteps.

We have grasped at life and found death.
No, we are not in Eden, and we cannot find our way back.

But in Christ,
you would lead us out of the wilderness back to the garden:
to a world washed clean
a world filled with the glory of the Lord as the waters cover the sea.

Lord, continue your new world in me.

Readings

Genesis 1:26–31; Genesis 2:4–9; Isaiah 11:6–9; John 1:1–5, 14;
Romans 8:18–25; Revelation 22:1–5

Silence

Prayer Activity

Look at some aspect of nature and delight in it. Feel your oneness with it,
your unity in a common creation with a common Creator. Try to return to this
oneness several times today.

Garden – Creating

And the Lord God planted a garden in Eden, in the east; and there he put the man whom he had formed. Out of the ground the LORD God made to grow every tree that is pleasant to the sight and good for food, the tree of life also in the midst of the garden, and the tree of the knowledge of good and evil.

~ *Genesis 2:8, 9* ~

Living God,
Today I remember

That you
Are in the business of planting,
Of sowing that seed
Which births fruitfulness and life.

Today I remember

That Eden is not so much
A lost garden from the ancient past,
As one that beckons to us
From the emergent future.

Today I remember

That you have set us here
To work with you
Towards that future,
As stewards of the earth
And not as owners.

Today I pray
For all who seek to cherish
The earth that you have
Put into our hands.

Prayer Activity

Set in your prayer corner a growing plant. Read Psalm 1. Meditate on the theme of roots and fruits in your own life.

Garden – Recognising

Supposing him to be the gardener, she said to him, 'Sir, if you have carried him away, tell me where ...'

~ *John 20:15* ~

Lord God,
It was on a green hill far away that we think of you on that cross.
A red bloody day when the sky turned black ...
but on a green hill.
And when you stood before Mary on that first Easter day
We think of you in the green garden with the empty tomb –
Not because the scenery is described but because you are:
and you were thought to be the gardener.

In the garden of your world, God,
We build things out of things you grew.
We snatch at life that has taken time to be.
We trample on detail and intimate design
And hammer a cross to stand on a green hill.

But beneath it all and about it all is your greenery, God,
Your life force to be reckoned with,
Your breath blowing butterflies in the breeze,
Your water of life nourishing and replenishing,
Your sun warming and comforting seed and creature.

Yes, you are the gardener, God,
Down to earth – planting and pruning
But waiting patiently too
For Mary, and us
to recognise the gardener,
Then hear the teacher,
then receive the saviour.

Readings

Genesis 2:10–17   *The Garden of Eden*
John 20:11–18   *In the garden*

Prayer Activity

Take some old photographs of people you know, especially family, and look at them. Try to see particular characteristics or immediately recognisable features. What things have changed over the years and what makes them instantly recognisable? How do we overcome our lack of recognition of Jesus in those around us?

'Come, let us go up to the mountain of the Lord ... that he may teach us his ways and we may walk in his paths.'

~ Micah 4:2 ~

Immortal, invisible, God only wise:
    so far beyond me, so near to me
        with your love in Jesus your Son
as I thank you for the commandments of old:
    laws given for my good on Mount Sinai,
        I confess that down in life's valley,
        I have ignored or broken them;
    and that sometimes they have broken me
        made me less than what I could be.

Living God, forgive me
    for not taking rest from work and not taking time out for worship.
Forgive me from turning aside to other gods: gods of human making:
    power & pounds; sex & success; money & machines.
Forgive me for venerating such false idols.
Forgive me for thinking and speaking against my neighbours,
        and for any envy of their good fortune;
    and for not thinking and doing enough for those near to me.
Maybe I do not kill or commit adultery or steal,
    but forgive me for murderous and lustful feelings
    as for thinking I might take something that is not mine.
And, Lord God, forgive me for breaking
    the new commandment, given by your Son:
    to love others ... even my enemies.

Merciful God, set Christ's Cross between my soul and my sins ...
    as I am contrite, assure me by the Holy Spirit that I am pardoned,
    healed, restored, forgiven.
And by Christ's grace raise me to new heights
of fresh obedience and good and glorious living.   AMEN.

Prayer Activity

As you might stand on a mountain and survey everything, take time to survey your life and how you might better live it. With fresh vision of what could be, descend to the valley of everyday life and in God's strength attempt it!

Mountain – Blessing

The spirit of God has made me, and the breath of the Almighty gives me life.

~ Job 33:4 ~

Told on a mountain – traditionally a place of meeting with God
Told as a series blessing – blessings that turned normal expectations upside
down
Told at the beginning of his ministry – in a form that held echoes of the
book of Deuteronomy

Blessed are those who are poor in spirit
Who rely on God for their breath, for their inspiration

Blessed are those who mourn, for they shall be comforted
Who open up to their emotions in a safe way, facing their truth and the pain
Feeling their depths, waiting and watching

Blessed are the meek, for they shall inherit the earth
Who discover and digest the truth of our smallness in the grand scheme of
things

Blessed are those who hunger and thirst for righteousness, they shall be
filled
Who honour the longing inside for truth and justice for ourselves and others

Blessed are the merciful, for they shall obtain mercy
Who embrace God into their very depths, into the womb of their being
Enabling an expansion of love, born of darkness within us
A wellspring of the living God

Blessed are the pure in heart, for they shall see God
Who are prepared to work through pain that confronts us in our lives
Willing to go into the depths and chaotic unknowns and still hold faith in
Divine love
Then something within us increases our intimacy, our seeing the one who
made us.

Blessed are the peacemakers, for they will be called the children of God
Who make space, and take time to allow the experience of love, joy and
hope
Helping people to know that we all belong, that we are all loved, all
valuable
Called into relationship with the One who made us

Blessed are those who are persecuted because of righteousness, for theirs is the Kingdom of heaven.

Blessed are you when people revile and hate you, your reward is great in the Kingdom of heaven
Who learn truly to not be affected by other people's expectations and demands
Able to tolerate the backlash of disrupting, settled patterns that no longer give life
And willing to let go even of our own image of ourselves
So that your Presence moulds us so much we are able to push through unnecessary boundaries
Living heaven here on earth.   AMEN.

... those who love God must love their brothers and sisters also.

~ 1 John 4:21 ~

On pavements packed with pushing people,
In cities that never sleep,
In the roar of traffic and the glare of lights,
You speak ...
Love one another.

Among the streetwise and the tourists,
Between the natives and the immigrants,
Inside the shops and the restaurants,
You speak ...
Love one another.

In the crowded square and the darkened alley,
In the gorgeous galleries and the dirty gutters,
In the noise of so many different languages,
You speak ...
Love one another.

God of love,
In the honesty of labour and in the creativity of the Arts,
In the gathering of the nations and in integrated community
May we speak love, to one another.

Readings

Acts 2:1–13	*Pentecost unity*
Acts 16:11–34	*Diverse converts*
Galatians 3:23–9	*All children of God*
1 Thessalonians 1:2–10	*Church thanksgiving*

Prayer Activity

If you have a hymn book at home, flick through it until you find a hymn from another country and culture. Alternatively, open your kitchen cupboard and find foods or ingredients from other places and traditions. Think about the new flavours and styles these other cultures have given you and thank God for the variety and diversity that enriches our world.

The Holy Spirit

A wind from God swept over the face of the waters.

~ Genesis 1:2 ~

Spirit of God,
like a wind you swept over the earth
while it was still a formless void.
We can only imagine what it can have been like to watch the earth take
   shape and form –
but you were there, before the beginning of time
you were with God and you were God.

Spirit of God,
you are our helper, enabler, comforter, supporting us in times of trouble and
   distress.
In our world today, you interpret for us the Word and inspire your people,
prompting us to pray for others and leading us into community.

As at Pentecost, break down the barriers in us and around us in the world.
We pray that you would continue to be with us throughout our lifelong
   journey with Christ;
may we always be aware of you
and thankful for you.

Readings

Psalm 51	*A prayer of forgiveness*
Matthew 1:18–25	*A story of Jesus' birth*
Luke 2:25–35	*Simeon blesses Jesus*
Luke 11:1–13	*The Lord's Prayer*
Acts 2:1–12	*Pentecost*

Life

In God's hand is the life of every living thing.

~ Job 12:10 ~

Lord God, in whom we live and move and have our being,
    understanding that life is not our right but your gift,
    realising that we are not owners but stewards of creation,
    appreciative that you temper the wind to the shorn lamb,
        that you feed the ravens,
        that you mark the fall of a sparrow,
        that your fatherly care is over all things and people,
    help us also to care –
        for all creatures,
        for the well-being of others,
        and for ourselves: our bodies … our minds … our souls.

Lord God, source of truth and life,
    enable all who help to create life:
        men and women in procreation,
        obstetricians and midwives,
        researchers into matters of fertility,
    to act wisely and responsibly.
    Direct the work of all who seek to unravel the mysteries of life:
        biologists and psychologists,
        and all who enhance human life.
    Help farmers and shepherds and vets,
        all who deal with your creatures, to be considerate
    and help each and all to know the Good Shepherd
        in whom is abundant life …
    and ever to choose him and his way.   AMEN.

Readings

Genesis 1:24–31	*The creation of life*
Deuteronomy 30:15–20	*The call to choose life*
Job 10:8–13	*Acknowledging God as creator and preserver*
Luke 12:22–30	*Life more than food*
John 10:11–15	*The Good Shepherd who gives abundant life*
Acts 17:22–8	*The God who gives life and breath*

Prayer Activity

Try to get a time of silence and then: listen to your breathing … your heart beating … sense your eyes blinking … your blood flowing – and wonder and give thanks for the marvel that you have been given life.

Stewardship

God saw everything that he had made, and indeed, it was very good.

~ Genesis 1:31 ~

From this beautiful creation
to the diversity of our living,
we are your stewards of love, O God.
From the spoils of this planet
to the offerings of our lives,
we are your stewards of love, O God.
From the abundance of Nature
to the giving of our being,
we are your stewards of love, O God.

May we live life fairly,
hold it lightly, love it gently,
so that balance is encouraged
and justice revealed
in all we say and do
from our possessions
to our talents,
from our politics
to our religion.

So we pray for those who flaunt their pride and those who offer humility,
those who desire more and those who long for the least,
those who hoard everything for themselves and those who long for
   equity.   AMEN.

Readings

Psalm 85	*Righteousness and peace will join hands*
Proverbs 15:15–17	*Rich and poor*
Jeremiah 22:1–9	*A message to the king*
Luke 15:11–32	*The Lost Son*
Acts 4:32–3	*Sharing possessions*

Prayer Activity

Focus on some part of your body (head, heart, back, face, etc.). Feel it, become aware of it. Think of what it does and what you do with it. Do you care for it, push it too hard, take it for granted? Think of how you use it in your life and how it is used in your care for others: supporting, encouraging and strengthening. Focus on this part of your body throughout the day and reflect on that experience.

New Growth

If a tree is cut down, there is hope that it will sprout again.

~ Job 14:7 ~

Prayer for Reflection

Yes, Lord, that may be true of a tree –
it's one of nature's laws.
But what happens when things die in my life?
– when the warmth of a relationship ebbs away,
– when the vitality of my faith diminishes,
– when I lose someone
    round whom my whole existence has revolved,
– when I have to leave everything behind
    and go to a new place and start all over again?

Yet we also are a part of your creation.
It is natural that our bodies and minds
    will repair themselves.
But in our case there is even more –
for you have entered into our bodies and minds
and defeated death and loss and despair for ever.

Keep before me today the noble tree of Calvary,
the faithful cross that brings glorious victory.

Prayer on Today's Theme

We pray for the natural world,
created to renew itself and to renew us, your creatures.
We confess the forests destroyed and seas polluted,
the litter on the streets
    which shows how much we squander,
the leaking landfill sites,
    barely enough for their purpose,
the creeping desert dust
    which swallows agricultural land,
the toxins which pierce the safety net
which surrounds the earth.

Teach us all, Lord, to tend your creation,
so that when a seed dies,
it will fall on an earth fit to bring it to rebirth.

The Word of God

The scriptures ... were all written for our instruction, in order that through the encouragement they give us we may maintain our hope with perseverance.

~ Romans 15:4 ~

Prayer for Reflection

Lord, the Bible is full of people
who found encouragement in a word from you:
when the Israelites turned from you,
    you sent them manna from heaven,
to a tongue-tied Jeremiah you offered fluency,
to suffering Job you offered a new relationship,
you called a disciple who denied you, your rock,
and persuaded your weary friends
    to cast their nets again.

As I take up my Bible,
release my imagination
that I may enter into the world of Scripture,
and, seeing you through the eyes
    of peasant and prophet,
    matriarch and maid,
find you in its pages
and discover you in my heart.

Prayer on Today's Theme

Encourage, Lord,
    those who have the Bible on their bookshelf
    but never in their hands;
those who turn its pages with their fingers,
    but do not write it on their hearts;
those who can quote it from memory
    but do not live out its love in their lives.
Support, good Lord,
those who explain the Scriptures to others,
translators who make your Word
    come alive in many languages,
those who share God's word
    with those who have never heard it;
those who take pride
    in designing and printing its pages.

May they all
     like Jeremiah receive the Word they are to speak,
     like Thomas see and believe,
     like Mary treasure its message in their hearts.

Remembering God's Word

I promise to keep your words.

~ Psalm 119:57 ~

Lord of the Word, in the pages of scripture I find:
    comfort,
    inspiration,
    warning,
    hope,
    forgiveness,
    rejoicing,
    love.
Help me to remember where the words are,
and to take them to heart,
and to keep them by me,
and to ponder their meaning.

Lord of the Word,
more precious to me than gold and silver
are the words you have woven into my heart and soul.
May they be landmarks along my pilgrim life,
pointing me to places of blessing and schools of learning.
May they shape the song of my life,
that I may sing the melodies of heaven whilst living here on earth.

In all I do this day, guide me, Lord, in your way, along your path,
by your word and through your love.
In Jesus' name. AMEN.

Prayer Activity

Psalm 119 goes on and on! The psalm talks about the word and the statutes and the commands and the precepts and the law. The Psalmist delights in all of these, a deep desire that they be truly inside one's being. But there are lots of frustrated moments when he is desperate, asking God for help to be able to live worthily. A time-honoured way to allow truths to travel from head to heart, from mind to spirit, is simple repetition of sacred words and texts so that the 'word' becomes a living thing within you. This psalm was meant to be memorised; in each eight-verse stanza every line begins with the same letter of the Hebrew alphabet, and there is a stanza for every letter of the alphabet. Try memorising a psalm or repeat favourite prayers, e.g. the Lord's Prayer, or, if you prefer, hymns. Try to do this several times today or even on the hour every hour. What difference does it make to your day to have this rhythm?

When God Speaks

The voice of the Lord is powerful.

~ Psalm 29:4 ~

Mighty God,
by whose voice the world was shaped,
the rivers, seas and oceans began to flow,
the sun, moon and stars scattered across space,
and all that lives came into being:
speak to us now.

Mighty God,
by whose voice
your purpose of grace is made known,
your Son is commissioned in ministry,
your people are called to service,
and your love is spoken to a world that is slow to hear:
speak to us now.

Speak with power,
to break the chains of pain and suffering,
to break the chains of debt and hunger,
to break the chains of loneliness and fear,
to break the chains of guilt and sadness.

Speak with power, to make us strong, *and all cry 'Glory!'*
Speak with power, to give us peace, *and all cry 'Glory!'*
Speak with power, to let us live, *and all cry 'Glory!'* AMEN.

Prayer Activity

Look and listen for the voice of the Lord today. Look expectantly, listen attentively. Look and listen in people, in nature, above you, below you. Prepare to be surprised and allow the blessing from God to flow when you recognise his presence. Let yourself experience being bathed in blessing, his voice, his sound showering you with love.

Babel

'Come, let us build ourselves a city and a tower with its top in the heavens, and let us make a name for ourselves.'

~ Genesis 11:4 ~

Spirit of God,
you moved upon the face of the waters.
The Word of command brought light, distinctiveness and life from chaos.
Creator God, Babel is a problem, for there you initiated confusion,
scattering people, bringing misunderstandings.
You saw at Babel the pride of hearts to build and dominate others,
to challenge you, so you sent confusion of language.
I pray for understanding between people – beautiful clarity of language.
I pray for understanding between communities and nations,
wonderful harmony of intent.
Lord, am I wasting my time when it was you who sent confusion of
language?
Will there ever be harmony and understanding?
But then I realise at Pentecost you reversed the confusion of Babel.
By your Spirit,
each heard in his own language the great things that you have done,
and the possibilities are real for change and unity.
Lord, with humility and reality,
I pray for this chaotic fractured world of misunderstandings and barriers
that you love totally.   AMEN.

Prayer Activity

Think of something that draws you close to God and meditate upon it. Think
of something that makes you feel far away from God and meditate upon
it. Finally, consider if you wish to make any changes or resolutions as a
consequence of your meditation.

The Lord's Prayer

Blessing

The peace of God rule in your heart.
The love of God rule your actions.
The joy of God be yours in full measure,
Today and always.

Jacob

*'How awesome is this place! This is none other than the house of God,
and this is the gate of heaven.'*

~ Genesis 28:17 ~

Lord of everywhere,
there are times and places you have surprised me
with an intimation of your special presence and I thank you for it.

I think of Jacob,
fleeing from his brother's threatening vengeance,
taking a stone for a pillow, dreaming,
and meeting you face to face;
of Columba, voyaging from Ireland,
landing on Iona, a sacred place.

I think of times and places where I too have had a sense of the eternal
presence, especially in contemplating the Cross where Christ laid his
sacred head.
when I have felt the pledge of saving love, and that heaven was nearer to
me.
For such blessings I pour out my gratitude.

Forgive me, Lord God,
my dim apprehension when I have not recognised you,
my poor prayers when I have failed to hear you,
my inadequate service when I have not followed you.
Forgive me for my sleeping faith, for my passiveness.
Remind me that Jacob *wrestled*,
that Columba *journeyed*,
that Jesus *struggled* in prayer in the Garden.
Remind me that faith can be hard,
its consequences demanding, but also that those who persevere to the end
will be saved. AMEN.

Prayer Activity

Remember a place where you have experienced the closeness of God's
presence. In your imagination go there now. Bring your difficulties and talk
to God, wrestle with God, then – whether resolved or not – let go; rest; wait
for God to show you the next step.

Joseph and his Family

And he kissed all his brothers and wept upon them; and after that his brothers talked with him.

~ Genesis 45:15 ~

God,
in Jacob, you show us – love that has favourites breads jealousy
in Joseph, you remind us – vision without sensitivity creates
    misunderstanding
in the brothers, you teach us – that wrong turns need righting.

God, your love story is not hearts and flowers, not idyllic and easy.
Your love story is:
    slow but sure
    watching and waiting,
    enduring and exciting.
Your story is life and death,
    Birth and grief,
    Cross and tomb,
    Full and constant.

Unconditional God,
thank you for the opportunities that people will have today:
    to talk things through,
    to meet again after time apart,
    to draw lines under grudges and let go of bitterness.
Thank you for the healing moments where people can:
    Weep in remorse,
    Sigh in relief,
    Relax in relationships
    smile at new people
    and feel known and loved – loved and known by you. AMEN.

Prayer Activity

Thinking of Joseph and his family, is there anyone in your family or circle of friends that you have not spoken to for a long time? Why is this? Is there any hurt or past regret? Hold this before God and ask for the grace to make moves of reconciliation and restoration.

Horeb

*Moses came to Horeb, the mountain of God. There the angel of the
Lord appeared to him in a flame of fire out of a burning bush ... he
looked and the bush was blazing, yet it was not yet consumed.*

~ Exodus 3:1–2 ~

*'Go out and stand on the mountain of the Lord, for the Lord is about
to pass.' ... the Lord was not in the wind ... the Lord was not in the
earthquake ... the Lord was not in the fire ... after the fire a sound of
sheer silence.*

~ 1 Kings 19:11–13 ~

Lord, the rational mind cannot
encompass these strange events.
However, this was a place of encounter and revelation.

Whilst reason limits, symbols have power.
Horeb – high above our understanding.
Wind – mysterious in its source of power.
Earthquakes – shake proud human foundations.
Fire – consumes and purifies.
Silence – speaks what words cannot utter.

Help us, Lord, to revisit
these symbols that coalesce
around Horeb,
with the honest questioning of Moses,
with the obedience of Elijah,
with the obedience of both.   AMEN.

Moses

Never since has there arisen a prophet in Israel like Moses, whom the Lord knew face to face.

~ Deuteronomy 34:10 ~

Lord God,
how long we have travelled;
how many the false dawns;
how often the dead-ends.

To the land of promise we pin our hopes.
We move our tired feet,
we climb the stony mountain,
we lift up our eyes,
we look for the Lord.

And still we come, for the vision is there, and the promise is sure –
that we will see our God face to face,
and delight in hearing our name called,
and marvel that in the Promised Land
there is room for us.

We pray today
for those who journey with us along the way,
for those who lead, and those who guide,
and those who protect us on the road,
for those who have gone ahead,
and for those who have yet to come.
May we all, in God's good time, climb the mountain, see the land of
     promise and cross over.   AMEN.

Prayer Activity

Imagine climbing up a mountain. Is the path rough or smooth? Is the way easy or hard? From the mountaintop, see in your mind's eye a distant land, the place where you want to be. What does your promised land look like? How will you get there? Who will travel with you?

The Promised Land

*'I have come to deliver them from the Egyptians, and to bring them
up out of that land to a good and broad land, a land flowing with milk
and honey.'*

~ Exodus 3:8 ~

'A land flowing with milk and honey' –
a proverbial saying in ancient times and to us as well.

To a desert, nomadic people the words
spoke of promised nourishment and plenty;
of nature supplying their every need,
body and spirit no longer struggling to survive,
blessed ease amidst life abundant.
Lord, the metaphor still stands brimful of hope:
hope that life can be better for me, my family, for the community and for
   all!

Is the promised land over the next hill? Through the next valley?
On the other side of sickness, disappointment, grief, frustration, toil,
   unemployment, lost love?

Or do we have foretaste now, Lord?
Like the grapes, the figs, the pomegranates that the spies brought back?
Lord, give us eyes to see.

In our present are signs of heaven.
The promised land beyond is here today
 in all that sustains our hope, in all
that is gathered in that promise-laden word:
       LOVE

Prayer Activity

In a quiet, relaxed mode (sitting in your favourite chair) think of the foretastes
of the promised land that you have experienced. Picture them (in childhood,
in relationships, in your favourite place), take time over them. Let your
happy memories be like bubbles of energy released into the stream of life.
Thankfulness empowers and is itself a foretaste of the promised land. The
harbinger of blessing still to come.   AMEN.

Sinai

*On the third new moon, after the Israelites had gone out of the land of
Egypt, on that very day they came to the wilderness of Sinai.*

~ *Exodus 19:1–2* ~

Lord God, from freedom to trial, from joy to disappointment, it is a familiar
pattern.

God of the wilderness, uphold us!
Uphold us through those long stretches where we are tested:
the painful places, the frustrating places, full of sands of doubt and rocks of
disappointment.

Dear God, in the deserts of life we often feel like giving up.
You know that the burning sands scorch belief and breed rebellion in Israel
and in us.
Yet in our better moments we know that Sinai is the place of revelation.
Self-knowledge is born there, false identity is stripped away.
Me and mine, arrogance and pride, lose their once directing power.
Higher things, purer dreams, God-given visions, become manna to the soul.
The water of life bursts forth from the rocks
and we drink with joy.

Prayer Activity

Picture a stream of water flowing in the desert (draw this picture if you like).
Imagine that you are drinking from this cool, refreshing stream. Think of
Jesus teaching that he is the living water. As the water refreshes your tired
body, so Jesus refreshes your weary spirit, bringing soothing, contentment
and the beginning of new vitality.

David

'I have seen a son of Jesse the Bethlehemite who is skilful in playing, a man of valour, a warrior, prudent in speech, and a man of good presence; and the Lord is with him.'

~ *1 Samuel 16:18* ~

Today I ask myself what it means for you, Lord, to be with me.
I wonder if others think
'The Lord is with him, or her'.
Is it to do with how good I look,
how successful I seem to be, how confident I appear,
how strongly I stand up for the right?

Today I think of those who look weak and worn,
who have lost self esteem and strength, for I know I've been there.

When we see goodness,
surely we cannot help but think of you with gratitude.
But when it all falls down around us,
when life turns upside down,
when everything that gives us security and confidence is stripped away,
what do we think then?

Maybe we think of ourselves, only, in self pity.
Maybe we should think of David,
shepherd boy – talented and full of potential,
king – grieving and shamed in the midst of power and privilege.

Surely we *still* think of you,
Almighty God, creator of all gifts and individuals,
who in Christ, came to touch and heal all fragile life.   AMEN.

Prayer Activity

Take a few quiet moments to reflect upon the word 'gift'. Think of gifts you have received, think of talents in your life and in the lives of others. Now think about gifts you have given to others. Everyone has something to offer to life and to God. As you identify what you have to give today, ask God for the strength and grace to use your gift wisely.

The Temple

Yet the Most High does not dwell in houses made with human hands ...

~ Acts 7:48a ~

Down through the ages, Ancient God,
generation after generation
has sought to build a dwelling for you:
to try and capture something of your ways,
to contain the presence of your holiness.
In Ark and in Temple,
in Synagogue and in Sanctuary,
people have strived to create environments
where the 'holy' might be encountered:
environments of nourishing imagery and evocative silence,
places surrounded by art and word and song,
atmospheres filled with grace and kindness.

Incarnate God, dwelling within us,
you have given each of us a temple of our own,
a place where your Being encounters our being.
Enable us to recognise and affirm your life within us.
Help us to create environments that are good for us and for all:
places where human encounters meet with divine experience,
atmospheres in which the holy and the human merge.
God within us, God beyond us, God around us:
blessed be your Name forever.

Prayer Activity

Jesus encourages us to experience our bodies as temples of the Holy Spirit.
Holy Spirit can also be translated as 'holy breath'. Breathe in as if receiving
'holy breath'. Breathe out, letting go of self-destructive thoughts or feelings.
Treasure your capacity to have God within you.

The Tent of God's Love

... who forgives all your iniquity, who heals all your diseases.

~ *Psalm 103:3* ~

The One who is life shows us the Way –
may my heart welcome you.

Your form is strong and powerful, reassuring and refreshing and renewing,
affirming the past, connecting me with my ancestors,
accepting my smallness and my futility;
asking me to embrace that,
to be content to 'be' that frail one,
and at the same time
to open myself to your wonder and power,
to move beyond individual human limitation
into the family of your love of peoples and of creation.

You take me up to the stars,
you make me see your embrace of all that is.
Your power of holding and containing knows no limit.
There is nothing beyond you.

You are what makes the greenness of the earth.
You are the grower that births all life into being,
mothering all, nurturing all.

May your mothering and fathering power be present in me.
May I rejoice and let you breathe new life into me.
May my body which you have made
be the birthplace of your Spirit.   AMEN.

Prayer Activity

Allow the images of a tent and a cloak to speak to you. Think and feel nature
embracing you, enfolding you, and notice the physical changes in your body
as you do so. You might like to put a cloak or similar garment around you for
this prayer time, or imagine doing so. As you leave the house today, pause,
and look at the sky as a tent encircling you. How does that change your
normal experience of leaving home?

Heaven

Then I saw a new heaven and a new earth.

~ Revelation 21:1 ~

Lord,
what is heaven? Where is heaven?
Is the idea not sheer escapism?
A sugary day-trip from reality:
fluffy clouds, harp-playing cherubs, celestial choirs?
But perhaps these images, bland and anaemic, are not the true images?
For you would show us heaven
by bringing us down to earth.
You would point us to an empty tomb, the shifting of rock,
new creation encountered on a country road
and at journey's end in broken bread
and poured-out wine:
solid, tangible, real.
You would call us from the shadows to the light, from the ethereal and
  wispy
to the solid and eternal.
Lord, make us to be of more use on earth by drawing us closer to heaven,
that in our common life we might foreshadow a world in which
the old boundaries, barriers and limitations are no more.
May we feel the new creation already straining through the old and weary
  world: heaven beckoning us forward.

Prayer Activity

What brings you a glimpse of the sparkle, the wonder of heaven? Ponder that.
Then feel yourself as the meeting place of heaven and earth – a creature of
earth who, in Christ, can open a doorway to heaven. Allow that encounter to
give birth to something new.

Hell

I am alive forever and ever, and I have the keys of death and Hades.

~ Revelation 1:18 ~

I thank you, Lord, that you have the keys to all the dreadful places
I wander to
or fall into.
You have the keys to places we fear:
places of woe,
pain, loss.
You have the keys to every hell in this world and the next.

Lord, why should anyone want to go to such places?
Yet there is something in all of us
that gravitates to these dark regions
in the soul, in relationships,
in affections, mind and will.

But you have the keys, Lord. Hallelujah!

Risen Lord, unlock the doors to every dungeon of the spirit.
Unlock the doors of every hellish place:
places of resentment, jealousy, envy, hatred, isolation, poverty and death –
these and more.

Now that the doors are open,
draw me with your light, love, forgiveness,
goodness and grace.
Let me see and truly know that I am and ever will be loved.
I leap for joy in your love and power.

Readings

Psalm 16; Matthew 16:18; John 12:32

Prayer Activity

Memorise a text meaningful to you from one of the readings given for this day. Keep it in your mind and heart as a reminder of the sovereignty of God over all the dark places that frighten us.

In God's Memory

They think in their heart, 'God has forgotten, he has hidden his face,
he will never see it.'

~ *Psalm 10:11* ~

O Lord my God,
Remember me, remember me.
I am being torn apart;
people talk about me behind my back;
I know I am far from perfect, but their words hurt.
Remember me, remember me.
I am not being given a fair hearing;
the people that I trusted have turned against me.
Nobody understands.
Remember me, remember me.
My family know me too well;
they say nothing but look accusingly;
I feel so alone.
Remember me, remember me.
And where are you, Lord,
when my words turn to ashes in my mouth,
when my mind is in disarray and my thoughts are jumbled?
Remember me, remember me.
O Lord my God,
when I cannot speak or think for myself,
when the world seems against me and even you yourself appear to be far
    off,
hidden –
stand beside me,
tower over me,
wrap yourself around me,
to keep me safe from fears, real and imagined.
Today and every day,
O Lord my God,
Remember me, remember me.   AMEN.

Prayer Activity

God is always present for us. This is both our theological belief and the witness of Christians throughout the ages, so when God appears to hide, we question what is going on. One way of looking at this experience of God hiding is that it allows questions to come to the surface within us and helps us to face things which are difficult. Hold the truth of God's presence in one hand, hold the experience of God hiding in your other hand, and see if you can allow a dialogue to emerge like the one in the psalm. If it helps you, write down your dialogue, create your version of this psalm. Then ask God for discernment. Which questions are you being asked to continue wrestling with? Which are you being asked to let go of and simply leave in God's hands? Finish by asking for whatever you need to take you further in understanding and love.

Anna and Simeon

... or mine eyes have seen your salvation, which you have prepared in the presence of all peoples ...

~ *Luke 2:30, 31* ~

There is subversion
in waiting,
in the tenacity of those who hope
and dare to long
for revelation,
for justice,
for truth.

And subversive beyond that
is when old eyes recognise,
fulfilled in a newborn,
the hope they have been harbouring for generations.

May we see in each new generation,
the evolving of the world,
in lives that will carry on our story,
with the chance for a new revelation of Gospel.

The subversion of old age,
is the placing in each younger generation,
the ongoing story of faith,
and the whole hope of the Gospel.

May we recognise what is good to pass on,
and the right time in which to pass it.

Prayer Activity

Spend some time considering words of parents and grandparents you remember years after they have been spoken and how they have revealed wisdom to you. How has what a previous generation said, shaped you? What has been wise and what has needed to be left behind? What has been unwanted baggage and what has influenced you in the direction of your life?

Incarnation

And the Word became flesh and lived among us ... full of grace and truth.

~ John 1:14 ~

When you put on flesh and we share breath,
when you put on flesh and we walk together,
when you put on flesh and we laugh and weep with you,
    God,
may I recognise these as holy:
each a moment of incarnation, where you have held me especially close,
knowing me and my needs, giving yourself to my pain and joy,
loving me completely in my incompleteness.

God, may I linger in these moments, touching the promise that is given of
    an ever-present love
given fully and lavishly, painstakingly,
and let that love shape my being, holding the promise close to myself,
 trusting it as fully and lavishly as it is given.
And may the world hold it too.
May my friends and family know of these moments,
my community and neighbourhood discover this promise,
and each person, no matter where they are,
know of a God who put on flesh for them.

Prayer Activity

Make a diary today of where you have discovered love present: people you have met, places you have been, conversations you have had, stories you have heard. Also consider the places and people you heard about today that seem to be without love. How can you bring God's love to them, through awareness, commitment, telling their story and putting flesh on the promises of incarnation?

Affirmation – Jesus' Baptism

'This is my beloved Son, in whom I take delight.'

~ Matthew 3:17 ~

Heavenly Father,
when at the font where water symbolises new hope after death
and washing stands for setting free from sin, we praise your holy name.
To us, for us, the miracle seems fresh again
as each new life is claimed by you and each soul called to follow on.
We are affirmed by you, named by you, given love and promise
and hopes of worlds to come.
Your great Spirit descends once more to visit us
and all who witness with blessing and peace.
At your baptism, another step was taken, Lord Jesus:
you heard the Father's voice.
Remind us now of power through symbol –
of water for freedom and naming for acceptance;
that time when we were claimed by you to follow and to serve.   AMEN.

Readings

Isaiah 43:1–2; Jeremiah 31:31–4; Ezekiel 36:24–8; Matthew 3:13–17;
John 1:31–4; Romans 6:1–4

Silence

Prayer Activity

Remember a time when you experienced God especially close, when you
knew yourself to be valued and precious. If it helps, also sing or imagine
singing a favourite hymn or chorus. Notice how the remembering, the singing,
changes the sensations in your body and your feelings. Allow God's light to
flood your being.

Lord's Prayer

Blessing

The Lord bless you and keep you;
the Lord make His face to shine upon you, and be gracious unto you;
the Lord lift up His countenance upon you, and give you peace.   AMEN.

~ Numbers 6:24–6 ~

River Jordan

*Then Jesus came from Galilee to John at the Jordan, to be baptised
by, him.*

~ Matthew 3:13 ~

Baptise us with your presence, Eternal God.
Cleanse us with your life, Christ Jesus, our Friend.
Set us free in your power, life-giving Spirit.

Rooted in the River Jordan are the souls of countless millions:
men, women and children baptised and brought into communities of faith.
Washed, cleansed and watered, affirmed and encouraged,
you assure us of your love, O God.

God within and God beyond:
calling us, individually, into life with you;
calling us, collectively, into life with each other;
calling us, eternally, into life with your Saints;
    baptise us with your presence,
    cleanse us with your life,
    set us free in your power.

Readings

Matthew 3:1–17; Mark 1:1–15; Luke 3:1–22

Prayer Activity

Imagine being beside a river. What attracts your attention: the sound, the flow
of the water, a pool? Meditate upon that and how that aspect of the water is
bringing you life. Dedicate that awareness to bringing life to other people
today.

Tax-Collectors/Sinners

'Why does your teacher eat with tax-collectors and sinners?'

~ Matthew 9:11 ~

I'm glad you did, Jesus,
eat with tax-collectors and sinners, that is.
I'm glad heaven makes space for outsiders and that grace is shaped like a
   table
and invites the world to dine.
I'm glad you made friends with the conspiring, the forgotten,
the broken,
the radicals,
that you went home with the terrorist and the fool, for I find myself more at
   home there
than among the clean linen
and polished halos of the saints.

Such generosity is heaven's gift to the world,
such openness is heaven's desire for the world,
such willingness to hope is heaven's bounty to the world,
such radical inclusion is heaven's intent for the world,
such readiness to accept is heaven's language for the world,
such strength to love is heaven's justice in the world.

Eat with me, Jesus,
a banquet of inclusion,
and may my living,
my faith, my love,
be as generous and as open,
as yours.

Prayer Activity

Take a sheet of paper and draw a circle on it. Write around the circle groups
of people, or names of individuals, that the world excludes for one reason
or another. Pray for them and, as you do, write the name of the group or the
individual within the circle, symbolising their gathering into God's love.

— Liberation – Jesus Heals the Dumb Man —

... the dumb man spoke ...

~ Matthew 9:33 ~

Lord of the Word,
I praise you this day for the joys of speech,
the words and sentences that have shaped my life:
my naming at baptism
and the promises said then;
my first faltering words
as the door to the treasury of language opened wide;
my family and friends and teachers
who encouraged those early words.

I thank you for the miracle of speech:
kindly things that are said to soothe and comfort;
stirring words which quicken my heart;
enlightening words which illuminate my mind;
for promises spoken and meant;
for pledges of love and commitment;
for words and sayings I have memorised
that guide my daily path and shape the way I am.

Oh Lord,
your word sets free the whole world,
calling light from darkness,
sound from silence,
hope from despair.
Speak to me today that I might hear
the word that frees,
the word that cheers,
the word that encourages.
By your grace,
when I have cause to speak,
may these words find themselves in my speech too.   Amen.

Readings

Exodus 4:10–17; Proverbs 15:1–4; Isaiah 6:1–8; Matthew 9:32–4;
John 1:1–14; James 3:1–12

Silence

Prayer Activity

It is hard for us consistently to hold on to the belief that Jesus can help transform us from the inside. Take your sense of restriction or inadequacy. Take what weighs you down or makes you rigid inside and invite God to soften and transform heavy moralism and old pains. Breathe in God's new life. Let the Spirit bring release from within.

Jesus Heals Peter's Mother-in-Law

'So he took her by the hand; the fever left her ...'

~ Matthew 8:15 ~

Lord, it seems so simple, so natural,
a wee touch from you and all is well.
There are friends whom I would love to see restored,
up and about again — a wee touch from you?

Minor ailments, recurring problems, terminal illness, a wee touch from you?

Your touch demonstrated the power of a life lived in God.
Transforming.

My touch can be less dynamic,
hesitant, with small faith;
embarrassed,
but
with potential.

Free me to be willing to pray
and identify with others by touch,
knowing that I may be a channel of divine grace
and human care appropriately expressed.

We pray for those whose experience of touch is painful and unloving
and whose lives are blighted because of this.   AMEN.

Readings

Matthew 8:14–17; Mark 9:38–41; Philippians 2:25–30

Silence

Prayer Activity

Place a hand or hands on yourself wherever you have pain, tension or stress.
(If you cannot reach, use your imagination!) Or recall any situation or thought
which pains you. Relax, let your breath flow in and out; breathe in the Holy
Spirit, breathe out your pain. Pray.

Lord's Prayer

The Disciples Sent out to Heal

He ... sent ... them ... with authority ...
~ Mark 6:7 ~

Lord God,
when we are hesitant, when we are trembling,
when we do not think we'll find the words or know what to do,
you come to us –
with the firmness that we need,
with the steadiness that sees us through,
with the purpose that gives us direction.
Your reassuring hand upon our shoulder helps us find the authority we seek,
to think and act and speak.

For those who bear responsibility today,
in the world of politics,
in the classroom,
in the courts,
in the hospitals,
in the relief centres.
in the workplace.
May your blessing and power, your wisdom and compassion,
your clarity and vision, guide and enlighten.
Help each one to step out in faith and act with a confidence,
which shows that though we walk on earth our footsteps find their echo in
    heaven,
that your will be done through us.   AMEN.

Readings

Exodus 4:10–17; Joshua 1:5–9; Joel 2:28–9; Mark 6:7–13; Acts 1:1–11;
Romans 8:37–9

Silence

Prayer Activity

Jesus taught his disciples to be rooted, gave them basic practical advice,
and challenged and encouraged them to move beyond their experience and
expectations. Stand, or imagine yourself standing, preferably in the open air
(or imagine being outside). Explore the experience of being rooted and stable,
with feet on the earth, and at the same time open your arms outwards and
upwards, reaching beyond. Try doing this while meditating on this story of

empowerment. Try doing this while meditating on the strength of the ground beneath your feet or on the bones which hold up your body.

Lord's Prayer

Blessing

May God, the source of all perseverance and all encouragement, grant that you may agree with one another after the manner of Christ Jesus, and so with one mind and one voice may praise the God and Father of our Lord Jesus Christ.

~ Romans 15:5–6 ~

Siloam

Jesus said, 'Go, wash in the pool of Siloam' (which means Sent). Then he went and washed and came back able to see.

~ *John 9:7* ~

Lord God, Siloam was ancient even in Jesus' day.
A place of cool water in steady supply,
stone surrounded, refreshing.

How did you do it, Lord?
Special spit, or curative clay?
Did Siloam have particular powers?
Or were you looking for simple obedience and trust that the man born blind
    might see,
and glory be given to God?

I also am blind to your purposes,
myopic to your working
but yet you work
in minds and hearts and bodies.
refreshing, restoring, healing.
Heal, I pray, my particular form of blindness that with fresh eyes
I will see the world
and humbly before you
give glory to God.

I ask that dreary Pharisees and sceptics today would be confounded
by the gentle confidence of disciples who recognise,
that though once blind,
now they see, because of Jesus,
who by the living water of his Spirit is at work
bringing glory to God.   AMEN.

Prayer Activity

Ask God to show you where you are blind, and ask for healing, for wholeness and for sight. Choose one of your five senses today and make an effort to appreciate it throughout the day.

Blessing

> May God delight you
> with the beauty of the world,
> the beauty of people,
> and the beauty of his Son.   AMEN.

Walking on Water

Between three and six in the morning he came towards them, walking across the lake.

~ Matthew 14:25 ~

The wonder of God's love,
always there for me, always understanding,
always ready to greet me, even seek me ...

The wonder that you come to me in the storms of life,
that you understand my fear, meet me there
and that you challenge me to move beyond,
to discover more of my own potential.

I wonder why there are stars in the sky?
I wonder why daisies close at night?
I wonder why it snows?

I wonder where I fit in?

I wonder at the strange coincidences that make me stop
and realise that I am part of something so much greater
than my rational mind can understand.
I wonder if I can open myself to so great a mystery?

Can I let myself be captivated by the wonder of love, of beauty, of mystery?
Can I open my heart to new possibilities, to saying yes and yes and more?
Let me trust the unknown, the darkness, the turmoil, the void, the lostness
    with you,
allowing these experiences to be birthplaces of wonder.   AMEN.

Readings

Isaiah 45:1–8; Proverbs 8:22–9:11; Matthew 14:22–33; Matthew 17:24–7;
1 Peter 1:1–12

Silence

Prayer Activity

Imagine being there in the boat in the storm. Watch your own fear, your relief, your enthusiasm. Can you look at the different 'bits' of yourself at this moment, the mixture of being human – your strength, your weakness? Hear all the different voices inside. Then 'out of the storm' let Jesus show you the next step.

The Healing of a Canaanite Woman

... the demon had left her.

~ Mark 7:30 ~

Help us now to focus on you and close out any influences that do not come
from you.
Help us to include in our prayers those we find it difficult to pray for and
those we try to ignore.

We pray for our society and think today
of the emotional damage and physical difficulty
people experience through negative influences on their lives.
We pray for those driven by money and greed,
those brought up in homes of deceit and abuse,
those controlled by dependency on drugs, alcohol, gambling.

As Jesus drove out demons,
we remember today those who need your renewing, forgiving spirit.
Those who are guilt-ridden,
those who are obsessive,
those who are wrong without realising.

God, who came among us as Jesus to touch and heal,
be in the situations and hearts of those today who cannot accept help from
people,
who find it too painful to be spoken to and too embarrassing to be touched.
God, in unbelievable power – break into our prisons.
God, in unspeakable forgiveness – cleanse our heavy hearts.
God in the Living Son – touch and heal all that is broken.   AMEN.

Readings

Psalm 98; Matthew 8:28–34; Mark 7:24–30; Mark 9:14–29

Prayer Activity

Jesus says 'ephphatha', which literally means 'be opened'. Repeat to yourself
this word – ephphatha – and feel the sound. Place your fingertips on your
heart, and on the syllable *tha* open out your arms and hands. Thus you embody
Jesus' prayer 'be open'. Repeat several times.

A Paralytic Healed

'Never before ... have we seen anything like this!'

~ *Mark 2:12* ~

All-seeing Lord,
it is not hard to imagine your eyes, their piercing gaze,
seeing through words and thoughts, into hearts and souls.
Seeing the real needs, knowing the real requests,
sensing things as they truly are.

Today we pray for insight into what is happening
around us and
within us.
The real feelings behind the words and the looks,
the real meaning of the silences.
As we look and listen, may we feel and think,
so that we might help, or comfort, or keep silence, or speak out.

We pray for others who use such skills:
the doctor in the surgery,
the carer in the home,
the teacher in the classroom,
and all who blend intellect with intuition,
perceiving what lies beneath the surface,
bringing to light what would otherwise remain dark.

All-seeing Lord,
may we who watch see with your eyes.
All-hearing Lord,
may we who listen hear with your ears.
And with your subtle perception and intimate power,
read the sights and sounds of humanity aright,
bringing your blessing and love to bear.   AMEN.

Readings

1 Kings 1:9–20; 2 Kings 4:8–37; Proverbs 2:1–15; Mark 2:1–12;
Hebrews 10:19–25; 1 Peter 1:3–9

Silence

Prayer Activity

Jesus so often brought wisdom. He saw beneath the surface. He revealed the stuck or paralysed place inside people. In what area of your life are you asking him now to give you wisdom and to help you to 'walk' into new life? Stay with the feeling of being stuck, explore it, ask for release.

Lord's Prayer

Blessing

See us, Lord, and bless us;
hear us, Lord, and bless us;
know us, Lord, and bless us;
that through your seeing, hearing and knowing we may be understood,
    accepted and redeemed.   AMEN.

Nourishing

Then Jesus ordered the crowds to sit down on the grass. Taking the five loaves and the two fish, he looked up to heaven, and blessed and broke the loaves, and gave them to the disciples, and the disciples gave them to the crowds.

~ *Matthew 14:19* ~

Lord,
In my mind's eye,
I see them spread across the beach, a great sea of humanity:

The smug and the struggling
The respectable and the reprobate
The pious and the perplexed –
I see them in their diversity.

Yet I also see them even if only for a timeless moment,
Under the blessing hands of Christ woven into one garment,
Fashioned into one people.

Did the smug and the struggling touch hands as bread was broken?
Did the respectable and the reprobate
Look into each other's eyes as fish was passed around?
Did the pious and the perplexed recognise in each other a shared longing?

Lord, today I pray for my own congregation.
May we who are so like that crowd on the hillside be fashioned by the hands
  of Christ
Into a sign of hope for a despairing world. AMEN.

Prayer Activity

Place a loaf of bread on your prayer corner. Touch it, smell it. Think of the labour that went into producing it – from the farmer to the baker. Think of the nourishment it brings. Think of those who have no bread. Meditate on Jesus' words, 'I am the Bread of Life'.

Emmaus

'What are you discussing with each other while you walk along?'

~ Luke 24:17 ~

Gracious God,

when we gather together — even just two or three,

when we speak of you in company,

often we are so engrossed in what we are saying, or singing, or praying, that we miss you in our midst.

When tragedy hits, when we lose a loved one, when our world changes beyond recognition,

sometimes we talk in jumbled, panicked ways and don't mean what we say.

When hope fades and faith is too hard to manage, sometimes we trudge on, numb and hardened to the journey.

Jesus,

not only do you walk alongside us,

you want to know how we feel, what we think, what we are saying about things that happen.

And just as we feel the warmth of the sun emerging, just as we cannot look right at it,

your presence helps us to take time to realise you are there in so many ways.

Bless each step we take as you stay with us day and night.   AMEN.

Readings

Luke 24:13–35; Acts 2:1–13

Silence

Prayer Activity

Reflect over your last twenty-four hours and look for any missed opportunity where you failed to recognise Jesus. Stand back and see the bigger perspective on your personal concerns and problems. Let your heart treasure, and burn, with any realisation that comes from this prayerfulness.

The Transfiguration

He took Peter, John and James and went up a mountain to pray.

~ Luke 9:28 ~

You really are the God of surprises.
It was just an ordinary day:
a sunny morning,
perfect for a walk
into the hills.

It was to be a day of quiet,
rest
and renewal.

That was the idea.
It seemed safe,
predictable
and straightforward.
But then,
life is not really like that when it is lived with you, is it?

For in your presence,
the ordinary becomes extraordinary,
the predictable day
becomes the very gate of heaven,
and even a scraggy gorse bush
burns bright with the glory of God.   AMEN.

Readings

Psalm 8; Luke 9:28–36; 2 Corinthians 3:12–18; Revelation 1:9–20

Silence

Prayer Activity

Pray with your body, expressing devotion and awe. (This can also be done as effectively with your imagination.) For example, you might go down on your knees, head on the floor, even a complete prostration if that feels right. Try repeating this several times. Then take some time to notice the effect on your body, mind, emotions and spirit.

Fields

At that time Jesus went through the grainfields on the sabbath; his disciples were hungry, and they began to pluck heads of grain and to eat. When the Pharisees saw it, they said to him, 'Look, your disciples are doing what is not lawful to do on the Sabbath.'

~ Matthew 12:1, 2 ~

Living Lord,
As I look out upon your world,
I see so many lives
That are stunted, constricted and blighted
By the rigidity of religion
And the pretensions of piety.

And then I look at Jesus
And see one who is gloriously
And marvellously free,
I see one who is utterly human –
And yet God present to us,
The very Glory of God
Smiling out from a weathered face.

As the disciples cavort and caper
Their way through the cornfields,
(Breaking human regulations,
But fulfilling the law of God)
You show us your joy
Breaking in upon religion's sobriety,
Your festivity gate-crashing,
The dour gatherings of the smugly pious.

Lord, I pray that in my life
And in the life of the world,
There may be a true breakthrough
Of that humanity and liberty
Which mark the place
Where the Christ has walked.   AMEN.

Prayer Activity

Use your imagination. Piece together in your mind the scene of Jesus and his disciples in the cornfields. Imagine the landscape, the sights, the sounds, the smells. Now focus closer on Jesus and the disciples. Focus on how they are walking and on their facial expressions. Then do the same with Jesus' opponents. Reflect. Pray.

Cana

On the third day, there was a wedding in Cana of Galilee.

~ John 2:1 ~

Lord, I picture you dancing at the wedding:
no dour onlooker,
frowning in self-righteous judgement, no hide-bound kill-joy,
disapproving of such frivolity.

Rather, you were in your element, revelling in the celebration.

But then,
joy *is* your natural element.
This is who you are:
the wellspring and source of all joy,
bringing the swirling colours
of your Kingdom dance
into the grey funereal shabbiness of our respectable religion.

You come to change, to transform and to transfigure,
that what we are might give way to what you would have us become.

Today I think of all for whom the life of faith
is grey and shabby, bland, watery and joyless.

May they know you present
as the One who dances at weddings.

Prayer Activity

What do you want to ask Jesus to transform? What in your life is bland, watery or joyless? Jesus came to bring abundant life. Ask for what you want with passion and clarity. Then, like Mary, leave it with him. Ask that you may recognise his answer to you.

The Resurrection

'I have seen the Lord!'

~ *John 20:18* ~

Risen Lord,
in the darkness of the rock-carved tomb,
when it seemed no dawn would ever come,
in mystery
you rose again,
transforming the world around you
and giving new meaning and purpose
to the children of the promise.
In your transforming touch
things begin to blossom,
hopes begin to grow
and all around is changed.

Looking at our lives and our world today –
    where there is staleness,
    where there is dull routine,
    where there is the imprint of bad habit,
with your transforming touch
come and bring that newness again.
In the circle of family and friends,
in the workplace,
in times of rest and leisure,
    where comfort has become restriction,
    where familiarity has brought contempt,
weave into the fraying fabric of our world
the new thread of hope
to help all shine and shimmer
with the promise of the new.
New beginning, new possibility,
new opportunity, new life
transformed by you. AMEN.

Readings

Matthew 28; Mark 16; Luke 24; John 20–1

Wind and Fire

The day of Pentecost had come, and they were all together in one place ... They were all filled with the Holy Spirit.

~ Acts 2:1, 4 ~

Spirit of love and power,
we praise you for the miracle of wholeness:
the wholeness of togetherness,
of communication,
of listening.

Spirit of Pentecost of then and now,
take from us all power that would
control others or promote self.

Holy Spirit, open our heart to the enrichment of
inclusiveness, understanding,
and power purified by love.   AMEN.

Prayer Activity

Take any experience of inadequacy, whether current or in your memory. Keep this in your mind and at the same time feel your breath by lightly placing a hand on your abdomen or heart. (Or, if you prefer, be aware of your breath as it goes in and out at your nostrils.) 'Holy Spirit' could have been translated as 'Holy Breath'. Breathe in the life from God, breathe out all that holds you back. Let God tell you what you need for your next step of faith.

Lord's Prayer

Blessing

God grant you the grace that doesn't flee
the purifying tongues of fire.
God grant you the grace of being
open to the winds of change.
God give you the grace that speaks
in every language,
the grace of Jesus' love,
active in heart and mind and tongue.   AMEN.

Damascus

Now as he was going along and approaching Damascus, suddenly a light from heaven flashed all around him.

– Acts 9:3 –

Lord Jesus Christ,
the road that wends its way before me, the turns and corners,
hills and valleys
provide you with opportunities
to meet me
when I least expect you.

In the midst of anger your calming presence.
In the midst of laziness your sharp rebuke.
In the midst of grief your soothing comfort;
in the midst of fear your steady hand.

And in such times
you stop me in my tracks
and make me look again
and check the way I go.
And in such times you turn me round
to face the way that you would have me go.

Lord, at the cross-road times of life, when there are many paths,
point me in the right direction.
Help me see, clearly, your way forward,
and with faith in my step
may I find my way to you.   AMEN.

Prayer Activity

Imagine a light from heaven flashing all around you, or relive a memory of experiencing God as light. Paul's experience turned his life around. Use this to help you when you feel swamped by old, dysfunctional patterns of behaviour – your own and other people's. Let the light shine and notice the difference it makes, even if that difference is just momentary. Start now by exercising your imagination.

The Conversion of Saul

'Tell me, Lord', he said, 'who are you?'

~ Acts 9:5 ~

Lord Jesus,
along the way, at unexpected turns,
in darkness, and in light, you meet us.

When minds are closed shut, when hearts are stony and hard, you meet us.
You take a hold of our lives.

Open up to us what is really there – we cannot turn away.

Today, when we forget, or fail to look,
or are not expecting, surprise us –

With a word, a sign, a touch,
a reminder that you are still there.
Though we may have forgotten you,
you have not forgotten us,
a hands-on, speaking, involved God,
threading through our lives remembrances of glory,
intimations of things still to come.   AMEN.

Silence

Prayer Activity

Imagine being there at Paul's conversion. With whom do you identify in the story? Allow your imagination to take you there and experience what is going on. How does it make you feel? What questions arise? Through your imagination and your curiosity, let God speak.

Lord's Prayer

God is not far from each one of us. For 'In him we live and move and have our being'; as even some of your own poets have said, 'For we too are his offspring.'

~ *Acts 17:27b–8* ~

Mysterious God,
in the multiplicity of things you are to be found.
Where peoples and cultures encounter each other,
whenever diversity is celebrated and individuality respected,
you are present in the synergy of our song.
> *In you, O God, known and yet unknown, we live and move and have being.*

In the vision and in the vibrancy of world faiths,
whenever people search for meaning in life
and are able to recognise your life in others,
you are present in the synergy of our song.
> *In you, O God, known and yet unknown, we live and move and have being.*

In the good use of science and technology,
in the growth of civilisations and in the politics of plenty,
in the benefits of education and in the working for health,
you are present in the synergy of our song.
> *In you, O God, known and yet unknown, we live and move and have being.*

In the searching for answers, in the asking of questions,
in the discourse of thinkers, in the dialogue of friends,
in the hospitality of strangers and in the intimacy of lovers,
you are present in the synergy of our song.
> *In you, O God, known and yet unknown, we live and move and have being.*

Prayer Activity

In an increasingly multicultural world we have responsibility to build peace. Reflect on a recent encounter you have had with another culture. What were your honest reactions – interest, confusion, irritation, fear? Speak to God of your questions and emotional reactions.

Eternal Life

Even though our outer nature is wasting away, our inner nature is being renewed day by day.

~ *2 Corinthians 4:16* ~

We can't imagine a life without the body;
how can there be life without a body, without senses, movement, people
  around us?
Yet how many of the really important things happen when the body is still?
– having an imaginary, loving conversation with someone who is absent, or
  who has died:
– taking a decision which changes your life or the life of others around you;
– letting someone do something for you that you are incapable of doing for
  yourself
so that they grow in the service of God.

God beside us, God within us,
God before us, God beneath us,
God surrounding us,
do you need us to have hands before you can give us gifts?
a brow before you can bless us?
a stomach before you can nourish us?
Sometimes we feel so confined by our earthly tent. We groan with
  frustration.
Painful limbs or pain-filled memories stop our tracks, and we long for the
  'house not made with hands'.

For you, God, there is no frontier between life and death.
Christ is our passport, our courier, our border crossing.
For you the living and the dead are one,
the cloud of witnesses as real as the day,
waiting to welcome us to your side.

Readings

Psalm 103:8–18	*As for mortals, their days are like grass*
Ecclesiastes 3:9–15	*A sense of past and future*
John 14:1–7	*'I am the way, the truth, and the life'*
2 Corinthians 4:13–18	*Our outer and our inner nature*
2 Corinthians 5:1–11	*A house not made with hands*

Beach – Dawning

Jesus said to them, 'Come and eat.'
~ John 21:12 ~

The new dawn shakes itself awake,
pulling apart the night with yellows and golds;
and in the freshness of this thin light,
the beach seems crowded with resurrection.

Hereon the edge of things:
between shore and land;
between dark and light;
between home and adventure;
I meet you face to face,
and staring into eyes
that confront me with images of crucifixion and death,
of darkness and things unimaginable,

I can see beyond,
as you have done,
into a reflection clear with the new promise of eternity,
and with sand between my toes,
the smell of fish on my fingers,
spray on my face,
and salt in my mouth,
we share a makeshift breakfast –
a sacramental moment,
that builds with light, and truth,
and love,
for in my heart I know you are alive!

May every morsel I share with the world this day,
contain as much Good News as this.

Prayer Activity

Be there on that beach. Feel the smells and the sounds, the sun or wind
on your face. Take yourself towards a small beach-fire and there is Jesus
preparing breakfast. Eat with him. What would you say to him? What does
he say to you?

Praise and Thanksgiving

Holy God

Our Father in Heaven, may your name be hallowed.

~ Matthew 6:9 ~

Prayer for Reflection

Names ...
I use a dozen, a hundred a day:
my family, my friends,
my colleagues;
names in the news,
names to remember,
names to call,
names on the tip of my tongue.

And all quite ordinary.

And yours, God,
perhaps shortest of all,
but none more special.

Hallowed be your name.

Prayer on Today's Theme

Today, Lord,
I remember those who introduced me to you.
It doesn't matter if some aren't here now;
you can tell them the lasting effect
they have had on my life.

I remember also
those who regularly preach the Gospel in public,
and those who say a word for you in private.
And I remember those who try to keep the faith
in places where your name is cursed,
or in the close company of somebody who suffers
from an overdose of bad religion.

Let my prayers
encourage those who speak in your name;
and let your Holy Spirit
inform and guard their conversation.

Our Father in heaven,
hallowed be your name,
your kingdom come, your will be done,
on earth as in heaven.
Give us today our daily bread.
Forgive us our sins
as we forgive those who sin against us.
Save us from the time of trial
and deliver us from evil.
For the kingdom, the power,
and the glory are yours now and forever.

~ The Lord's Prayer ~

Adoration

You shall love the Lord your God with all your heart, and with all your soul, and with all your might.

~ *Deuteronomy 6:5* ~

Prayer for Ourselves

Can you really be the one true God,
when so many other gods
clamour to add colour and excitement to my life
and capture my undivided attention?

Can you be Light for my world,
when I am happy to be dazzled
by the bright promise and glamour
which seems almost within my reach?

Can you be my Good Shepherd
when I am happy to throw myself
into the arms of the first self-help package
which offers me warmth, success and security?

But yes, Lord, it must be you.
And this I come to know for sure
as soon as I taste the disappointment
and see through the glamour
and hear the hollow sound
of all the world's feeble promises.

Help me to love you with all I have.

Prayer for Others

God, we thank you
for those who give us the words and the ways
to express our adoration:
hymn writers who give us images and arouse our passion,
poets who dig deep into our souls,
artists who open our eyes to beauty, colour and form,
musicians who lift us to the heights,
writers who help us reflect on our human condition.
Bless those who have lost the capacity to adore, because their senses have
    been dulled,

or their lives become focused in on themselves, because they do not know
   you,
or their vision of your glory has become obscured.

Celebration

Praise him for his mighty deeds;
Praise him according to his surpassing greatness.

~ *Psalm 150:2* ~

Amazing God, there is no-one, nothing like you.
How blessed we are to know of you
and to be able to have a relationship with you.

Everything around us seems to speak and sing and show us your loveliness.
As part of your creation we want to join in the song of praise,
yet all our best instruments and sweetest voices
blended in harmony couldn't express the feeling of our hearts,
the joy of our souls at knowing you!

But let us try, God,
let us breathe your name and shout our excitement
and make sure we are heard.
God, we cannot contain you,
we cannot help our praise.   AMEN.

Readings

Psalm 150; Isaiah 43:1–8; John 2:1–13; John 20:1–20; Ephesians 5:1–3

Prayer Activity

Join the dance in your imagination. Have a ball! Let your imagination run riot. Dance with animals, trees, musical instruments and anyone you want to be there. Is there a pattern to the dance? What sort of place do you find yourself in? What colours are strongest? What does the music sound like? Give yourself the freedom to 'be there' and enjoy taking part and/or watching what is happening. At the end, reflect with God how this has changed, or not, your mood, your feelings, your thinking. Find a word, picture or gesture to mark the end of the dance for the moment.

The Lord's Prayer

Blessing

With a spring in your step,
and a hope in your heart,
express joy in this day
and embrace the gifts you have been given,
through Jesus Christ our Lord.   AMEN.

Exuberant Appreciation

Great is the Lord and greatly to be praised.

~ Psalm 96:4 ~

Glory, Glory, Glory!
Declare his glory among the nations.

Loving Father,
I declare your glory in this room now,
as sunlight illuminates the already vivid flowers in a vase,
glorying in the brilliance of your world.
Praise to you
for the variety and beauty of everyday things.
Praise to you
for your love expressed in Christ.
Praise to you
when the mind glimpses new insights of faith.
Praise to you
when words run out and glory fills the soul.

Gracious God, I praise you for who you are,
enable me to glorify you
and enjoy you forever.   AMEN.

Prayer Activity

'Bow down.' Literally or in your imagination offer this devotional act of bowing down or kneeling. Find the connections kneeling this gesture of adoration and praise and the exuberant aspects of this psalm. What happens when your praise is focused in this way?

Acceptance

Here I am! Send me.

~ Isaiah 6:8 ~

Prayer for Reflection

I'm not much to look at, Lord.
I don't always get things right, either.
What on earth do you see in me?

And yet you call me by name and lead me out!
Wonderfully, miraculously, I am made in your image!
Praise be!
Let me remember with joy and humility
    that you love me just as I am.

Prayer on Today's Theme

O God,
be with all whose spirit is always striving
    for the unreachable and unattainable,
who are always crying for the moon
    or grieving over spilt milk.

Be with those who refuse
to accept the constraints of their circumstances –
    the prisoner in the cell,
    the patient in the ward,
    the paraplegic in the wheelchair –
that they may press on to achieve what seems impossible.

Gratitude

Your unfailing love is better than life; therefore I shall sing your praises.

~ *Psalm 63:3* ~

Prayer for Reflection

For this day
of this month
of this year ... thank you, God.

For my body,
my mind,
my spirit ... thank you, God.

For my past,
my present,
my future ... thank you, God.

And because,
in the mystery of your kindness,
you who gave me life and time
also give me your listening and your love,
accept my deepest gratitude
through Jesus Christ my Lord.

Prayer on Today's Theme

Today, God,
I ask you to remember in your love
those for whom a new day or a new month brings no joy;
those for whom light has turned to darkness,
    or confidence to confusion.
    or faith to despair.

I do not ask you to make them suddenly happy;
I ask you to help them discover that you understand,
    and that you have friends, of whom I am one,
who care and hope and pray.

'I am the Bread of Life'

~ *John 6:48* ~

Prayer for Reflection

It takes me so long, Lord,
to plan the meals and balance the diet;
and buy the groceries and cook the food.

And mealtimes are not always a joy,
especially if I feel the need of company,
or cannot enjoy the food for keeping the peace at the dinner table.

I need more to sustain me
than what my money buys and human hands prepare.
I need to identify a deeper hunger,
and to give you time to nourish my soul.

Prayer on Today's Theme

Help us, eternal God,
provider of all nourishment,
not to be greedy.
Prevent us from craving tomorrow's bread before today's is eaten;
and keep us from demanding more faith before we savour and cherish
what you have already given us.

Be gentle
when you touch bread.
Let it not lie
uncared for, unwanted.

So often
bread is taken for granted.

There is such beauty in bread:
beauty of sun and soil,
beauty of patient toil.
Wind and sun have caressed it;
Christ often blessed it.

Be gentle
when you touch bread.

~ *Anon* ~

Nourishing

Prayer for Reflection

Lord, I thank you for the food you set before me.
Living as I do, life is a feast;
but I remember that for others life is a famine.

You nourish us not just with bread,
    but through the beauty of nature,
    through poetry, and music, and art,
and best of all by your Word,
    Jesus, the bread of life.
Help us to feed on him by faith
and to hold him always in our hearts.

Prayer on Today's Theme

Jesus, living water,
we pray for those whose lives are parched,
who thirst to know, to learn, to be loved, to be wanted.
We pray for those whose lives are arid,
who thirst to control, to manipulate, to stay on top,
who live in a desert of their own making,
believing they are always right, keeping others at arm's length,
smug in their own self-sufficiency.
    You are able to slake all thirsts with with the water of life,
    springing from the wells of divine love.

Nourishment

'At twilight you shall eat meat, and in the morning you shall have your fill of bread.'

~ *Exodus 16:12* ~

Prayer for Ourselves

Generous God,
what nourishment you give me!
The earth feeds me, sun, wind and rain refresh me,
families and friends sustain me in love.
It is not only material things that nourish me:
there is the beauty of nature,
the richness of poetry, art, and music, the excitement of play,
the quietness of relaxation;
all feed my spirit.
Above all I am fed by the very Word of God,
and nurtured by my life in the church.
Thank you that you care for me and sustain me, body and soul.

Prayer for Others

We lift to you our sisters and brothers who are hungry
because the crops have failed, the well has run dry,
and relief has not yet reached them.
We pray for those who enjoy worldly wealth
but whose souls are parched,
whose eyes are closed to the beauty of creation,
whose ears are deaf to your Word.
May your church reach out to all,
as we remember how you fed hungry people with bread and fish,
and spoke a word of love and reassurance to the rich and powerful.
Help us to work for a world
where your many gifts to us are shared by all.

Jesus and Peter – the Surprise Catch

'Put out into deep water ...'

~ Luke 5:4 ~

Lord, your voice of command is crystal clear, but we fear the deep waters.
The security of the shallow waters causes us to keep our eyes on the shore.
Lord, give us courage to sail into the deep, knowing that you are present
  with us.
Help us to believe that in deep waters there is food for the soul:
the food of trust,
the food of dependence upon you,
the food of cooperation with each other,
food we could never dream of.   AMEN.

Readings

Exodus 16:13–35; Luke 5:1–11; Hebrews 11:1–13

Silence

Prayer Activity

Imagine looking deep inside your body. Where in your being do you
experience or sense 'God within'? (If this is not easy or obvious to you,
start by imagining a sacred or holy place inside your heart.) Stay with that
sense of the holy, healing place inside you and listen and look. Here you
might 'catch' the presence of God. What today is there to surprise you? What
'abundance of fish', what answer to a problem or question where, like Peter,
previously you have had no success? Look for the great treasures in the deep
places of your soul. Like Peter, be prepared to try again and look beyond your
expectations.

Lord's Prayer

Blessing

God's blessing be upon you
as you set sail for your journey;
God's strength sustain you
when the waves of fear oppress you.
God's love fill you with the surprises of his grace;
and God's Spirit nourish your soul
with the bread of faith and trust.   AMEN.

Encounter – the Picture Clears

'I see people – they look like trees, but they are walking about ...'

~ Mark 8:24 ~

Lord,
happily this blind man had a friend to bring him to you.

We thank you for those who led us to you,
long ago,
recently.

Lord, you took the man away from the public gaze to minister to him.
You minister to us in the private places
of heart and life.

Lord, you restored the sight of the blind man gradually.
Happily the restoring of our lives is ever ongoing.   AMEN.

Readings

2 Kings 5:1–19; Psalm 23; Mark 8:22–6

Silence

Prayer Activity

Normally your eyes look outwards, but now in your imagination let your eyes look inwards. Imagine them travelling from your head down through your body, observing any pain or tension of mind, of body, of emotion, of spirit. Invite God's love to bring release and new life. Talk with God, ask for more understanding to see more clearly.

Lord's Prayer

Blessing

> The Lord bless us with friends that are true,
> the Lord bless with his healing touch,
> the Lord bless us from beginning to end,
> and in the gift of each new day.   AMEN.

Jewels in the Crown

For what hope or joy or triumphal crown is there for us, what indeed but you?

~ 1 Thessalonians 2:19 ~

Prayer for Reflection

Does this mean, Lord,
that I am part of your success story?
That all my attempts to live the Gospel
    have actually added up to something?
That my faltering love,
    my intermittent concern for social justice,
    my fumbling attempts to share my faith,
    my tuneless song and my stilted prayer,
    even my honest doubts
have somehow brought the Kingdom closer?

Will I be a jewel in your crown today?

Prayer on Today's Theme

Today I thank you, God,
for those whose life has been a success story;
who have found ways of relieving pain,
who have persuaded people not to enslave others,
who have helped build a fairer society,
who have inspired people with great ideals,
who have taken the Gospel to unlikely places,
who have spent their lives in prayer
    and shown us the way into the heart of God.

A Thing of Beauty

Take the impurities out of silver and the artist can produce a thing of beauty.

~ *Proverbs 25:4* ~

Prayer for Reflection

Though someone in my childhood
may have told me I had no voice,
still let me sing for you.

Though someone in my past
may have told me I could not draw,
still let me make for you,
    or bake for you,
    or mend, arrange, design
    something beautiful.

You are the great artist,
who sang the world into being,
and you did not make me in your image
to be feckless and dumb.

Prayer on Today's Theme

Thank God for poets and painters,
    drummers and bagpipemakers,
    seamstresses and silversmiths,
    Celtic harpists and home-bakers,
    potters and flower-arrangers,
    sculptors and landscape gardeners.
Thank God for all whose skill and imagination brings beauty out of silence
  and shapelessness.
Thank God for all artistry
as it strives after perfection
and so imitates our one Maker.

Almighty Creator, maker of all things,
the world could not express your glory
even were the grass and the trees to sing.

You have wrought such a multitude of wonders
that they cannot be equalled.
No language can express them,
no letters can contain them.
Yet it is not too great a toil
to praise the Trinity.
It is not too great a toil
to praise the Son of Mary.

~ Ninth-century Welsh ~

Roots

You have accepted Christ Jesus ... Be rooted in him, be built in him.

~ Colossians 2:6, 7 ~

Prayer for Reflection

Lord of all life and living,
I am deeply grateful
for the love, warmth, and security of my first home;
for the stability of parents, grandparents,
and all who set me on the path to you,
guiding and supporting me through my earliest years.
I acknowledge the wonder and the promise of my birth,
the opportunities to develop,
the widening experiences of life,
    some joyful,
    others challenging,
in this your gloriously rich and wonderfully expansive world.

Prayer on Today's Theme

Help, O God,
all who feel cheated and disadvantaged
by the ordinariness of their background.
Remind them how down-to-earth was your Son's birth,
yet how glorious was the life, death, and resurrection
that followed.
May all come to know
that the bottom may be a good place to start.
Reassure them with the knowledge
that your love always surrounds them,
and that to the end of their days
their home is in you.

❧

We pray today that those who represent the Kingdom's promise in the structures of our common life may find renewal both from fellow members of the church as well as from those whom they meet; and that, in speaking for Christ in the institutions they serve, they may also speak in turn to the church on behalf of the life of the world, reminding it of the urgency of the message it bears.

Praise

The earth is the Lord's and all that is in it.

~ Psalm 24:1 ~

Today, O mighty God
many of us will be living
as if the world were ours to rule.
In homes, communities and nations
we will treat our environment as if it were infinite,
and all at our disposal.

Forgive us in your mercy,
mend our faulty perceptions,
restore us to right understanding
and open our spiritual eyes to the glory of your kingship.
Transform our lives, which are yours,
our churches, which are yours,
our communities, which are yours,
and our world, which is yours.

We give you our praise, Almighty God, through Jesus Christ,
King of Kings and Lord of Lords.   AMEN.

Prayer Activity

The gates or doorway spoken of in Psalm 24 refer to the gates and doorways
of the Temple in Jerusalem. To go under these gates, to enter those doors,
was very special. Can you imagine what that would have been like? As you
go through any gateway or doorway today, recall what was special about
these entrances so long ago. Can you lift up your head? Our understanding
as Christians is that our bodies are temples of the Holy Spirit. Can you allow
yourself to feel special, crowned, part of a kingdom, a royal person, a holy
nation? You are part of this ongoing tradition!

The Lord's Prayer

Blessing

Live to the praise of Christ's glory
and enjoy his world, a precious heritage.

Praying

'This is how you should pray: Our Father in heaven ...'

~ *Matthew 6:9* ~

Prayer for Reflection

It is prayer time again, Lord,
time to bring you my shopping list,
'Do this, fix that, and, oh yes, bring peace to the world.'
So much I ask Lord, and how self-centred I sound.
But you have taught me how to pray,
> to find space and time to hear your voice,
> to be still and know that you are God.

You have already told us the secret of prayer,
how we needn't adopt special postures,
or use particular words,
nor wait for emergencies,
but how we must walk with you,
> be guided by you, be lived in by you,
> listen for you day and night,
– indeed, say *Our Father ...*

Prayer on Today's Theme

Lord, stretch out towards those who cannot pray:
those for whom prayer is merely a routine,
those who use prayer as a substitute for action,
those who are proud of their prayers,
those whose prayers do not carry over into daily life,
those who feel no-one prays for them,
those who feel they have no-one to pray to.

Time for God

Jesus sat down, and when his disciples had gathered round him, he began to address them.

~ *Matthew 5:1* ~

Prayer for Reflection

I sit down, Lord,
     to watch television,
     to write a letter,
     to mend clothes,
     to rest my feet,
     to listen to music,
     to read the paper,
     to shut my eyes and forget.

You sit down, Lord
     to wait for me
     to be ready for you.

Help me, among the other things
     for which I sit,
     to remember you
     waiting for me.

Prayer on Today's Theme

I think of those who will chase the clock today,
     as if there were no tomorrow;
     and those who will watch the clock today
     as if the best were lost in yesterday.

And I think of children keen to speak
whose parents have no time to listen;
and troubled people with a story to tell
which nobody wants to hear;
and those who see time as the enemy
of their ambition,
     their ability,
     their complexion.

Teach us, God of eternity,
     to be kind to time,
     so that time can be kind to us.

Thanking God

Let them thank the Lord for his steadfast love.

~ Psalm 107:31 ~

Almighty God,
We come to you with grateful praise.
    It is good to give thanks to the Lord.
We praise you for the times you found us in the lost places of life.
    It is good to give thanks to the Lord.
We praise you for the food and drink that sustain us.
    It is good to give thanks to the Lord.
We praise you for your healing power.
    It is good to give thanks to the Lord.
We praise you for accompanying us as we travel.
    It is good to give thanks to the Lord.
We praise you for the work we can do in the world.
    It is good to give thanks to the Lord.
We praise you for calming the storms of life.
    It is good to give thanks to the Lord.
We praise you for setting us free from sin and death.
    It is good to give thanks to the Lord.
We praise you for your creative Spirit at work within us.
    It is good to give thanks to the Lord.
We praise you for calling us home to be with you forever.
    It is good to give thanks to the Lord.
Almighty God,
We come to you with grateful praise.
    It is good to give thanks to the Lord.   AMEN.

Prayer Activity

Find the repeating verses in Psalm 107. Say them to yourself frequently during this day. How are you affected by doing this? Glad, anxious about remembering, enjoying doing it, hating it, enjoying the sound and the rhythm, not especially liking these words? In as detached a way as possible, reflect on this way of praying and your reactions to God. See what you have learned. There is no right or wrong. Some people find this way of praying helpful and others do not.

The Feeding of the Five Thousand

'Give them something to eat yourselves.'

~ Matthew 14:16 ~

God of goodness, source of strength and wholeness,
in our efforts to follow you,
at times we feel weak and lack the energy to grow.
As we rest and are silent and stay for a while in your presence,
let us realise the areas of our lives we starve of attention:
our commitment to family and friends, our efforts in work and community,
and our quiet times focused on you in prayer and reflection.
Source of life,
may we relish this moment with you;
may your Spirit restore us,
your love enthuse us and in your acceptance build us up for the days ahead.
May we be able to give back to you
the very best of all that we are and all that we have.
God, we thank you for the miracle of sharing, for the blessings we can bring
   to others
and the signs of hope we can receive from them.
From now on, help us always to ask what we can give and can do,
rather than expecting someone else to do it.
God, develop our capacity for goodness that we may live
     lives that encourage those around us,
     lives that are nurtured by you.   AMEN.

Readings

Matthew 14:15–21; Mark 14:1–11; Philippians 4:10–13; Ephesians 2:4–10

Silence

Prayer Activity

Go to, or imagine, a favourite place in the country or in a garden and enjoy the abundance of life that is there. Set aside a particular amount of time and allow yourself this nurturing space. When you find your mind wandering, simply come back to the 'here and now' beauty and feed on it.

Lord's Prayer

Abundance

He restores my soul.
He leads me in right paths for his name's sake.

~ Psalm 23:3 ~

God,
you make us;
you give to us something new,
something better and stronger and lasting.
And yet we look for you in the old,
speaking of you in words
that our mouths churn out without thinking,
words we expect to have to say,
words we think have to be sung and heard.

But, God, you are alive.
Should we not be amazed that you provide all that we need each day?
Should we not find it overwhelming that you offer abundance, renewal and
    constancy in our lives?
Should we not feel your word tingling in our bones,
surging through our veins as you live with us
and in us and remind us of life's essence?

Surely goodness and mercy
will follow us all the days of our lives as we follow you?
Surely you are all we need? Amen.

Readings

Psalm 23; John 14:1–8

Silence

Prayer Activity

I shall want nothing. God renews life within me. Read Psalm 23 again, notice
which image or picture today renews your life so that you want nothing. Stay
with that image for at least five minutes, letting your body, mind and spirit
rest, be nurtured, feel, taste, touch and smell.

Harvest

For everything there is a season, and a time for every matter under heaven.

~ Ecclesiastes 3:1 ~

Constant God,
spring, summer, autumn, winter –
this is the pattern of our lives.
Easter, Pentecost, Harvest, Christmas –
these are the seasons of our Church.

Today, I think of spring
    – fresh starts, green shoots, hope, new life.
I give thanks for summer
    – bright sun, fresh air, rest and recreation.
And I remember now autumn
    – glorious colours, cleansing breezes, hands gathering crops.
For the winter will come and there will be frost, bitter winds, bare trees;
    times will be hard,
    life will show signs of death.

Tomorrow – when life begins, all over again,
help me, God.
When work seems futile, when time feels short, when relationships are
    lost –
show me the new thing, push me forward, love me back to reality –
for you really are the same
    – yesterday, today and forever.

Prayer Activity

Life today is often full of electronic communication, convenience food and ready-made products to consume. Notice the intricacy of things made for you and by you – plant some seeds, bake or cook food to eat – use your hands to create, mend or decorate something today – and as you do, praise God for the sheer detail of his provision and care.

Fertility

Every valley shall be lifted up ...

~ Isaiah 40:4 ~

O God, often, often we want you to come down –
    some glorious cataclysm:
    an end to human hunger and suffering;
    an end to tyranny and terrorism;
    people, acknowledging you, raised
        from valleys of despair
        to bright mountains of hope.
Yet, praise be, that kingdom has begun:
    in Christ your glory was and is revealed.

We thank You that in Him
    we are given the new creation for a new world;
    a promise for peace and plenty;
    an agenda for a new age.
Forgive us for our failure to attempt it.
    The farmer has to tend the seed,
        but we have not attended your will;
            the seeds of Christ's planting often lie dormant;
            the seed of his redeeming Word has not been well sown.
O God our Father who gives life to the seed,
    speed the plough – that there may be a harvest for all;
    speed the Church – that your Word may be widely sown;
    and speed us – that we may bear fruit in our living:
        so may the valleys rejoice
        and the Kingdom come. AMEN.

Readings

Psalm 65:9–13	*God's bounty in the harvest*
Galatians 5:22–6	*The fruit of the Spirit*
Luke 8:4–15	*The parable of the sower*

Prayer Activity

Observe and marvel at the growth of seeds planted in good ground. Ask if you are sufficiently planted 'in Christ' and are open enough to the outpouring of the Spirit.

Garden – Loving

I have entered my garden, my sweetheart, my bride.
I am gathering my spices and myrrh;
I am eating my honey and honeycomb.

~ Song of Songs 5:1 ~

Tell me,
who would take an eternity
choosing the million flavours of peach
and not notice it pass?
Only you, my Creator.
Who would consider the patience it takes
to harmonise the subtleties of a flower's perfume
time well spent?
Only you, my Creator.
Who would celebrate that it took not a moment sooner
to compose the sound of bird song?
Only you, my Creator.

Creator,
may I find time to celebrate in your garden of wonder,
to slow down this moment of heaven
that sweeps me off my feet in love for you
from some holy recognition
too deep for words.

And if a burden is too great,
or a pain too fresh,
may that same garden wait for me
to bloom once more
into the life you shape for me,
that I might see in the waiting
the place of resurrection
calling me.

Prayer Activity

Imagine the life of a single flower and its life cycle, watching it grow day by day and then die and give up its life. Reflect on the cross and what Jesus did for us all, giving his own life. The dead flower now waits for its seed to grow a new shoot, a new plant to burst through the ground: imagine Jesus in the tomb about to do the same.

Healing

He said to her, 'Daughter, your faith has made you well: go in peace'.

~ *Luke 8:48* ~

Lord, teach me how to experience your healing Love.
   Flow in me and through me and around me
      in a way that feeds me,
         strengthens me,
         reassures me,
      transforms me, lets me grow.
Allow your healing Love to flow through me to others
   in quiet ripples of gentle love,
      in waves whose force
      I do not know or understand.

Enable me to trust that a phone call made at
      an appropriate moment,
  a chance meeting in the street,
    a word spoken in the passing,
      can be a miracle.

Let me listen to your Word
knowing that some Bible stories
will change my life,
bring healing in me –

healing which also means wholeness, an integration in me:
heart speaking to mind,
body teaching me intuitive skills,
   a readiness to allow your creative Spirit to mould me
anew.

Readings

1 Samuel 16:14–23	*Music bringing healing*
Mark 2:1–12	*From paralysis to walking*
Luke 8:40–56	*Your faith has cured you*
Luke 13:10–17	*You are rid of your trouble*
2 Corinthians 5:11–17	*You are a new creation*

The Senses

Creator God, continually you renew the gift of life in giving us senses with
which to savour it to the full, and through their power you deal graciously
with us.

When you looked at the new-created world and *saw* that it was good,
you showed that you meant us to see beauty in all things and all people;
and when Jesus singled out Bartimaeus the beggar and made him see again
he was calling us to look upon others and see the real person underneath.

Because you are a God who *heard* the cry of your people
so we are to hear not just those who please but those also who disturb us;
and when Jesus said to the deaf man, 'Ephphatha',
he opened our ears not just to hear sounds but also the silence beyond.

As you *smelled* the incense burned by a grateful people
so our bodies are given to worship you and not for seeking sensation;
and when the house was filled with the aroma of precious ointment
Jesus called us to a life of generosity rather than self-gratification.

As God wrestled with Jacob till dawn and *touched* his thigh,
so you bless us as much during the struggle as when at peace;
and when the woman touched the hem of Jesus' garment,
so we learn that we do not touch for taking but for healing.

As God *tasted* the offering of Elijah and exposed the false gods,
so we relish the life offered by the one true bountiful God;
and when Jesus shared the bread and wine with his disciples,
he offered us a foretaste of life when all are reconciled in his kingdom.

Remove from this earth, Lord, senseless slaughter
which does not savour the riches given to us in others.
Curb the appetite which craves fulfilment
and turns the globe into a supermarket for the rich.
Silence the pulsing air which surrounds us with noise, preventing us hearing
the voice of need,
even our own need.   AMEN.

Teaching, Enabling

For it is God who is at work in you, enabling you both to will and to work for his good pleasure.

~ Philippians 2:13 ~

Lord God, where would we be
if there were no teachers or enablers —
those who play an important part
in shaping the people we are today and will be tomorrow?

As Christ lived and taught, people realised and recognised God among
    them,
so today we thank you for all whose patience and tireless efforts
help us to learn new things in a way that is easy for us to understand.

As Christ inspired and healed, people found they were capable of things
    they never dreamt of,
so today we thank you for those who enable,
for their ability to see something in us which they are able to help us to
    shape
and hone into a special gift.

Lord, it is no easy task to teach or be an enabler for others
and we give you thanks for this wonderful gift
and for the many people in our world who are blessed with it.
May they be aware of their gift and use it to inspire
all the people you lead them to, for your glory.   AMEN.

Prayer Activity

Look back and think of someone who taught or enabled you to do something.
Give thanks to God for that person. Are you still in touch with them? Why not
contact them and tell them how much what they did meant to you?

Gentiles

After greeting them, he [Paul] related one by one the things that God had done among the Gentiles through his ministry.

~ Acts 21:19 ~

Love: large enough for all.
Love: broad enough for everyone.
Love: deep enough for the world.
Love: broken for the sinner.
Lover: being born among outsiders.
Love: rising for us all.

Love cannot be contained within any system, or held exclusive to any one
   religion.
She cannot be tied down with definitions, or explained by any one culture.
Love cannot be fenced in by any particular group, or owned by any
   denomination.
She cannot be copyrighted by one body, or held ransom by any particular
   history.

Love can only be for everyone, or it cannot be love.
She loves beyond barriers of:
race or language; sexuality or lifestyle; culture or heritage; religion or
   politics.

God of the Gentiles, help me welcome love into my heart, my mind, my
   decisions;
help me welcome love into my relationships, my choices, my family;
help me welcome love into my neighbourhood, my community, my world.
God of the Gentiles, may I live a love big enough for all.

Readings

Jonah 3:1–10	*A prophet to the Gentiles*
John 4:1–26	*The Samaritan at the well*
Acts 10:9–16	*God's big picnic*
Acts 10:34–43	*Peter's breakthrough*
Romans 9:19–26	*God's anger and mercy*
I Corinthians 12:12–14	*One Body*
Ephesians 5:1–6	*The Plan*

Prayer Activity

Reflect on the communities that are divided on religious or cultural grounds. Simply be present with these things rather than say things about them. Be present and let the images linger in your mind for a while. Conclude by repeating the first stanza of today's prayer.

Blessing

> May God's grace curve towards you and yours,
> may the sky stretch for a thousand acres about you,
> may the land forever hold you and give you life,
> and may you share this blessing of heaven, always.

Prophets

God has spoken; who can but prophesy?

~ Amos 3:8 ~

Lord God, we thank you for the prophets of old –
    Isaiah, Jeremiah, Ezekiel and the glorious rest:
men with a message; men who feared you but no other:
    those who spoke of your plans and purposes –
    railing against idolatry and defection
    condemning the ills of society
    challenging the complacent
    arousing all to do justice, to love kindness and to walk humbly with
        you.

Lord God, we thank you for latter-day prophets,
    who also interpreted the times, discerned the future;
a Martin Luther King … a George MacLeod
    who like the Old Testament prophets
    had a dream, a vision, that gave hope and comfort not least as they
        witnessed to Jesus:
    the Messiah, the Christ, promised of old.

Lord God, we thank you for John the Baptist,
    the wild wilderness preacher,
the last of the old prophets; the first to proclaim Jesus:
    the Lamb of God who takes away the sin of the world.
We thank you for all who preach your living Word
    with all who often, in some dry desert place, witness to Jesus:
on whom was laid the iniquity of us all.

Lord God, thanking you, above all, for him:
    whose chastisement made us whole, with whose stripes we are healed:
Jesus Christ the supreme prophet, who can lead us through every
    wilderness,
speak to men and women in our day and raise up many who will prophesy
    and proclaim your Word in Christ.   AMEN.

Prayer Activity

Recall Isaiah's temple vision and the question: 'Who will go for us?' Think of
some need within the Church or without: can you say 'Here am I, send me'?

Blessing

> Guide me, O thou great Redeemer,
> Pilgrim through this barren land;
> I am weak but thou art mighty;
> Hold me with thy powerful hand.   AMEN.

> *~ William Williams 1717–91 ~*

Mary and Martha

Martha, Martha, you are worried and distracted by many things ...

~ Luke 10:41 ~

You know me, Lord, so well.
I have seen the depressing sinkful of dishes, and heard the laughter from the
    sitting room
Where the TV is; and I have wondered how I got landed with all this to do.
    Again ...
And sometimes, I've said so. Vociferously.

And I have done the dishes in a quiet house, and my mind has fled
To some happy or sad thought, but something real, something urgent
That the rhythmic swish of the dishcloth in my hand has set free.
And I have started, as the water from the still-running tap
Spills out of the bowl, or jumped when, in my hand,
The cup runs over.

You know me, Lord, so well.
Sometimes I am Martha, with my worthy agenda and my sense of being
    taken for granted;
My hectoring sense of all that needs done, that no one is doing, that drives
    me to ginger up and chivvy along.
The humdrum has to be got through first.
Then comes the good stuff ...
And sometimes it is given to me to be Mary.
To be grasped by a moment when eternity strikes down into time,
And time must yield.

Then the humdrum is charged with meaning, and not just the meaning of its
    own flat demands.
For you, Christ, are here. Now.
Help me to grasp your presence. Now.
To 'Be still, and know that I am God ...' Now.
Maybe the dishes can wait ...

Prayer Activity

Sit quietly, and look at your surroundings. Just stop completely. Marvel at the
fact that it's all there. Accept it as it is. Then, in a way that seems appropriate
to you – greet the presence of Christ in this reality.

Prodigal Son and Father

... let us eat and celebrate; for this son of mine was dead and is alive again; he was lost and is found!

~ Luke 15:23, 24 ~

Father God,
For giving me more than my share,
For allowing me to go my own way,
For letting me be my own person,
Thank you.

Yet in independence,
    when my world has chaos all around,
    when I have made bad choices and have nothing and no one to turn to,
    even when others ask why you do,
Thank you for waiting for me.
Even when I think I know best, and lose myself,
thank you for finding me.

Thank you, that though I feel far from home,
    You are never distant,
Though I close off and focus on other things,
    You are always open and unconditional in your embrace.
Though I am 'prodigal',
you are,
unyieldingly,
love.

Prayer Activity

The word 'prodigal' has come to be thought of as a negative term for someone who is 'long lost' or misguided and off the straight and narrow. However, 'prodigal' really means 'lavish' or 'extravagant'. While this can be seen from a negative perspective in terms of the son in the story, in terms of the prodigal father there is a much more positive understanding. Think of the 'prodigal' aspects of your life and hold both negative and positive feelings before God.

Faith and Devotion

'I am what I am'

Prayer for Reflection

I am ...
a child,
a parent,
a valued customer,
a supporter,
a non conformist,
a right winger,
a left footer,
a treasured friend,
a single mother,
a graduate,
a grandfather,
a voter ...

... all these
and more,
and most important,
and better than all,
I am
yours.

Prayer on Today's Theme

Have pity, good God,
on those who cannot live with themselves,
because their past looms too large,
    or their relationship is a mistake,
    or their work is a compromise,
or because
    no one has said, 'You are good to be with';
    no one has said, 'Come and visit me';
    no one has said, 'I love you'.
And in all of us,
eradicate the long miles
between what we are and what we should be,
until, like Jesus,
our performance lives up
to our potential.

Christ be with me, Christ within me,
Christ behind me, Christ before me,
Christ beside me, Christ to win me,
Christ to comfort and restore me;
Christ beneath me, Christ above me,
Christ in quiet, Christ in danger,
Christ in all the hearts that love me,
Christ in mouth of friend and stranger.

~ *St Patrick* ~

'And you, who do you say that I am?'

~ Luke 9:20 ~

Prayer for Reflection

... the Son of God, the Saviour, the Messiah, the Christ;
... the teacher, the healer, the debater, the disturber;
... the one who listened to women, the one who played with children,
... the one who outraged his friends, the one who loved his enemies;
... my friend, my disturber, my listener, my Lord!

Prayer on Today's Theme

A thought today
for those who translate the Bible into foreign languages and contemporary
    English;
a thought for those who teach and study scripture and theology;
a thought for those who preach, write or broadcast the message of the
    Gospel;
a thought for those who argue Christian principles in awkward places.

For all these people, Lord,
may a living relationship with you
inform and guide all they say about you.

No voice can sing, nor heart can frame
nor can the memory find
a sweeter sound than thy blest name,
Saviour of humankind.
Jesus, our only joy be thou,
as thou our prize wilt be;
Jesus, be thou our glory now
and through eternity.

~ Twelfth Century ~

We pray today that in those nations where to speak openly of Christ can lead
to persecution, the quality of Christian lives might preach the Gospel in the
absence of words.

'In Truth I Tell you, I am the Door'

~ John 10:7 ~

Prayer for Reflection

There is no way in except the door.
Sometimes, I imagine that the good I do is enough;
or that the prayers I say are sufficient;
or that the religious experience I once had is all that matters.

But underneath I know
that my virtue and my prayers and my past
– no matter how perfect –
are no substitute
for you, Jesus Christ,
the door to heaven
here and hereafter.

Prayer on Today's Theme

God liberate those
wrongly imprisoned behind locked doors
by governments or families.

God liberate those
who sit behind locked doors fearing the outside world,
living, perhaps, in private squalor.

God liberate those
whose door no one knocks
because everyone is too busy to notice who are ignored.

And if my hands or my words can help your process of liberation,
then use them.

Thanks be to you, Lord Jesus Christ,
for all the benefits you have given us,
for all the pain and insults
you have borne for us.

Most merciful redeemer, friend, and brother,
may we know you more clearly,

love you more dearly,
and follow you more nearly,
day by day.

~ St Richard ~

~ John 14:6 ~

Prayer for Reflection

Puzzled,
I wonder where to go;
confused,
I wonder what to believe;
cautious,
I wonder how to live.

Meanwhile, you, Jesus Christ,
walk into the future,
communicate the deepest truths,
and behave with complete integrity.

This is your uniqueness
on which I can rely
utterly.

Prayer on Today's Theme

Remember in your kindness, Lord, those who teach the faith to children,
    for their warmth may reflect yours;
those who argue the faith with teenagers, for their interest may reflect yours;
those who prepare worship for folk who have limited abilities,
    for their compassion may reflect yours;
those who say prayers in prisons, for their faith may reflect yours.
Remember, Lord,
all your servants who are called to listen, counsel, befriend and heal;
let theirs be the kingdom of heaven.

My God, I choose the whole lot:
no point in becoming a saint by halves.

I'm not afraid of suffering for your sake;
the only thing I'm afraid of is clinging to my own will.

Take it, I want the whole lot,
everything whatsoever
that is your will for me.

~ Theresa of Lisieux ~

Faith (1)

Faith gives substance to our hopes and convinces us of realities we do not see.

~ Hebrews 11:1 ~

Prayer for Reflection

Lord, you never asked people to pretend
    that something was there that wasn't;
you never asked them to invent
    things that weren't true.
But you did ask them to use their imagination
    – not to create fantasies,
but to break out of attitudes that were just a habit
    and didn't lead anywhere.

You never said faith would have to do
    until the real thing came.
You did say faith could be small,
    but that it would grow.
And you said that when we believed in you,
    loss and death and endings
    could bring new life just as much as beginnings.

Help us to believe in you
so that trusting what we know
we may be able to trust what we cannot know.

Prayer on Today's Theme

I pray for people for whom nothing seems real,
the shock of seeing their home reduced to rubble,
    fields scorched, family members killed,
but who still believe.

Faith (2)

Peter answered him, 'Lord, if it is you, command me to come to you on the water.'

~ Matthew 14:28 ~

Lord, I am just like Peter:
for I too am so often a turmoil
of believing and doubting,
of faith and denial.
Like Peter walking on the waves, I step out in faith
but then I look down and panic;
I take my eyes from you and begin to sink.

To me also you say,
'Why have you so little faith?'

Perhaps I need to learn the lesson that Peter himself learned:
that you, Lord, are on the inside of my believing
and that faith is not about having the strength to hold on to you
but having the humility to be held.

Today I remember all who need to know the strong grip of your hand upon
theirs.

Readings

2 Kings 6:15–19	*The vision of faith*
Matthew 14:22–33	*The practice of faith*
Matthew 15:21–8	*The persistence of faith*
Hebrews 11:1–3	*The essence of faith*

Prayer Activity

In the language which Jesus spoke, Aramaic, the sense of the word faith is captured in the colloquialism, 'Go for it'. In what area of your life are you seeking that sort of energy and courage? Reflect and make this into your own prayer in words that also express expectancy of some form of answer.

Affirmation – the Touch that Healed

'Daughter, your faith has healed you ...'
~ *Luke 8:48* ~

The moment she touched your garment, Lord,
she knew healing, change;
you affirmed her in precious relationship.

How splendid, a double blessing:
for the body and the fearful vulnerable soul.
But her need and input mattered
to enable your work to be done.

I'm grateful that you accept me in just the same way,
your beloved child, with my acorn of faith.
Thank you for those who encourage and affirm in my everyday places,
who let me know I'm accepted.

There are many who have been crushed by life experience
who believe they are of no value to anyone.
I pray for your grace
to cherish them through the love of Christ,
heart to heart.   AMEN.

Readings

Psalm 139:13–18; Jeremiah 31:1–3; Luke 8:40–56; John 17:7–10;
Hebrews 13:5–6

Silence

Prayer Activity

Jesus said 'Talitha cum' to Jairus's daughter. 'Talitha' means 'little girl',
or 'one who has not fully realised their potential'. 'Cum' means 'get up' or
'come forth'. Imagine cradling in your arms a part of yourself which you
sense God is calling forth into fuller potential. Open your arms and release
yourself into his love and care.

Ask, Seek, Knock

Ask, and you will receive; seek, and you will find; knock, and the door will be opened.

~ Matthew 7:7 ~

Prayer for Reflection

It is so simple, Lord,
yet I spend so much of my life
avoiding it.

I fret and worry,
rather than ask;
I expect things to fall in my lap
rather than seek;
I stand with my hands behind my back,
rigidly independent,
rather than knock on heaven's door.

Teach me, Lord, to trust, to move, to lose my stubborn independence,
so that I can ask, seek, and knock,
as you intended.

Prayer on Today's Theme

Have mercy Lord,
on those who have been questioning for a long time, and have found no
   solution.
Have mercy, Lord,
on those who have been looking for a long time, and have yet to discover
   what they need to find.

Have mercy, Lord,
on those whose knuckles are raw with knocking
      at the doors of earth
      or the gates of heaven.

Answer their prayer;
or teach them to pray
for the right thing,
and to be patient.

Faith – a Man Struggles with Belief

'I believe; help my unbelief!'
~ Mark 9:24 ~

Lord of faith, so often I struggle with what to believe:
the loose ends,
the unanswered questions,
the eternal 'Why?'
Too often I have little to say to those who ask
and find myself with the same doubts.
Why this tragedy?
Why that death?
Why the unfairness?
Why the disappointment?

I believe, but help my unbelief!

When I struggle with things too great,
when I feel unequal to the task,
when I reel from blows,
when the world goes dark,
take me by the hand, lift me up, that I may arise
and see the brightness of a new day, the colours of creation,
the power of faith at work.

For me, and for all who struggle with their faith,
bring that touch of belief which banishes the shadow of doubt,
that I may see, that I may believe.   AMEN.

Readings

Psalm 22; Psalm 27; Psalm 42; Mark 9:14–29; 2 Corinthians 4:6–18;
2 Corinthians 12:7–10

Related Prayer Activity

Let all the waves of your emotions have their full effect. Notice the most
dominant emotion within you at this moment. Whether you are joyful or very
sad, let the emotions flow over you like a waterfall. Value your emotions,
experience them as fluid and flowing – bring life, energy and sparkle – like
a waterfall. Let go and let God show you what to do next, how to allow the
emotions to flow.

Doubt

How long, O Lord, will you leave me forgotten,
How long hide your face from me?

~ Psalm 13:1 ~

Prayer for Reflection

How strangely comforting, Lord,
that so many of your servants
have doubted you.

So,
if I cannot always see the sense
    of your Word;
if I do not always feel confident
    about my faith;
if I wonder where your love is
    in the face of pain and death;
I am not the first.

A great company of saints and martyrs
has felt this way before me.
Now, in your presence,
they see face to face
and know as they are known.

Teach me, like them,
not so much to fear doubt
as to see it
    as a sign of the mystery of life
    and a door to discovery.

Prayer on Today's Theme

In a world where sometimes it seems
that few follow Christ,
and the fascination with exotic beliefs
or with astrology
impedes the Church's witness,
I pray for candles in the darkness.

Raise up, O God, a visible presence
of writers, poets, artists, actors,

broadcasters and debaters
who, in public life and in their own way,
will say a word for you.

And may the measure of their witness and of mine
be not how successful we seem,
but how faithful we are
to the One who never doubts us.

Lord, make me an instrument of your peace.
Where there is hatred, let me sow love;
where there is injury, pardon,
where there is doubt, faith;
where there is darkness, light,
where there is sadness, joy.

~ *St Francis of Assisi* ~

Commitment

Commit your ways to the Lord; trust in him and he will act.

~ Psalm 37:5 ~

Prayer for Reflection

In imitation of my Saviour,
this day I commit into your hands, O God,
>   my deepest hope, my greatest fear,
>   my fondest friend, my farthest adversary,
>   my health, my conversation,
>   my wealth, my imagination,
>   my life, my love,
>   my spirit.

Do not cradle me gently as if I were not meant for this world;
rather hold me firmly
that I may be faithful in my commitment to you
and to all your people.

Prayer on Today's Theme

Today I remember, Lord,
those who have yet to throw in their lot with you.

Some enjoy talking about you,
but would not risk talking to you.
Some should be close by your side,
but the wrong word at the right time
>   from one of your followers
>   has kept them at arm's length.
Some are aflame with great ideas,
but have yet to find the bridge
>   from conviction to commitment.

For them I pray,
and for all who dither on the doorstep of discipleship,
that they may not fear to turn and face you
>   or take your hand
>   which is calloused with care.

Growing in Faith

God guides the humble in right conduct and teaches them his way.

~ Psalm 25:9 ~

Prayer for Reflection

God and Source
of all knowledge and understanding,
gladly I remember those who,
from my earliest years,
showed me the way and the truth and the life
of Jesus Christ.

Some by their songs,
some by their stories,
some by their smile or generosity,
        daring or quietness,
pointed to Jesus
and nourished my discipleship.

Now, as an adult,
may I be true to the nourishers and nourishment of the past,
by daily developing my knowledge and understanding of you
so that I may show and share a mature faith with others.

Prayer on Today's Theme

Lord Jesus Christ,
you understand what it means
both to teach and to learn.

Bless, then, all those who,
whether in school, college or church,
inform minds and nurture wisdom.
May all who lead playgroups,
teach infants or teenagers,
educate students,
prepare the disadvantaged
for the life of the world,
sense their privilege
and know their worth.

May those who teach
never stop learning,
and those who learn
cherish the truth
as a precious gift of God.

God, the Source of Confidence

'Come', my heart says, 'seek his face!'
Your face, Lord, do I seek.

~ Psalm 27:8 ~

The Lord is my light and my salvation;
whom shall I fear?
The Lord is the stronghold of my life;
of whom shall I be afraid?

Lord,
I like these words of confidence,
and the note of trust that runs through the whole psalm.

Joyful trust! Confidence! The absence of fear!

If my father and mother forsake me,
the Lord will take me up.

God help me to live a spirituality of dignity and quiet strength,
mature in reaction to the things that test me daily.

You are my stronghold,
I don't need to be afraid.
You heal my wounds
and help me to be brave and strong
time and time again.   AMEN.

Prayer Activity

Where are you safe with God? In church, at home, out walking, listening
to music, lighting a candle, in your own heart? Imagine being there. Allow
the feeling of safety to surround you and then let it permeate your body,
your bones, your muscles, heartbeat, your breath. Embrace and enjoy the
sensations of safety. You have cells forming in your body every moment;
bathe them in love.

Steady Trust

You who fear the Lord, trust in the Lord!

~ Psalm 115:11 ~

Heavenly Father,
I want to trust in you,
but idols of materialism impinge.
You, Lord, know my humanity.
It's what sent you to Calvary.
Forgive me for Jesus' sake.

Lord Jesus,
I want to trust you more
but I can't see what you are doing
in the world, even my bit of it,
and I get nervous.
Forgive me for wanting to be in control.

Holy Spirit,
I want to trust you even more,
but I don't know what that might mean.
Forgive me for my fears.

Triune God,
give me a simple trust,
that knowing you more day by day I will be content,
for Jesus' sake. AMEN.

Prayer Activity

Give glory to God's name. One way of doing this is the repetition of the name
of God. This is not a pointless repetition. In our stressful world where we
have to be alert so much, this is a way of resting the mind. Doing this allows
God to speak from the depths, cutting through the chatter of our minds. The
part of our mind which chatters to us with endless lists of things to do, to sort
out, is held steady by the simple repetitive sound (really *listen* to the sound).
A single word seems to be the best for most people. Try any of these —
Jesus, God, Love, Our Father, or the Aramaic words Jesus would have used
Maranatha (meaning 'Come, Lord') or *Abwoon* (meaning 'Our Father').

Strength

Be strong and stout-hearted, all you whose hope is in the Lord.

~ Psalm 31:24 ~

Prayer of Reflection

I think of friends, staunch and true,
upon whose strength I have depended,
on whose shoulders I have wept,
who have listened into the wee small hours;
always there when I have felt broken-hearted,
building me up,
so that, burning with a new hope,
I have been made strong again.

Help me, Lord,
to recognise when someone needs my help.
Show me where in my life and experience
I can find the resources to rebuild another person's life,
and what life experiences of mine
        would stand in the way of my helping.
Help me to bring these to you
        and find forgiveness
so that I do not keep inflicting them on others
        and causing them to stumble.

Prayer on Today's Theme

I give thanks for people in all walks of life,
who pass on their strength
both to those who know them well
and to those who have never met them,
people whose work and whose generosity has affected the lives of many.
I pray for those who lack strength of character,
because of the way they had to grow up,
because of damaging experiences,
or because that's the way they are.

Encourage them, Lord,
        as you encouraged Zacchaeus:
show them that all have a place, and all are loved.

Sea of Galilee

Immediately he called them; and they left their father Zebedee in the boat with the hired men, and followed Him.

~ *Mark 1:20* ~

What an amazing and exciting place the Sea of Galilee must have been,
place of miracles, where Christ lived and taught,
where lives changed dramatically,
a special place that marks the beginning of ministry and
adventure ... but I've never been.

And yet, God, I feel as though I have.
I've known that passion and urgency of doing your work.
I've heard you call my name and knew what I had to do.
I've thought how natural it seems to drop everything and to follow and go
with you wherever.

I realise there are times when I lose sight of you and don't so much follow
as fumble in the dark.
Sometimes I've wondered about what I'm doing and have counted out the
cost.
I want to hear your call again.

God lead me to a place today where I can listen for your voice,
where I can remember the conversation of faith,
where I can revive my enthusiasm,
and realise the ministry and mission you have given to me.   AMEN.

Prayer Activity

In your heart feel your sense of calling. Live and move today as if you were being drawn forward from the heart, following Jesus into our everyday activities. Peter frequently found in his life that Jesus moved from the ordinary activity into the extraordinary awareness of God's presence in his life. Open your heart today and find God taking you beyond your expectations.

Disciples

*And Jesus said to them, 'Follow me and I will make you fish for
people.' And immediately they left their nets and followed him.*

~ Mark 1:17–18 ~

Lord Jesus, you said 'Follow me' and they did;
the twelve chosen to be your closest disciples, and others, adding their
    experience to the group.

Today we reflect on this assortment of people from everyday walks of life,
none of them highly educated or religious, nothing particularly special about
    them.

Yet, Lord, you saw their potential;
you saw past the labels of tax-collector and fisherman,
you saw in them what they could and would be.

It would have been wonderful to be a fly on the wall
listening to all their conversations and discussions:
what did they speak about in private?
were they always serious?
did they have a laugh every now and then?
what were their private thoughts about you, Jesus, whom they followed?

You see the potential in each of us and call us to 'come and follow'.
Help us to leave everything behind and immediately follow you, today and
    every day.

Readings

Mark 1:16–20	*Calling of the first disciples*
Matthew 10:1–15	*The twelve disciples' mission*
John 8:31–59	*True disciples*

Prayer Activity

The disciples were fortunate in that they could speak to Jesus in person, face
to face. Close your eyes and imagine that you are sitting with Jesus. Is there
something you would like to talk to him about? Tell him now and sit quietly,
enjoying being in his presence.

Calling

And Jesus said to them, 'Follow me and I will make you fish for people.'

~ Mark 1:17 ~

Where the waves lapped against the shore,
as salty, sandy hands tugged at nets and slippery fish,
when the working day was in full swing,
Jesus came, and the familiar was soon cast aside.

And yet, God, it seems so absurd that those men downed tools and followed
your son.

What convinced them?
What made them leave so much and take up so much?
Today we, too, grapple with that challenge.

So help us recognise that compelling communication you had and have with
your people,
for in Jesus you spoke to the heart of working communities;
farmers and fishers, those who worked with their hands;
you spoke and they understood beyond words,
hearing you the maker and the worker of wonders.

So that's the call to us today too, typists and teachers, scientists and social
workers ...

Maybe not to down tools ...
but to bring your transforming presence into what we are already doing.

To notice that, as we teach – we hear the patience of Jesus,
As we write – we know the creativity of Spirit,
As we care – we nurture your compassion,
As we make and communicate and order – we begin again our journey
where something in you overwhelms something in us,
making us follow no matter what or where.

Prayer Activity

Reflect on three very different ways people earn a living, for example, by
working with their hands as a joiner or builder, using their minds as researcher
or technician or by expressing creativity as designer or artist. How might God
speak to them in these tasks? What do you do that links you to the nature
of God without words and what qualities from God do you need to work
today?

— 'I am among you as one who Serves' —

~ Luke 22:27 ~

Prayer for Reflection

Lord Jesus,
all my intuition tells me that I, like Peter, don't want *you* to wash *my* feet;
I would rather wash *yours*.

Like Martha, I would feel happier doing something for *you*;
than think of you doing something for *me*.

But how can I know how to serve
    unless I have been served?
How can I know how to love
    unless I have been shown love?
How can I share the Gospel
    unless I have let you tell me what it is all about?

Prayer on Today's Theme

A blessing today on the servants.

A blessing on those who cook and clean, and clear up, and change babies,
    and wash clothes, and make tea, and sing whiles.

A blessing on those who tend ungrateful relatives, and listen to bores,
and re-mend what has been torn again, and repeat the wisdom
which one day their children will remember and cherish.

A blessing today on all your domestic servants, Lord, who go down on their
    knees in the company of Jesus.

Bless to me the thing
    on which is set my mind,
bless to me the thing
    on which is set my love,
bless to me the thing
    on which is set my hope;
O thou King of kings,
    bless thou to me mine eye.

~ Gaelic Traditional ~

Women around Jesus

*Many women were also there, looking on from a distance; they had
followed Jesus from Galilee and had provided for him.*

~ *Matthew 27:55* ~

Lord Jesus, when you walked the earth you didn't just call men;
you called women too and encouraged them to follow and learn from you.

Let us ponder for a moment on these women:
women who followed and provided for you.
They were fortunate, given an unusual opportunity to leave their homes and
follow their Messiah, to walk and talk with you.

You made them the centre of attention, Jew or Gentile,
you healed them, had compassion for them, discussed weighty matters with
them.
When you rose, it was to women that you first appeared. Surely there can be
no greater affirmation.

Still today women have continued to follow you, sometimes quietly in the
background, sometimes not so quietly.

Women today play many roles,
no longer just homemakers, wives and mothers, sisters and daughters.
We pray for women who still have to fight hard to be allowed to step out of
their homes and into all walks of life to make their voices heard.

Readings

Luke 8:1–3	*Some women accompany Jesus*
Luke 7:36–50	*Jesus forgives a sinful woman*
Luke 24:1–12	*The resurrection of Jesus*
Matthew 9:18–26	*Life and healing*
Mark 7:24–30	*A Syrophoenician woman's faith*
John 2:1–11	*The wedding at Cana*

Prayer Activity

Think of the women who have been with you on your journey: mother, sister,
friend, colleague. Take a moment to think of what makes these women special
for you, then thank God for them and ask his blessing on them.

Andrew

(Andrew) first found his brother Simon and said to him, 'We have found the Messiah'.

~ John 1:41 ~

Living God,
there is something reassuring, something solid about Andrew.

He was the quiet fisherman,
always introduced as 'Simon Peter's brother', and quite happy to be so.

Yet, I remember how he was the one
who first brought Peter to Jesus,
who brought about that meeting
which brought Peter to the forefront of the disciples,
and gave himself a lesser part.

I admire his humility,
his readiness to play a supporting role,
his willingness to work in the shadow of his gregarious brother,
and his desire to bring others to Jesus.

Teach me to be a servant Lord.
that I might know the liberation of humility
and the joy of introducing others to you.

Prayer Activity

An ancient tradition of the church is that of the 'Jesus Prayer'. This originated in the Egyptian desert in the 4th century. The prayer runs as follows: 'Lord Jesus Christ, Son of God, have mercy on me, a sinner.' Quietly (within yourself or out loud) repeat the prayer in rhythm with your breathing, as follows: (breathe in) Lord Jesus Christ, (breathe out) Son of God, (breathe in) have mercy on me, (breathe out) a sinner. At first, try this for five minutes at a time and gradually increase up to twenty minutes. This is a time-honoured way of quieting mind and body to focus on Christ.

Thomas

Thomas answered him, 'My Lord and my God!'
~ *John 20:28* ~

Accepting Lord, when doubt and question and uncertainty
fog my mind,
and I cannot discern the way to go,
or what to believe or whom to trust,
> emerge with your truth from the mists of doubt,
> and show me your way.

When faith is hard,
and trust in what was once secure is shaken,
or shattered,
and I am left incoherent with fear, or guilt, or grief,
> emerge with your truth from the mists of doubt,
> and show me your way.

When, of all your followers, I am most like Thomas,
and want to touch and hold and not believe till then,
when my eyes and mouth are open,
but my heart and mind are closed,
> emerge with your truth from the mists of doubt,
> and show me your way.   AMEN.

Readings

Job 38:1–18; Psalm 14; Proverbs 9:1–12; Mark 9:14–29; John 1:1–18;
John 20:24–9

Prayer Activity

When we are in doubt it often feels as if the earth beneath our feet is shifting
and we are in danger of losing our footing and falling. Sit comfortably in a
chair, placing your feet firmly on the floor. Feel the sense of solidity. As you
feel this solidity repeat slowly the words, 'I know that my Redeemer lives'.
Repeat this several times and allow the rhythm of the words to add to the
sense of solidity under your feet.

Peter

... for we cannot keep from speaking about what we have seen and heard.

~ Acts 4:20 ~

Lord God, who gave the Word and everything came to be,
I bless you: for good and wise words ... for words of warning ... for
   forgiving words ... for words of tenderness and love... for words of
   encouragement and hope.

Lord God, I thank you for all who have so spoken to me: poets and
   philosophers and preachers, lyricists and broadcasters and journalists, yes,
   and true and loving friends.

Lord God, who gave the Word in the person of Jesus, a friend indeed, I bless
   you
for his words of life with all their assurance and promise; for that Word in
   Scripture that is sharper than a two-edged sword, for that Word that, read
   and proclaimed, is bread for the soul.

Lord God, there are so many words around and sometimes we do not hear
   you.
Often I speak so much that I do not hear what matters.
Help me, by your Spirit, to listen ... especially to you –
not least to that Word of the Cross that is wisdom and power.

As I bless you for all who have told me of the Saviour's love –
parents and teachers, writers and ministers –
help me, by that same Spirit, to speak of what I have seen and heard,
ever to put in a good word for Jesus Christ,
to tell of him in whom alone is my health and wholeness.   AMEN.

Prayer Activity

How do you cope when someone is challenging your faith or Christianity
generally? What do you think inside? How do you feel inside? Are you
defensive or do you want to attack? Explore your reactions and talk with
Jesus about how helpful your way of reacting is for yourself and others. Is he
asking you to attempt a different approach?

Discipleship

My Father is glorified by this, that you bear much fruit and become my disciples.

~ John 15:8 ~

Prayer for Ourselves

I know the warmth of your love in my life, Lord,
and want to bear fruit that will bring you glory,
but I know there may need to be painful pruning
if the fruit I bear is to be good fruit.
I lay my life before you, the Gardener.
Help me not to regret what you cut away
or resent what you rearrange
but to welcome your tending of me
that I may grace your garden
and be a refreshment for others.

Prayer for Others

We pray for those who have been hurt and bruised,
those who have not been able
to grow to their full potential,
those who have yet to mature,
to blossom and bear fruit,
those in younger years
that all their vitality and energy
may not go unharvested,
those who are weary in well doing
who feel their efforts come to nothing,
those who work hard
but do not see the fruits of their labours,
those who labour but to little purpose,
those who claim too much
for what they are able to produce.

Service

Do you love me? ... Feed my lambs ... tend my sheep.

~ John 21:15–17 ~

Prayer for Ourselves

Of course I love you, Lord!
I hoped it was obvious.
I care for my family,
I help my neighbour whenever I am able,
I never avoid a collecting can.

Yet you keep asking, 'Do you love me?'
Show me the kind of love you mean.
Bring home to me what it means to show your love,
not just when opportunities lie to hand,
but to break through into situations
where your love seems a foreign currency.

Prayer for Others

We give thanks for those who love you
in reaching out to the hungry,
the hurt and the wounded ones.

We pray for those whose duty is to serve,
    members of local congregations,
    professional and volunteer carers,
    those who have learned to face themselves
        so that they can give counsel to others.
Strengthen them as they stand with those in need.

Fellowship

God is faithful; by him you were called into the fellowship of his Son, Jesus Christ our Lord.

~ *1 Corinthians 1:9* ~

Prayer for Ourselves

When you created us, God,
you created us for fellowship with you.
Even when I want to hide from you,
    you come looking for me;
in Christ you brought me back
    into your company.

But I am not your only child, Lord.
For in Jesus also you reconciled
all people to yourself
and made us for each other,
living in a community of love.

When I try to live as if you don't matter,
or as if I am the only person in the world,
call me back to you
and bring me face to face with my neighbour.

Prayer for Others

Hear our prayers, Lord,
for those who have wandered from you,
for those who are searching for you,
for those who have a restlessness,
    that they may find rest and peace in you.
Hear our prayers, Lord,
for those who have broken fellowship with others,
those who try to go it alone,
that they might realise how much they need you, and need others too.

He bids us build each other up;
and gathered into one,
to our high calling's glorious hope
we hand in hand go on.

~ *Charles Wesley (1707–88)* ~

Uncertainty

I will tell of your name to my brothers and sisters; in the midst of the congregation I will praise you.

~ Psalm 22:22 ~

I love to tell your story, God –
proud of your power,
pleased at all your praiseworthy deeds.
I love to stand with the faithful,
remembering those of the past,
hopeful of those still to come.
I love to shout and boast of you,
contented among your people, strong and true.

But when I am alone I whisper my doubts,
I hide my disappointment that you don't seem near,
I am ashamed that the mocking and jeering about you
does bother me because it hits a nerve.

Sometimes, I cannot boast,
sometimes, I believe their scorn,
sometimes, I feel like nothing because I see nothing of you.

When I feel abandoned and when I feel triumphant
let me look ahead, God.
Let me remember moments of clarity,
and let me be
somewhere in between the sure and the shaken.   AMEN.

Prayer Activity

Often we feel God is not there. Sometimes this is because our fear, distress and anger is in front of us and we are trying to fight it, get rid of it, sort it. It stands in our way like a blockage between God and us. It can lead us to condemn ourselves, and hear other people condemning us by word or implication. Our fear, distress and anger thus grow bigger and bigger; they self-perpetuate. All we can see and feel are strong emotions. They are 'in our face'. 'Our world' becomes our emotive state. Suddenly I see God; something shifts, my perspective changes. God has turned me around, to a new horizon. Now all my emotional energy is behind me; my fear is motivating me to bring changes into my life, my anger is giving me energy and direction, my distress is helping me to stay on course, close to God.

The Emmaus Road

*As they talked and argued, Jesus himself came up and walked with
them.*

– Luke 24:15 ~

Yes, Lord, I've been there:
the day after the funeral,
when the whole world seems
to be painted in shades of muddy grey.

I've been there
when the road is long,
the steps are heavy,
and the best thing that my friends can do
is walk beside me.

I've been there:
but I see now that *you* were there,
walking by my side.
You were the unseen companion:
the one who rekindled
the Spirit's fire,
who opened the Scriptures once again,
and met me
in the breaking of the bread.

Open my eyes to see you today.
I remember all who walk the road of sorrow, that their hearts be warmed
    within them.   AMEN.

Readings

Exodus 3:1–6; Job 38:1–18; Jonah 4; John 20:24–9; Acts 9:1–19;
Revelation 22:1–5

Silence

Prayer Activity

Imagine being there at Paul's conversion. With whom do you identify in
the story? Allow your imagination to take you there and experience what is
going on. How does it make you feel? What questions arise? Through your
imagination and your curiosity, let God speak.

Defending the Faith

Always be ready to make your defence when anyone challenges you to justify the hope that is in you.

~ *1 Peter 3:15* ~

Prayer for Reflection

Thank you, Lord,
for this clear mandate to witness to you,
    wherever I am,
    whoever I'm with,
    at all times, to all people.

But this is not a licence to browbeat,
to bludgeon people into believing
    with loquacious monologues
    and an insufferable goodness.

Help me rather to treasure the Good News in my heart,
    my life, and my conversation,
that others may recognise what their hearts yearn for
    and what their lives desperately seek.

Prayer on Today's Theme

Remember, Lord,
those whose responsibility is to defend the faith,
scholars, monarchs, preachers, religious broadcasters,
who must ever find new words to touch the heart,
new styles of presentation to arrest the attention,
ever-renewed conviction to persevere in their task.

I pray for those lost for lack of a faith,
those who cling to an immature faith
    which one day will not stand the test,
those who feel on the fringes of faith
    but put off finding out more
    or who are put off by the Christians they know.

Renew your Church, Lord,
    until it unmistakably can declare
    in whom it lives and moves.

Drama

The storm was raging unabated, and our last hopes of coming through alive began to fade.

~ *Acts 27:20* ~

Prayer for Reflection

Thank you, Lord, for a Gospel
not only found in the quiet, devotional moment,
    when the mind can appreciate it at leisure,
but encountered in the dramas of life,
    when body and mind together
    grapple with tensions and troubles
    and grasp for something to hold on to.

Teaching patiently on a hillside,
listening thoughtfully in a kitchen,
praying in a garden,
    but also head to head with the Pharisees,
    in the cut and thrust of the court room,
    in the face of the shouting crowd,
    in the agony of execution,
you, Jesus, lived out the Gospel.

Be with me today
    when the hours hang heavy
    or when things are happening so fast
    that there is no time even to think.

Prayer on Today's Theme

I pray for those whose day will be full of drama,
    facing a sheriff,
    going through an operation,
    waiting for news,
    being involved in an accident,
    discussing a divorce settlement,
and all those also who wish
    something would happen to them.

Let them feel your arms around them,
    that they may not sink.

When they heard these things, they became enraged and ground their teeth at Stephen. But filled with the Holy Spirit, he gazed into heaven and saw the glory of God.

~ *Acts 7:54–5* ~

'Glorious things of thee are spoken', the ancient hymn declares,
and yet, God, terrible things have been done to those who declared your
    name.

We wrestle today with the thought of dying for our beliefs, with the idea of
    suffering for our faith, being persecuted to death.
For we are of a world that often believes nothing and that at best mocks
or has pity on those with passion and the courage of conviction.

So may we reflect now on those from the Bible who faced rage head on,
who did not back down but kept on proclaiming and who in pain, with death
    approaching,
remembered Christ, and with faith, in reverence and complete surrender to
    your cause of love, cried: 'Lord, receive my spirit, do not hold this sin
    against them.'

As we recall that group of biblical martyrs
who let their lives end for your glory to shine through,
let us learn how to stand strong and make our lives count for Christ in this
    day.
Let us pray for those who boldly go and suffer the consequences
– who do things we would never do for the gospel.
But above all, let us regain and relive the passion of Christ, love that is the
    be-all and end-all,
and glimpses of resurrection that bring life to our dead places,
colour and experience and courage behind our locked doors.

Prayer Activity

Scared? What of? Of whom? Let Jesus receive these fears and anxieties from you, and ask him what he would do.

Falling Away

You must persevere in your faith ... and never ... be dislodged from the hope offered in the gospel you accepted.

~ Colossians 1:23 ~

Prayer for Reflection

Lord, my faith is so precarious sometimes.
It doesn't need much to make me fall by the wayside:
    a pompous office bearer at church,
    something I don't agree with in the sermon,
    a discussion with an unbelieving friend,
    the death of a child,
    a natural disaster,
    things going wrong in my own life.
Is the hope of the Gospel just make-believe?

Help me to remember that,
    even when I feel estranged from God,
God has made me no longer a stranger to him
but has reconciled me in the dying and rising of
    Christ.

Prayer on Today's Theme

Thank you, Lord,
for those who in past years
have given my faith a firm foundation,
because in the midst of setback, poverty, grief,
and in the times of great rejoicing,
they became convinced above all things
that you were there with them
and would always be with those
    who would follow them
    and all who would follow us.

Holy Will

Your kingdom come. Your will be done on earth as it is in heaven.

~ Matthew 6:10 ~

Prayer for Reflection

Holy God,
when a child dies in the womb
    or lives for only an hour,
      is this your will?

When a life full of energy
    is cut down in its prime,
      is this your will?

When a nation of people
    who have worshipped your name
    is ravaged by famine
    or decimated by war,
      is this your will?

I ask, Lord,
because such questions need to be asked.
And even if, on this side of time,
no answer is evident,
I want to know that you hear my prayer.

Prayer on Today's Theme

To the watching ones, the waiting ones,
who yearn for a new day
and are prepared to work for it,
your kingdom come.

To the weary,
    those bent beneath dull routine,
    those whose horizons narrow daily,
    those who are too tired to pray,
your kingdom come.

In me, in my church,
by me, by my church,
through me, through my church,
and – if need be – despite us,
your will be done.

Bystanders ask for a Sign

'What sign can you give us, so that we may see it and believe you?'

~ John 6:30 ~

Lord Jesus, we are a difficult lot –
demanding what we perceive as rights,
measuring you by our standards,
dragging you down to our level,
refusing to budge an inch until
you have satisfied us, bowed to our will.
The miracle is we can see at all,
or hear at all because of the blindness of our eyes
and the deafness of our ears.
All around us are signs and symbols
of the wonders produced by faith and hope and love,
all around us the handiwork of a Creator's hand,
the imagination of a Creator's mind.

And in the world
wherever faith triumphs in the face of doubt,
wherever hope springs up from the ashes of despair,
wherever love breaks through the barriers of hate,
the signs are there to see.
We lack the vision that faith brings
and ask your forgiveness now.

Help us to see what you are doing each day,
a new miracle, a fresh vision
in the ordinary and everyday
and rejoice that you always have the power
and the undiminished love for us
to put these signs in our way
in the hope that one day we will see and understand,
and then believe, and follow you.   AMEN.

Readings

1 Samuel 8; Psalm 14; Ezekiel 13; Mark 6:1–6; John 6:25–36; John 20:24–9

Walking on Water

He came towards them early in the morning walking on the sea.

~ Mark 6:48 ~

God, it seems your kingdom works the wrong way round.

We scratch out order and design in this world
and call it religion
yet find you in the uncharted.

Our holiness is found in routine in well-worked-out creeds
and fine-constructed buildings
and we call it faith
yet find you in the unpredictable.

We build sanctuaries that beautify symmetry
creating a space that restrains the unfamiliar
and call it your realm
yet you are found outside the boat.

May our fear of the unexplored be tempered by your voice through the
    confusion.
May our longing for solid ground be balanced by your call amid the waves.
May our need for a boat be lessened by your presence on the water and may
    our faith be not safe
but risky
that we dare to step into the unknown and find you where adventures are
    made.

Prayer Activity

Think of an adventure, a time you were away from the normal routine. It may
have been in a place you were unfamiliar with or somewhere you know very
well, but something different happened. Stay with that adventure and reflect
on a moment when you felt God's presence. Linger there, remembering it.
Spend some time remembering and enjoying the memory. How does that help
your day? Appreciate the memory.

Faith – a Centurion's Servant Healed

I am not worthy to come under your roof, and that is why I did not presume to approach you in person.

~ Luke 7:6–7 ~

Loving God,
often when we feel you near us,
we struggle to know how to receive your presence.
We are torn between the excitement of greeting you
    and the awareness that at times we have ignored you.
We are torn between the desire to tell you our deepest needs
    and the realisation that we have shameful things to admit.
We are torn between a faith that knows you are the one to hope in;
you are holy and good,
and we believe that we are not good enough;
we do not deserve your time and care.

Father, forgive us for talking ourselves out of the gifts you try to give us.
Forgive us for listening to the view others have of us.
Forgive us for holding back because we have decided what we deserve and
    are worthy of.

But save us, God, from putting ourselves above others,
from stressing our own importance and from hiding our true selves from
    you.
May our humility be real,
may our understanding be deep,
and may our faith in you be stronger than our self-doubts.   AMEN.

Readings

Joshua 1:5–9; Luke 7:1–10; Luke 18:9–14; Romans 13:1–5

Silence

Prayer Activity

Allow your hands to 'walk' forwards, placing one after the other as if they were feet walking. Continue this 'walking' gesture and at the same time hold in your awareness any situation where it is hard for you to have faith. No words are necessary — they may come. The gesture alone is a prayer, an act of faith.

Lord's Prayer

Blessing

> May the mind of Christ my Saviour
> Live in me from day to day,
> By his love and power controlling
> All I do or say.   AMEN.

A Crowd Reaches for Healing

They ... begged him to let them simply touch the edge of his cloak ...

~ Matthew 14:35–6 ~

We marvel, Lord, at such faith.
What would it mean for us to have this faith today?
Where are the fringes of your cloak for us?
Open our eyes, dear Lord,
so that we see how to touch you:
in places which are sacred,
in the Bible,
in the lives of our brothers and sisters,
in the needs of all your creatures.
Loving Lord,
the fringes of your garment are surely found
wherever there is a touch of compassion.   AMEN.

Prayer Activity

Be aware of any place in your body that is sore or tense, any thought or situation which is troubling you. Allow the light of God to penetrate and stay focused there, doing this for several minutes if you can. Reach out and touch that light ... feel the power of light and its warm gentleness ... like the fringes of a cloak.

Blessing

Bless the faith that reaches out,
Bless the touch that comes to you,
Bless both with Christ's own purity.   AMEN.

Transformation – a Woman made Whole

Take heart, my daughter, your faith has healed you.

~ Matthew 9:22 ~

Lord God,
where do we find that will to keep going, plodding along?
How do we manage at times to muster that momentum to move forward?
Why do we feel that desperation is overcoming our hope?
When will any release come, any comfort, any acknowledgement?
In the eyes of Christ – our courage is recognised.
In the heart of Christ – our cries are understood.
In the presence of Christ – our waiting is over.
Transforming God, be with those today
who do not dare to reach for you for fear of losing the little faith they have.
Be with those who see no way out, no other options;
be with those who have tried for so long and have given up.
Be with us, Father, as we move in places
and amongst people who can be affected by our words, our presence and
    our touch,
and let us give thanks for those who transform our world daily.
Help us take stock of progress made and new ways begun,
whilst expecting the next difference you will make in our lives.   AMEN.

Readings

Isaiah 43:18–19: Matthew 9:18–26; John 9:1–9; Romans 6:1–11

Silence

Related Prayer Activity

Clap your hands, snap your fingers (not something we normally do when
praying). Repeat and notice the effect on your mind, body, emotions and
spirit. Read the prayer again and see what has changed.

Lord's Prayer

Blessing

> Gracious God:
>   may we learn to expect more,
>   may we strive to respect more,
>   may we try to reflect more
> of your life-changing love, for Jesus' sake.   AMEN.

Trust

Prayer for Ourselves

Life is full of ups and downs.
One moment I am on a high,
    the next I feel at the lowest ebb.
At times I do not understand
    what is happening to me.
The odds seem stacked against me,
    disaster only a step away,
    and I feel quite alone.

Yet I know that wherever I am
you are there too,
waiting for me to call on you,
for you are faithful above all things
and utterly to be trusted.

Prayer for Others

We pray for those who have been let down
by family and friends,
those who can no longer trust a partner or spouse,
those who feel life has dealt them a bitter blow,
those who are angry at what has happened to them.

We pray too for those
whose work it is to bridge the gap
    between families in conflict,
    between nations at war,
    between the wealthy and the dispossessed,
    between refugee and host country,
    between people and their God.

May they all know that
nothing can separate them from your love,
and that if God is on their side
there is no one left against them.

Interruptions

Hope deferred makes the heart sick.

~ *Proverbs 13:12* ~

Prayer for Reflection

Why is it that just when everything is going well
something happens
which not only causes a delay
but makes me wish I had never started?

Why is it that when our hopes and visions
    receive a setback
it doesn't just dim them for a little
– we could cope with that –
but often makes them vanish altogether?

Yet, Lord, you are the continuous line
who runs through all our experiences,
waiting out our bad moments
    till we recognise the encircling arms,
patient as we gradually jettison
      our treasured ambitions
      and embrace the Kingdom's goal.

Prayer on Today's Theme

To those whose scars and wounds
are invisible to the naked eye,
your touch, Lord.

Upon those whose hurt is deep,
who carry secrets they can hardly name,
your strength, Lord.

Among those who wander
without direction or purpose,
your company, Lord.

Loyalty

It is for loyalty to the hope of Israel that I am in these chains.

~ Acts 28:20 ~

Prayer for Reflection

Being loyal is not always an easy task.
There are times when I must be loyal
– to my family when they are giving me a hard time,
– to my friends when we cannot see eye to eye,
– to my church when it seems to be going off the rails.

There are times when loyalty seems to count for little:
in a marriage that is turning sour,
in a business that is going wrong,
in a congregation dwindling in numbers.

Your son Jesus Christ was loyal to you.
Did he not carry out his mission to the end,
even though the end was a cross?

When you look for loyalty in us, may you find it;
and may we not look for more loyalty in others than we ourselves are
willing to offer.

Prayer on Today's Theme

I pray for those
who are finding it difficult to stay loyal:
to the one with whom they once pledged love,
in a job where others do not value their work,
when their minister seems to preach
a different gospel;
those who allow selfish motives
to break the bonds of loyalty,
those who can no longer be bothered.
Deal gently with those harassed
by a conflict of loyalties;
those who find it difficult because of many pressures
to pay proper attention
to those who have claims upon them:
aged parents or relatives,

neighbours and friends,
charities and people in need.

And watch over those whose loyalty
to their people, their nation, their beliefs,
has brought them imprisonment,
banishment, or persecution.

Discovery

Taste and see that the Lord is good!
~ Psalm 34:8 ~

Prayer for Reflection

You were there, Lord,
when I took my first stumbling steps,
when I first knew what the word 'friend' really meant.

You were there, Lord,
through my first youthful encounters with grown-up love;
when I found the one
    with whom I wished to share the rest of my life,
or when I embraced life on my own;
when I discovered that human love
    brings pain as well as joy.

You were there at all these times, Lord, by my side.
And I know that you will be with me
when I find that this life is the gate
to a richer, fuller experience with you.

Prayer for Today

God,
help those growing stale and staid.
Open their eyes to see the fresh beauty of each new day.
Open their ears to hear new sounds.
Open their minds to absorb new ideas.

Keep their hearts open to experience your vitality,
    your ever fresh,
    ever-refreshing love.

Help them to know that in you there is no ending
only everlasting renewal and beginning.

Anticipation

Those who look to the Lord will win new strength.

~ Isaiah 40:31 ~

Prayer for Reflection

Life is so rich, so varied, so puzzling, Lord:
always something to look forward to,
always something just around the corner.
Where will we go on holiday?
Should we look for a bigger house?
How will I feel when those I love leave me?

Help me to put my trust in you no matter what lies ahead.
Let me constantly be aware
that tomorrow is a time I may not have,
and today is the only day that I can live.

Prayer on Today's Theme

Be with all who are fearful of the future,
Lord of eternity:
those who are anxious about health, their own or others';
those who worry about money,
and whether they have enough;
those who fear what lies ahead
and are unable to talk about it.

They can talk to you,
and you are willing to listen to them,
no matter how small, or inadequate,
or ineffectual they may feel.
After all, you care even about the sparrows!

Patience

If we hope for something we do not yet see, then we look forward to it eagerly and with patience.

~ *Romans 8:25* ~

Prayer for Reflection

Lord, some of the things we do not yet see
are the things we want most:
    a world free from hunger,
    children free from poverty,
    a church free of divisions,
    a society free from injustice.

The good future we long for
    makes demands on the present,
taxing our patience,
calling on all our powers of persuasion,
so that people become ready
    to embrace reconciliation,
    and begin to live even now
        in the light of your promises.

Give us a stout heart for a steep hill.

Prayer on Today's Theme

I pray for those who live for their vision
– of hunger eradicated,
– of an end to torture,
– of peace and health for their clients or patients,
– of sinners taking Christ into their hearts.

I pray for those who once had visions and goals,
not for themselves
    but for their fellow men and women,
but who have become discouraged,
    soured, distrustful
    after so many setbacks.
Nourish what remains,
    that they may find that the smallest spark
    can blaze in the oxygen of your love.

Catching

Out of the depths I cry to you, O Lord.

~ Psalm 130:1 ~

The sea
The most mysterious place on earth.
New plants, new creatures still being discovered,
Treasure in the deep.

Yet I resist going into my depths –
Fear keeps me from possible wonder, delight and resource.

And you, God, understand this,
And Scripture both reflects this, and challenges me –
'Do not be afraid' said so frequently
As acknowledgement and a call to freedom.
May I, like Peter, be prepared to have a go at things,
Find myself occasionally out of my depths
But remain with my commitment – willing to recognise and run to God

And also willing to reflect on such memories,
Prepared to ponder hidden depths,
Opening myself to consider such mysteries as the huge catch of fish.

Whether the waves in my life are calm or wild today
May I ride them
And know that the tide always turns ...

Readings

Luke 5:1–11   *A previous catch*
Isaiah 45:1–8   *Treasures of darkness*
1 Samuel 12:16–25   *God who teaches rather than condemning*
Psalm 38   *God come close to me when I fail*

Resurrection

Just as day was breaking, Jesus stood on the beach; yet the disciples did not know that it was Jesus.

~ *John 21:4* ~

Lord, we believe: help our unbelief.
> The disciples did not recognise you at first.

No wonder – you were the last thing they expected;
> but you made yourself known as at the beginning, by the seashore.

Lord, come to us in your risen power in the everyday:
> as day breaks to give us new life and new hope,
> in our work to give us patience and perseverance.

Lord, we believe: help our unbelief:
> seeing not as Moses did at the burning bush
> hearing not as the disciples did beside the sea yet in the here and now
>> to turn aside with the eye of faith to behold the great sight
>> to take the plunge and acclaim you 'It is the Lord' –
> God in the midst.
> God with us – great and glorious wonder.

Lord, we believe: help our unbelief.
> With all our great islands of knowledge
> there are yet longer shorelines which blind unbelief cannot scan.

Help all people to discern you – in the midst, yes;
> and on the edges and the horizons of living,
> Lord of science and of all things.

Lord, we believe: help our unbelief.
As we would venture in faith in you,
when the sands of time run out
leave us not on the beach,
but take us to the eternal shore
to see you face to face and acclaim you
the risen and glorious saviour.   AMEN.

Prayer Activity

Think of a shore – of sand … of shingle … of stones: warm and pleasant or cold and wet. Comfortable or uncomfortable – an illustration of life. Howsoever, know that the Risen Jesus stands on whatever beach – with you always.

'I am the Resurrection and the Life'

~ John 11:25 ~

Prayer for Reflection

When it comes to my end, Lord,
I do not want to fear death,
I want to embrace it
like a woman longs to embrace
the child in her womb
after a safe delivery.

So, teach me to live deeply
and love deeply,
finding a place for loss
and a purpose in loss.

And may there always be in my heart an empty space
in which I anticipate resurrection,
until that day when you deliver me
from the fulness I have known
to the fulfilment which awaits me.

Prayer on Today's Theme

Holy Spirit of God,
go gently today
among those who mourn,
especially if it has been
a sudden death,
a cruel death,
an undeserved death.

Use my prayers and the
companionship of God's people
but not to provide cheap answers
to the mystery of death.

Rather, let those who weep know
that they don't weep alone;
let those who are bewildered
have the chance to express their confusion;
and let those who have no faith
lean on someone who has.

- 'I am he ... I who am Speaking to you now' -

~ *John 4:26* ~

Prayer for Reflection

To an unsuspecting woman
during an ambiguous conversation,
you, Jesus Christ,
revealed yourself as God's Messiah.

It was not within religious buildings;
she was not studying theology;
you were not preaching.

It was a mid-day meeting, when you were thirsty
and she had time to talk to a stranger,
that the most ordinary of places
became holy ground.

I ask today, Lord,
that you meet me as the mid-day Messiah
who converts the ordinary into the special.

Prayer on Today's Theme

Where today
people look for you in the wrong place,
or in their preferred place,
widen their horizons;

where today
people avoid you
because of embarrassment with their past,
or confusion about their beliefs,
widen their horizons;

where today
people shape you in their own image,
bringing you down to size
while imagining they are exalting your name,
become a stumbling block:

we need a saviour who is bigger than our beliefs,
not smaller than our best intentions.

Abraham and Isaac

*'Take your son, your only son Isaac, whom you love, and go to the
land of Moriah, and offer him there as a burnt offering on one of the
mountains ...'*

~ *Genesis 22:2* ~

If love is a good thing, why is it tested?
If family is so sacred, why is it hard?
If parenting is precious, why is it painful?
If you, God, always provide,
Why do we sometimes feel we will lose everything?

Thinking of Isaac; innocently asking 'Where is the lamb for the sacrifice?'
We offer our prayers today for vulnerable children
In our time, naive and trusting.

Thinking of Abraham; following without question,
Acting without hesitation, strangely focused
We offer our questions, our doubts and discomfort.

Thinking of Jesus; your only son,
Given to die because you loved us so much,
Christ who asks us to follow in costly ministry –
We ask today,
What is the cost?
What are the sacrifices we are prepared to make?

Prayer Activity

Call to mind a relationship or situation where there is a lack of trust. Offer
your concerns and your questions about this to God.

Blessing

> God,
> of immeasurable love
> of family beyond convention
> of trust beyond understanding
> bless through Christ your given son.   AMEN.

River Crossing

*As soon as the priests stepped into the river, the water stopped
flowing.*

~ *Joshua 3:15–16* ~

Living God,
if we never go down into the valley
and get our feet wet as we step into the river,
then we will never know what it is to risk everything,
and trust everything to your promises.

If we never go down into the valley
and face the Jordan getting our feet wet,
then we will never know what it is to imperil our faith,
and discover, deeper still, the certainty of love.

If we never stand by the water and get our feet wet,
then we will never know what it is to place all things in your hands,
and be held completely by you.

May we step into the water and reach the other side:
into all conflict and cross towards peace;
into all hunger and cross towards the table;
into all injustice and cross towards full living.

Readings

Joshua 3:1–17	*Crossing the Jordan*
Exodus 14:22–9	*The parting of the Red Sea*
Psalm 22:1–11	*Trusting God*
Mark 6:45–52	*Calming of the storm*

Prayer Activity

Today as you journey, to work, to the shops, to visit someone, or even as
you go from room to room in your own home, consider the crossing points
– doorways, pavement edges, the change from bed to floor, bus to pavement,
steps – and pause at each. Feel God's blessing as God crosses with you.

Ruth

'Where you go, I will go; where you lodge, I will lodge; your people shall be my people, and your God my God.'

~ Ruth 1:16 ~

Lord, so many people wander the earth,
nomads, pilgrims, asylum seekers …
we also are sojourners.
Where is journey's end? –
It is where so many in the past and present
have found a stay and a support,
and a way through the wilderness of life,
the one who is a refuge and a help.

To whom shall we go?
We turn to you, the God of Abraham, Isaac, and Jacob, the God and Father
    of Jesus Christ and our Father.
Help us make our way towards Christ –
Christ who had nowhere to lay his head but a cross,
Christ of the welcoming open arms,
Christ in whom countless seekers have found joy and peace,
Christ the Way who can lead us on to our eternal home.

Lord, we thank you for all who have come to you
        for your ancient people recognising Jesus as the Christ,
        for those of every generation who have followed him,
        for those coming from other lands and cultures
            who have, like Ruth, said,
        'Your people shall be my people and your God my God'.

O God and Father of all, remind us of the lonely and lost,
of those who flee from tyranny and oppression,
whether in distant lands or our own land.
Help us to be kindly, neighbourly and welcoming,
showing something of the concern and love of Christ.   AMEN.

Ruth and Naomi

So the two of them went on until they came to Bethlehem. When they
came to Bethlehem, the whole town was stirred because of them.

~ Ruth 1:19 ~

God, today we remember that
In a time when women only had status through men,
In a land where journeys were always long and tiring
And in circumstances that were risky and unconventional
Ruth clung to Naomi in loyal love.

And with the gleaning of a harvest,
And the reciprocated concern of Naomi,
A new bond was made and a new family begun.

So now we affirm families of our time:
For those bound by action not blood,
For those not recognised by some but admired by others,
For those trying to fit and live up to expectations,
For those journeying through tragedy gleaning something of a future.

Loving God,
By the telling of the story of Ruth and Naomi,
Teach us whom we should stand beside and cling to with devotion.
May all the bonds of love you forge in us be strengthened,
For this is your unexpected,
unconventional,
unconditional way that stirs us and moves the world.

Prayer Activity

There was of course another 'Bethlehem story' – read the Christmas story and
consider the people and the family there, reflecting on the unconventional and
unconditional aspects you recognise and relate to.

Blessing

May the God of Ruth and Naomi
bind us together with ties of love and loyalty
and may the peace of Christ unite us in hope and joy.   AMEN.

Joseph (husband of Mary)

*'Joseph, son of David, do not be afraid to take Mary as your wife, for
the child conceived in her is from the Holy Spirit.'*

~ *Matthew 1:20* ~

Lord, Joseph is portrayed as marginal to the gospel, with only scattered
   references.
However, within this limitation, we do know that he was of royal descent,
a son of David, born in David's city – Bethlehem – a carpenter to trade.

What sort of person was Joseph?
A conscientious Jew that kept ordinances and feasts?
We know he was good and kind;
learning the truth behind Mary's pregnancy,
he took her with him to Bethlehem, away from the slanders of neighbours.

Joseph must have taken Jesus to his heart, and was identified as his 'father'.
After the visit to the Temple when Jesus was twelve, we hear little more of
   Joseph.
Did Joseph feel marginalised and insignificant?
Or did genuine piety reconcile him to your divine will,
with a sense of wonderland peace?
Just like Mary!
Was he much older than Mary?
Did he die at 111 years of age,
when Jesus was only 18 years as tradition holds?
Whatever the truth, help us to learn from Joseph's life.   AMEN.

Prayer Activity

Think of times when you have felt undervalued, at work, in the family or in
the church. Picture Jesus coming to you with reassurance of your worth as a
human being, a child of God, one of his own loved ones.

Zacchaeus

'Look, half of my possessions, Lord, I will give to the poor; and if I have defrauded anyone of anything, I will pay back four times as much.'

~ *Luke 19:8* ~

Jesus, you said,
'Salvation has come to this house today' when Zacchaeus turned his life
  around. When we think of that story, so well known from Sunday School
  days,
it all seems simple and possible.

But it's not.

Sometimes, if we're brave and honest,
we know what it would mean, in real terms,
to make amends – not just to say sorry,
but to back it up with life-changing action.

Jesus, if you came to our house now,
what would you say?
For our part, we would be worried about the mess, what we had in for a
  meal,
how to show hospitality.
But you, Jesus,
you would want to spend the time helping us realise the kind of people we
  have been –
deceitful, greedy, selfish and unfair –
not because there would be anything we could do
to make it up to you,
but because you want us to put our house in order
that we might experience life in all its fullness.

With the fresh start you offer to us now,
help us find ways to turn things around
for ourselves, for others, for good.   AMEN.

Prayer Activity

As you clean or tidy anything at home today, think of some of the things that
worry or trouble you, clear the clutter, asking God to open new ways to begin
positive behaviour in your work, your leisure and in your relationships.

Stephen and Saul

...and the witnesses laid their coats at the feet of a young man named Saul.

~ Acts 7:58 ~

God,
even if I do not always find myself the bearer of eloquent words
that speak out clearly for the sake of justice,
and even if I never find myself
at the front of protest marches in the name of peace,
may you never find me holding the coats.

Even if I cannot shout as loud as my neighbour
in the ears of those who need to know the truth,
and even if I cannot always be singing in protest
for your sake and in the name of your love,
may you never find me holding the coats.

Even if I do not always speak out
on behalf of those who have been silenced by the powerful,
and even if I do always have the words to say
to those who wait to hear,
may you never find me holding the coats.

Instead, if I do not find myself on the frontline like this,
may I encourage with my blessing,
strengthen with my prayers,
nourish hope with my faith,
and hold with my love,
those who do.

Prayer Activity

Spend some time today searching through the paper or Internet for just one story of someone involved in non-violent protest. Read their story and pray for them and for those who gather round them in support and witness.

Blessing

Listen for the rejoicing of heaven, each time a word of love is spoken.
Listen for the encouragement of heaven, each time a throat is cleared.
Listen for the blessing of heaven, each time the kingdom is made known.

Barnabas

*When he came and saw the grace of God, he rejoiced, and he exhorted
them all to remain faithful to the Lord with steadfast devotion.*

~ *Acts 11:23* ~

Holy Spirit,
you are companion on the road, our confidante,
nudging us toward right decisions, our conscience and guide.

Spirit of God,
you are the one who gives comfort in sad times, inspiration in bleak times,
nourishment in times of deprivation.
So we thank you with all our hearts today,
and confess our need of you
to transform us and redirect us.

Loving God,
enable the fruit of your Spirit to be seen in us today.
Where there is turmoil,
may we bring peace and resolution;
where there is grief and disillusionment,
may we bring vision and hope;
and where there is lack of faith and when confidence is shaken,
may we be like Barnabas,
accompanying on the road,
encouraging and explaining,
giving the incentive to travel on.   AMEN.

Prayer Activity

If you think of a negative comment or insult as a slap or blow, then a
compliment or word of encouragement can feel like a pat on the back or
affectionate touch. As you meet and communicate with people today, practise
positive, affirming gestures and comments and notice the effect this has on
you, and them.

Our Life and Work

Rhythm

The heavens are telling the glory of God; and the firmament proclaims his handiwork.

~ *Psalm 19:1* ~

Your world proclaims you, O Lord:
in the unique fragile lace of a snowflake,
in the solidity of an oak tree,
in the vastness of the star fields,
in the rhythmic dance of the universe:

in pattern,
in order,
in symmetry.

Your song is chanted,
your praise is sung,
your glory is proclaimed.

In the lives of all who heed your Word,
in the labours of all who are shaped by your call,
in the actions of all who seek your Way:

there is a like pattern,
a recognisable order,
a familiar symmetry.

In small deeds,
in words of hope
in quiet ways:

your song is chanted,
your praise is sung,
your glory is proclaimed.

May this be true of my life today.   AMEN.

Prayer Activity

The rhythm of day and night, night and day, sunrise and sunset: this rhythm gives us life. Choose a verse from Psalm 19, or a favourite chorus, and repeat it several times during the day. Ask God to help you develop a rhythm that works for you, before meals, or every hour, or sunrise or sunset.

Who am I?

What are human beings that you are mindful of them, mortals that you care for them?

~ Psalm 8:4 ~

Lord, the universe is so vast!
As I think of distant galaxies
and the unfathomable reaches of deep space, like the writer, I feel so small.
Who am I amidst such immensity? What matter my hopes and fears?
What matter my joys and sorrows?
Am I any more than a drop of water in a vast ocean?
Am I any more than a tiny spark, glowing for an instant and then gone?

And yet, you tell me another story, of a Christ whose cry of victory
echoes to the furthest galaxy,
and of a cross in which atoms and distant worlds are held together.
This is your universe:
not infinite corridors of emptiness,
not endless tracts of void,
but the cathedral of your glory, pulsing with the vitality of your presence.

Who am I?
I am yours, called to reflect your glory.
What I do today, what I say today
will echo for good or ill beyond time into eternity.   AMEN.

Readings

Genesis 1:1–5; Job 38:1–7; Psalm 8; Romans 8:18–25; Colossians 1:15–21

Silence

Prayer Activity

Imagine yourself up in the sky looking down. Allow a sense of expansiveness, letting your imagination take you to the heavens. Enjoy it. Notice how small everything is on earth. What happens when you change perspective like this? Do you feel amazed, are you scared, do you laugh at how seriously we take ourselves? Do you notice? Talk to God about it. Come back in your imagination, and from within yourself look out at the world, allow things to come back to their normal size. What attracts your attention? Pray about it and listen for God's response.

Myself

I heard the sound of you in the garden, and I was afraid because I was naked; and I hid myself.

~ Genesis 3:10 ~

Prayer for Ourselves

How often do I find myself
hiding the real me
behind my own stubborn pride at home,
behind a display of competence at work,
behind a facade of respectability in church?

Lord,
why am I so afraid of being vulnerable,
or making a mistake,
ashamed to show that I am not perfect?
Grant me the humility to admit that I am created in your image,
     fearfully and wonderfully made,
that within me is sown the seed of your compassion,
          your spirit,
          your truth.

Teach me to love myself,
as you love me,
and then I can come out of hiding.

Prayer for Others

Creator God,
I pray for those who cannot love themselves.
Open the way of hope
to those who live in fearful and abusive circumstances.
Open the door of forgiveness,
to those who are ashamed of their past.
Turn your face
towards those who cannot raise their heads,
who have been stripped of dignity and power
through imprisonment, disability, abuse, prejudice;
those who have nothing to hide,
because they feel they have nothing left.

Lord Jesus Christ, who hung naked on the cross,
clothe them all in your mercy and love
and be their salvation.

Being Real

O Lord, you have searched me and known me.

~ Psalm 139:1 ~

I wonder, Lord, how many people know me?
How many people know me, the real me?
I am so good at acting – expert wearer of masks, talented adopter of roles:
the smile that hides my anger,
the laughter that camouflages my pain, the confident voice that veils my
    fear.
Only you know me as I am.
Nothing at all is hidden from you: the tangle of hopes and fears,
the tension of good and evil, the struggle of darkness and light.
You know me through and through,
you know what I have been,
you know what I am,
you know all that I can become.
Lord, help me to be real today,
to lay aside my masks,
to give up my acting routine.
to grow towards the authentic 'me',
to fullness of humanity in Jesus.   AMEN.

Readings

Exodus 33:7–11; Psalm 139; Jeremiah 1:4–10; Hosea 6:1–3; John 17:1–5;
Romans 8:18–27

Silence

Prayer Activity

As we come to God we let down the masks we normally need to deal with
aspects of everyday living. Ask God to help you to get to know yourself
better, your depths. Can you let God into those memories and corners where
you are ashamed or confused or in a rage? Can you voice that bit of venom
as at the end of Psalm 139? For us, like the writer, it often takes some time
before we can unmask the more distasteful bits of ourselves. These are often
initially cast outwards, blaming other people. Can you let God examine who
you are, without trying to sort yourself out? With God's help, offer yourself
God's compassion. Not being able to receive God's unconditional love can
result in self-condemnation, which perpetuates rather than heals, which
becomes repetitive, even addictive, rather than breaking through into new
possibility and new birth.

Talents and Abilities

For it is as if a man, going on a journey, summoned his slaves and entrusted his property to them; to one he gave five talents, to another two, to another one, to each according to his ability. Then he went away.

~ Matthew 25:14–15 ~

Lord, where was I when you gave out the talents?
It sometimes feels that I have no talents at all,
that I am not worthy to have even one talent.
Lord, have mercy on me.

I live in a world that praises talented people,
that raises them up and puts them on a pedestal;
often they forget that their talent is a gift from you.
Lord, have mercy on them.

We crave to be talented and to have great abilities.
Children long to be the next Beckham or Madonna.
Adults hanker after success and the fame it brings.
Lord, have mercy on us.

Lord, give us talents and abilities that we can use for others,
the ability to love our neighbour unconditionally,
the talents to care for our neighbours' needs.
Lord, have mercy on us. AMEN.

Readings

Exodus 35	*Sabbath regulations*
Deuteronomy 8	*People are given the land*
Matthew 25:14–30	*Parable of the talents*
2 Corinthians 1:3–11	*Paul gives thanks to God*

Prayer Activity

We all have talents and abilities, some we are aware of and some we use often. Sit quietly for a few moments and think of a time when you used a talent or ability that you may not have been aware of, and ask God to help you develop and use it.

Mephibosheth

Saul's son Jonathan had a son who was crippled in his feet. He was five years old when news about Saul and Jonathan came from Jezreel. His nurse picked him up and fled; and, in her haste to flee, it happened that he fell and became lame. His name was Mephibosheth.

~ 2 Samuel 4:4 ~

Lord, Mephibosheth's life speaks to me of brokenness and grace,
like that of children without limbs who are victims of land mines –
innocent victims of war, like Mephibosheth.

Thank you, God, for the grace we see in the heart of David,
when he seeks out the descendants-of Saul,
not to destroy the remnants of in enemy but to show kindness.

And for Mephibosheth to dine daily at King David's table was surely an end
to a life of shame,
and the beginning of self esteem, no longer a nobody but an honoured guest.

Deliver, O Lord, those who live with shame, often with deep roots in
childhood.
We thank you for the progress that has been made in overcoming the shame
that some people wrongly attach to mental illness, or AIDS or cancer.
Help us to learn the lesson of David's forgiving, generous and gracious
heart, and so free and empower every Mephibosheth.

Prayer Activity

As an intercessory prayer, turn to 1 Peter 2:6 and repeat to yourself the words, 'Whoever believes in him will not be ashamed'. Meditate on these words and think of anyone you know who is carrying a burden of shame. Imagine Jesus going to that person and taking the burden from them.

The Ford at Jabbok

The same night Jacob got up ... and crossed the ford at Jabbok.

~ Genesis 32:22 ~

It was a simple stream, Lord,
but surely also a symbol
of a deep ravine in Jacob's soul.

Jacob, the 'twister', was coming home on a journey of self-knowledge.
Reconciliation with the estranged Esau inspires both fear and hope.
The past is meeting the present, giving birth to the future.

Who is the wrestler?
Nameless with power to bless.
A stranger in the dark night, strong with power to wound, an imparter of
    wholeness.
The man said, *'You shall no longer be called Jacob but Israel,*
for you have striven with God and humans and have prevailed.'

Help us, Lord, to face our fears, bring us to new life through our wounds.
Take us over our personal Jabbok, even in fear and trembling.
Lead us to the blessedness of Peniel,
face to face with your living presence.   AMEN.

Prayer Activity

Reflect on some examples of woundedness giving life, for example the art of
grafting in horticulture, or the planting of 'slips' cut from trees for growing
hedges. Reflect on how these symbols are wounds that lead to life.

Blessing

> The God of power overshadow you.
> The God of might be in you.
> The God of strength preserve you.   AMEN.

Jacob's Well

Where do you get that living water?

~ John 4:11b ~

Lord of the living water,
images tumbling through history,
water that connects me with people of every age and nation and continent,

and with you,
Fountain of Life, well of depth, water that is still and moving,
moving and still.

Move me and still me, still me and move me,
that I may be part of the flow of your love, ever old and ever new.

Sparkling, recharging, refreshing, cleansing,
deepening, bringing clarity,
take me deeper into your living water.
Take me to the springs where your love wells up ...

Prayer Activity

As you breathe in, imagine a spring of water welling up within you, up and out the crown of your head, and as you breathe out, imagine this fountain of water cascading around your body. If you open your mouth as you breathe out, it can help to give the felt sense of water rushing around you.
Choose to do this for five or six breaths or for a few minutes.

Exasperation

He loved to curse; let curses come on him.
He did not like blessing – may it be far from him.

~ Psalm 109:17 ~

O God,
sometimes I get fed up with being nice;
I can't take any more 'churchiness' and tea and biscuits.
Sometimes I wonder
why people adopt a whole way of being
when they speak of you and to you?
Why do we leave our anger and frustration
and disgust and distaste at the door ready to pick up on our way out?
People have made a fool of me, cheated me out of what is mine,
judged me when their behaviour was much worse,
taken advantage of my forgiveness and walked all over me.
God, I wonder what you think about all that,
what you would have to say to that.

O yes – I turn the other cheek.
'Love your enemies' –
but sometimes, God,
I want to be real and say that swear word,
hit back, hate my enemy
because there's a reason why they are my enemy in the first place!

Sometimes I think revenge would be really good; release, compensation.
But what would make up for my pain, my distress, my humiliation?
What payback would be good enough?
Revenge – I'll leave it in your hands, God.
Make it good,
but don't make it too bad,
for there may be some people who don't like me!   AMEN.

Readings
Psalm 109; Job 3:1–26; Matthew 18:21–35; Luke 23:26–43

Silence

The Lord's Prayer

Blessing

Let the real love of God
enable you to be real,
to be honest, to be loving
to yourself and to others this day and always.   AMEN.

Guilt

For I know my transgressions, and my sin is ever before me.

~ Psalm 51:3 ~

God,
I carry the shame of mistakes,
I feel the dirt from the path I have chosen,
I see the lies I have used to hide behind.
I have been untrue to myself,
I have been unfair to others
but, Lord,
I cannot live in your sight this way.

In my fear and guilt, there is yet hope,
In my very despair and sadness
the way through is there.
You know my heart, o God,
and my desire to change.

Let me live without burden,
let me stand without shame,
let me experience the goodness I've glimpsed.   AMEN.

Prayer Activity

'Wash away my guilt ...' Hold in your mind something you feel guilty about
and imagine water washing over you and the guilt dissolving, washing away.
Do this for several minutes. 'Create in me a pure heart.' Find your own words
to express this prayer. Put your hands over your heart and know that you are
loved by God.

Blessing

God, get us back on our feet again,
let us walk in the way we used to know,
let us see the things we've missed before,
and wonder again at you.   AMEN.

When they call, I shall answer; I shall be with them in time of trouble.

~ Psalm 91:15 ~

Prayer for Reflection

It is when I am ill, that I call to you Lord,
to heal my body.
When I am well, I call on you less
to guard my health.

Forgive me
if I have taken for granted
your concern for my well-being.
Forgive me
if I have imagined
that Christians should never get ill.
Forgive me
if I have not cared for my body
as though it were the temple of the Lord;
and whatever the state of my mind or body,
let my spirit rejoice in your salvation.

Prayer on Today's Theme

On those who suffer
and wonder when there will be an end to pain
    ... have mercy, Lord.
On those who wait for an operation
or fear to discover the results of recent tests
        ... have mercy, Lord.
On those who have no peace of mind,
who seem to walk in ever narrowing circles
        ... have mercy, Lord.
On those who are avoided
because of the nature of their illness
        ... have mercy, Lord.

Guide the hands and the intelligence
    of those who heal;
prosper the work and research
    of those who seek new or better cures;
preserve the patience and skill
    of those who nurse and care;
and inform the minds
    of those who manage the nation's health.

Watch now, dear Lord,
with those who watch or weep tonight,
and give your angels charge over those who sleep.
Tend your sick ones, O Lord Christ,
rest your weary ones,
soothe your suffering ones,
pity your afflicted ones,
shield your joyous ones,
all for your love's sake.

~ *St Augustine* ~

Thoughtless words can wound as deeply as any sword, but wisely spoken words can heal.

~ Proverbs 12:18 ~

Prayer for Reflection

When I stop to think
of the power of speech,
it worries me, Lord.

Off-the-cuff remarks,
tongues dripping with honey,
judgemental silence,
grudged words of faint praise,
smug put-downs ...

... these can all come from the same mouth,
and sometimes that mouth is mine.

God help me to be as thoughtful with my speech
as Jesus was with his,
and, like him, to use my voice
for those people and causes
about which others are silent.

Prayer on Today's Theme

Be present, Lord,
to those who even today
hurt from cruel criticism made years ago.

Be present
to those who know that ending their silence
would help someone else be happy.

Be present
to those who today are expected to say a word
which may alter the course of one human's history.

In solidarity
and bringing strength and sensitivity,
be present, Lord.

Pigs and Pearls

Do not give dogs what is holy; do not throw your pearls to the pigs.

~ Matthew 7:6 ~

Prayer for Reflection

Here is a paradox, God.

You send your only son
into the world
to live at risk,
and to be handed over
to those who cared little for his words,
and less for his safety.

And yet you ask me
to take care of what is precious.

Do you request this
because I am not Jesus?

Or is it because the faith I have
was bought at a price,
and deserves to be honoured
with nothing less than everything?

Prayer on Today's Theme

Give to me and to all Christians, Lord,
that sensitivity, so evident in Jesus,
that we might know
what is the right word
      and when to say it;
what is the right action
      and how to do it;
so that the Gospel will not be misrepresented
      either by careless word
      or senseless action,
or Christ be ever short-changed
      by our thoughtlessness.

Grant this to me, your servant: Let me live so that I may keep your word.

~ Psalm 119:17 ~

Prayer for Reflection

God of all life,
in you is novelty and everlastingness, lavishness and simplicity.

In me, aware of the needs of humanity
    and of the limitations of the earth,
there is confusion over what to buy,
        what to preserve,
        what to destroy,
        and how to be a good steward
        of your resources.

Because good works alone do not lead to salvation,
make me open to the prompting of your Holy Spirit.
Then may I live wisely and well.

Prayer on Today's Theme

Save us, Lord,
    from the temptation to buy what we do not need;
    from confusing what we need with what we want;
    from wasting what we do not own,
    from owning what we will never use;
    from idealising the past as a golden age;
    from bequeathing our children a sorry inheritance.

Strengthen the arm and the will
    of all who, for the good of the world you made and love,
    challenge our greed
    and inform us about appropriate living.
    May their words gain a good hearing
    so that the world may have a good future.

Dorcas

Peter put all of them outside, and then he knelt down and prayed. He turned to the body and said, 'Tabitha, get up.' Then she opened her eyes, and seeing Peter, she sat up.

~ Acts 9:40 ~

Loving God,
Maker of heaven and earth,
you gave each one of us gifts;
gifts to help,
gifts to heal,
gifts to make,
gifts to teach.

Lord show us our gifts.
Give us strength and courage
to use these gifts
so that we too may help people
just as your other disciples did and do.

Even though our gifts
may seem small and insignificant
we know that you can use them
for greater things.

Lord, you brought life from death;
let us go forth in faith and trust
that your will be done –
even in us.

Prayer Activity

Everyone has gifts; some of us are more aware of them than others. God gave us all gifts that he meant us to use for ourselves and for others. Take time and think of one of your gifts. Now think about how you can use that gift today.

Beginnings

In the beginning the Word already was. The Word was in God's presence, and what God was, the Word was.

~ John 1:1 ~

Prayer for Reflection

O Lord of all creation,
you were with me from my very beginning.
You knew me before my parents did.
I have no memory of my birth,
but you knew me,
and loved me from the moment of my conception.

Help me not to forget that you are with me and for me at all new
   beginnings;
each new day,
each fresh challenge,
each new joy or sorrow.
I need fear nothing.
You are always there.

Prayer on Today's Theme

Where a baby is being born,
God be with the mother and father
as they welcome the gift of a new human being
and wonder what the future will bring.
Strengthen mothers who experience childbirth alone and unsupported.
Let them feel you near them.
Give courage and enthusiasm
to all this day who face a new start:
     young people in a new job,
     older men and women facing retirement,
     those moving house,
     all who are entering new relationships
     or breaking new ground.

Lord Jesus,
share their joy, calm their fears,
help them to remember how they are caught up
in the mystery of your birth.
Emmanuel! God with us!

Birth

You it is who fashioned my inward parts: you knitted me together in my mother's womb.

~ Psalm 139:13 ~

Prayer for Reflection

I praise you, God,
for my parents,
for my birth,
for those who first cradled me,
and for my name, given on earth,
      recorded in heaven.

I thank you for the mystery
of my life
and of every life.
We are made in your image,
stamped with your uniqueness,
companioned by your Son,
strengthened by your Spirit.

Thank you, God, for being God,
and for making me, me.

Prayer on Today's Theme

Today, Lord,
I remember those into whose lives
a child is soon to come.
Theirs is a waiting time of tiredness,
      apprehension,
      hopefulness.
May it end in joy
and in the cherishing of a wanted child,
especially should the baby enter life
incapacitated in any way.

And I remember those who fear they cannot have children
and in whose lives yearning and disappointment run deep.
May they never see themselves as inadequate
or be demeaned by the wrong kind of pity.
Rather, where there is no fruit of the womb,
may the fruit of the Spirit abound in plenty.

'I am the Alpha and the Omega'

~ Revelation 1:8 ~

Prayer for Reflection

You knew me
before I was born.
You shaped me
in my mother's womb,
and you saw me there,
growing in secret.
You called me into the world
and will call me out of it
to an even finer place.
Bless you, God.
Bless you.

Prayer for Today

God be present
in homes where a baby
is expected.

Be present to calm anxieties,
    to ensure sensible gifts
    are made and bought,
    to quicken love,
    to bond – albeit unseen – parent and child.

God grant a safe delivery,
    a healthy child,
    a happy family,
    a faith deepened by the miracle of life.

Children (1)

You are my hope. Lord God, my trust from childhood.

~ Psalm 71:5 ~

Prayer for Reflection

Lord Jesus, when you took a child
and told adults to become like her
if they wanted to enter your kingdom,
what did you mean?

Are we to be naive
    or to ask questions?
to be innocent or to be trusting?
to be shy or to sing?
to be docile or to be open-eyed?

Show me how to become
not the ideal child I imagine
but the real child you blessed.

Teach me, if I have done too much growing up,
how to grow down.

Prayer on Today's Theme

Your blessing, God,
on the children who play in the streets,
    who pass me on their way from school,
    who remind me of how I once was
    and who, even today, shape the face of tomorrow.

Your blessing, God,
on the children who have no sense of family,
    who are offered a DVD instead of conversation,
        a lollipop instead of love,
    and on those who suffer pain or loss
        enough to agonise an adult.

Gather them all to yourself
like a hen gathers her chickens,
and use your Church to be your wings.

And he took them up in his arms, laid his hands on them, and blessed them.

~ Mark 10:16 ~

O God our Father, after whom all fatherhood is named,
and in whose heart is the love of a mother,
we give thanks for children –
> for the pleasure in begetting them,
> for the joy in their safe delivery,
> for their trusting expectant nature,
> for the delight they so often bring.

O God the Son, who came as a little child,
we give thanks for your example and teaching –
> taking children into your arms,
> putting a child right in the centre,
> warning us against harming a little one,
> telling us in them of our need for humble trust.

O God the Spirit, by whom Mary conceived,
we thank you for your continuous activity –
> encouraging parents to love and care,
> teaching those who would teach,
> leading those who would lead,
> inspiring all concerned for the young.

O God, Father, Son, and Holy Spirit, bless all children everywhere.   AMEN.

Readings

Isaiah 9:6–7	*To us a child is born*
Zechariah 8:1–8	*A vision of the New Jerusalem*
Luke 2:1–7	*The birth of Jesus Christ*
Mark 10:13–16	*Jesus blesses little children*
Matthew 18:1–6	*On humility and not harming children*
Matthew 21:14–17	*The children's praise in the Temple*

Prayer Activity

Think back to your own childhood. Remember adults who were kind and supportive to you. Think of one or two children you know now: your own, some in your street, some you know and meet. How might you show you care about them? Give them perhaps some of your time or a word of encouragement or a smile?

Jesus and Children

*Truly I tell you, whoever does not receive the kingdom of God as a
little child will never enter it.*

~ *Mark 10:15* ~

Jesus,
children ran towards you and you welcomed them with open arms
reprimanding those who wished to keep them under control.

We have lived as children,
and have grown up leaving behind something of the
trust,
enthusiasm,
vulnerability,
curiosity,
imagination,
openness,
acceptance,
the playfulness of childhood.

We too often reprimand children,
'They don't behave.' 'They're too noisy.'
And yet we want children to be present –
'They are the church of tomorrow!'

Jesus, you call children to be part of the church
not because they are church of tomorrow, but
because the Holy Spirit speaks through them today
because they remind us of the essence of our humanity
because they invite us to become again the child we once knew
because we need to be like them
trusting,
enthusiastic,
curious,
imaginative,
open
accepting and playful
to enter into the kingdom of heaven.

Child Rearing (1)

Would any of you offer your child a stone when he asks for bread, or a snake when she asks for a fish?

~ Matthew 7:9–10 ~

Prayer for Reflection

The answer is No, Lord.

I would like to think
that I would be the kind of parent
who gave good gifts,
> thoughtful gifts,
> appropriate gifts.

I would like to think
that I would never abuse a child's trust.

But spoil a child?
Give him a banquet
when all he needs is a sandwich;
give her a toy shop
when all she needs us a doll?

May I who never intend
to abuse a child's trust
never be guilty
of spoiling the child's appetite.

Prayer on Today's Theme

With deep gratitude, let me remember with you, Lord,
those who, in my childhood,
gave me the best gifts ...
... those who let me appreciate honesty,
> those who let me feel belonging,
> those who identified my hidden talents,
> those who rubbed my knees when I fell
> > and dried my tears when I cried;
> those who made me want to sing 'Jesus loves me'
> > because those words so clearly
> > rang true for them.

If a child lives with security,
    she learns faith;
if a child lives with approval,
    he learns to like himself.
If children live with acceptance and friendship
    they learn to give love to the world.

~ author unknown ~

Teach a child how he should live, and he will remember it all his life.

~ Proverbs 22:6 ~

Prayer for Reflection

You laid an awesome responsibility on us, Lord, when you gave us children.

They trust quickly,
they try to please,
they ask a thousand questions.

They are too easy to cheat, to misinform, to betray.

Help me to respect children,
to offer them more than empty pleasures,
to know when to say 'no' firmly,
to remember that televisions and computers
have 'off' switches,
and that children need relationships
more than novelties.

Prayer on Today's Theme

Bless today, Lord,
all teachers of the young,
that their interest and instruction
may reflect your perfect example.

Bless all parents
that they may cherish their children wisely,
and live to see their care appreciated.

Bless all grandparents,
and let them find an advantage in their years.

And help us all to identify in children
the characteristics of your kingdom,
that we might learn from them and enter it.

Generations

Lord, you have been our dwelling place in all generations. Before the mountains were brought forth, or ever you had formed the earth and the world, from everlasting to everlastng you are God.

~ Psalm 90:1–2 ~

Help me, Lord, to hear these words as a promise.
We spend so much time and energy
being anxious about the Church's future.

You are the God of each generation.
I will write it out in LARGE LETTERS
and pin it up where I can glance at it, a constant reminder.

> *The days of our life are seventy years,*
> *or perhaps eighty, if we are strong;*
> *even then their span is only toil and trouble;*
> *they are soon gone, and we fly away.*

Help me, Lord, to hear these words not as pessimistic, but as realistic;
a mirror that reflects our mortality and dependence.
This prayer of Moses ascribes life, death, everything to your sovereign
   power.
Who can argue?
Our coming and going are boundaries that seem so arbitrary to human
   reason.
Love is the solace of this interim life.

> *Satisfy, us in the morning with your steadfast love,*
> *so that we may rejoice and be glad all our days.*

Readings

Psalm 90; Matthew 6:25–34; Matthew 18:3; 2 Timothy 1:3–5

Prayer Activity

Allow a memory of someone in your family or someone special to you, past or present, to surface. Reflect on what you value in them. What do they mirror in your own life? How have they helped you live? What light, what wisdom, what aspect of God do they shine into your heart? Treasure that in some way.

Co-education

People learn from one another just as iron sharpens iron.

~ Proverbs 27:17 ~

Prayer for Reflection

In this,
I take after my mother _____ ;
and in this,
I take after my father _____ ;
and for this,
I'll always bless my grandparents _____ ;
and when I remember who was around
when I began to work,
I realise what I took from them then _____ ;

Yes, people do learn from one another.
I just hope to God
that what others pick up from me
will point to my greatest teacher.

Prayer on Today's Theme

May the day come soon, Lord,
when our nation will learn from others it once colonised;
when our church will learn from other churches it once founded;
when I will learn from those I tend to patronise.

And if such a turnaround seems impossible,
sing to me Mary's song
about the way you intend things to be ordered.

Maturity

Train children in the right way, and when old, they will not stray.

~ Proverbs 22:6 ~

Prayer for Reflection

I do not always behave as a mature adult, Lord.
Often I act like a spoilt child,
insisting on my own way,
riding roughshod over the thoughts and feelings of others.

Sometimes I take the services of others for granted.
I am not always gracious to those who serve me,
in shops, on buses,
wherever I need the help of other people.

Help me to be child-like, never childish.
Let me never forget that you said
we must become as little children to enter your Kingdom.

Prayer on Today's Theme

Lord,
be with all who are struggling to be grown-up;
    the adolescent
    coping with bewildering physical changes
    and the complicated demands
    of approaching adulthood,
    those who have suffered the loss of a parent,
    the newly committed and the newly married.

When we feel small and immature,
help us to turn to you,
the Father and Mother of us all.

Relating

You must love your neighbour as yourself.

~ Leviticus 19:18 ~

Prayer for Reflection

I don't always love my neighbour, Lord.
Yet I know I have to work with colleagues,
                live with neighbours,
                thole my family.
Give me grace
to get on with the task of loving them as well.

I don't always love myself, Lord.
Yet I know you love me and accept me, warts and all.
Give me grace to get on with the task of loving myself as you love me.

Prayer on Today's Theme

Lord,
you teach us to love our neighbour as ourselves.
Show us the way to love your people.
Some of them can be hard to love
    (and that goes for me too)
but they are all your brothers and sisters:
    rich or poor, black or white, near or far,
    Christian or non-Christian.

Before we criticise others,
help us to remember
what it feels like to be criticised.
Before we find fault with others,
help us to remember
what it feels like to be found fault with.
Before we condemn others, help us to remember
what it feels like to be condemned.
Help us at all times to be like Jesus,
who went about doing good;
who was among us as one who serves;
who, even on the cross,
prayed that his enemies should be forgiven.

~ William Barclay ~

Emmaus and Strangers

When he was at table with them, he took bread, blessed and broke it,
and gave it to them. Then their eyes were opened, and they recognised
him; ...

~ *Luke 24:30–1* ~

May we gather round the table as strangers,
yet, in the sharing of bread,
discover we are sisters and brothers.

May we look into the eyes of travellers as strangers,
yet, in the sharing of a word,
discover we are companions on the road.

May we hear the confusion of journeyers as strangers,
yet, in the sharing of questions,
discover we are adventurers on the way.

Jesus, who meets us in the guise of stranger,
whose face is glimpsed in breaking open hospitality,
create among us countless meeting places:
in setting of table, in opening of doors, in sharing of food,
in offering greetings that we meet you in every stranger,
and in this sharing of Gospel,
discover our own place in the family of God.

Prayer Activity

Place an empty chair in front of you. Imagine it is Jesus sitting there. What do
you want to ask him? And what does he say?

Blessing

May eating together always make more sense than fighting,
may sharing what we have always make more sense than taking,
may asking our questions always make more sense than shouting our
    certainties,
and may breaking bread together always make more sense than division.

Community

Now the whole group of those who believed were of one heart and soul, and no one claimed private ownership of any possessions, but everything they owned was held in common ... There was not a needy person among them ...

~ Acts 4:32, 34 ~

Gracious God,
through Father, Son and Holy Spirit you demonstrate relationship,
in your creation – you display harmony and union,
in Christ – you nurture love and human connection,
in the Holy Spirit – you move us towards each other.

But our actions demonstrate: 'look out for number one', 'do your own
thing', 'every man for himself'.
God, so many things move us away from each other, into ourselves alone.
Life is often so self-gratifying, communication is often so faceless and
nameless, relationships often a source of stress and grief.

And so we eat alone, we keep our feelings to ourselves, we watch others
suffer and do nothing.

Loving God, direct us in our being together today.
Christ, forgive us and remind us of love's worth.
Holy Spirit, open our eyes to see beyond ourselves.

Readings

Numbers 11:16–17	*'Gather the elders of Israel'*
Deuteronomy 26:12–15	*Remembering the outsiders*
Matthew 5:1–11	*The Beatitudes*
Romans 12:3–16	*One body, many members*
1 Corinthians 12:12–20	*If one member suffers, all suffer*

Prayer Activity

The community of God (Father, Son and Holy Spirit) is often called the Trinity. Think of three parts of your life – perhaps work, friendships and leisure. Are these three things totally separate? How do they relate to each other? Offer in silence some thoughts about how these areas of your life help you to be together with others and with God.

Humdrum Relationships – Mary and Elizabeth

*In those days Mary set out and went with haste to a Judean town in
the hill country, where she entered the house of Zechariah and greeted
Elizabeth.*

~ *Luke 1:39–40* ~

Perhaps, Father, when first we set out on our journey of faith,
We thought we were saying 'Yes!' to something
That would make life different. Exciting. Constantly *alive* . .
And perhaps – God forgive us – *exempt*
From what ordinary life so often is.

Was ever a 'Yes!' greater than Mary's,
When she answered the angel, 'Let it be to me according to your word ...'?
And with her 'Yes!' she embraced a mother's life. The whole deal.
Pride, perplexity, vulnerability, anxiety, pain – yes, all that;
And so much that is just humdrum.
No exemption from the sheer messiness of incarnation,
And all that that big word might mean, for God's *mum*.

Where we cling to our illusions, Father, she dispelled hers.
Where we romanticise, Lord, she demythologized.
She went to talk to Elizabeth about being a mother. The *reality* ...

Help us, like Mary, to find the reality of Christ,
Where life is what life *usually* is:
> Doing what needs to be done, meeting needs that aren't ours;
> Little things, not exciting, not even very elevating,
> But scary in their sheer volume; more, we fear, than we can cope with.

We thank you for a commitment to us so total, an incarnation so complete
That 'Immanuel', 'God-among-us', meant this for Mary;
Hours, days, weeks, years, of humdrum motherhood.
Where, Mary might well have wondered, would God be, in all of this?
Then, unborn John danced his recognition in Elizabeth's womb.
Then, she knew.

Prayer Activity

Faced with something shatteringly new – in her case, motherhood – Mary
went straight to someone who would know and understand this new reality.
Who shares your reality with you? Who, just now, is asking you to share their
reality with them?

Humdrum Relationships – Sarah and Abraham

But Abram said to Sarai, 'Your slave-girl is in your power; do to her as you please.' Then Sarai dealt harshly with her, and she ran away from her.

~ *Genesis 16:6* ~

Sometimes, Lord, we know,
There is an incredible harshness to day-to-day life.
Hopes, expectations, dangerous dreams,
Grind together and shatter; love turns to hate, people behave very badly.
Shards and sharp edges wound and lacerate.

Life can be like that.
We dare not idealise, especially not in the name of faith,
As though life had to be simplified to fit our small vision of you.

That you in your faithfulness and love are gracious where we are not –
Is this not the heart of our faith? And if it is not, Lord, let it be.

Sarai was insecure; Abram was weak; this is how they were.
From spat to vendetta, was this the family of your exalted promise?
Is this soap opera really the story of your covenant?
Help us to turn the question round, Lord.
'Does God really love real people?'
'Can God really love unlovable people?'

Free us from sanitised versions of faith.
Free us from that sundering of God from human reality
That makes us censors of the story.
Free us from the dark suspicion
That you can only deal with the nice, respectable bits of us,
Or that God is prim and easily shocked.
Challenge us with your realism, that sees us as we are,
And deals with that.

Prayer Activity

Take a mirror. Look into it. Who do you see? What do you know about who you see? Knowing what you know, can you love and accept what you see? Can you see someone whom God loves? Now visualise someone with whom you have difficulties getting on. See their face framed in the mirror. Ask the same questions. Bring the answers honestly to God.

Humdrum Relationships – Peter and Dorcas

So Peter got up and went with them; and when he arrived, they took
him to the room upstairs. All the widows stood beside him, weeping
and showing tunics and other clothing that Dorcas had made while
she was with them.

~ *Acts 9:39* ~

Into the community of the Resurrection,
Into the fabric of daily life,
Death has come.
Across the web of relationships,
A cold hand has brushed,
Tearing the fabric, sundering the weave.
The silver cord is cut.
Its power is brusque, violent, summary.
Death is real.

Her hands wove, and sewed, and stitched, and her life was woven in with
   theirs.
Now they finger her work, remember her skill, touch what her hands had
   touched.
We do this, we of finite flesh and blood.
When death takes away, we cling to what we have left.

Into the torn web
Comes Resurrection.
Not at the edge or the end of life
But in its midst.
Gently mending what is torn and sundered,
Renewing, healing, consoling and transforming,
Reweaving, mending the fabric of belonging.
Its power is patient, intricate, painstaking.
Its power is love.

Whether we live, or whether we die, we are the Lord's.
Knitted together by his love, we are his living body.
We have no need to cling, for we have been grasped,
And here, where death is real, more real the life that conquers death,
That life we're called to live, each day.

Prayer Activity

Eat a pleasant seeded fruit. Pick out a seed. Contemplate its packaged,
inhibited life. Relinquish it to the soil somewhere. Imagine the life that can
spring from it.

Love (1)

There is nothing love cannot face; there is no limit to its faith, its hope, its endurance.

~ *1 Corinthians 13:7* ~

Prayer for Reflection

What is it that drives human behaviour?
Greed certainly, ambition too, not to mention fear.
Yet for many it is love that is in the driving seat:
    health professionals;
    mothers, marriage partners, politicians even;
    people who go into the firing line for aid agencies;
    rescue workers, reformers.
Truly, love does make the world go round.

Behind it, Lord, is your love
which embraces the whole world,
and all its awkward people.
Help me today to reflect that love.

Prayer on Today's Theme

Give hope, O Lord,
to those whose endurance is stretched to its limit,
the parent with the fractious child,
the child with the difficult parent,
the employee who is exploited but fears losing her job,
the volunteer whose willingness is taken for granted.
Challenge those who never see things through,
who give in when things don't go their way.

Help us all to fix our eyes on Jesus,
who lived beyond love's limits,
who knew faith from both sides,
who endured to the end
to become our living hope.

Love (2)

I led them with cords of human kindness, with bands of love ... I bent down to them and fed them.

~ Hosea 11:4 ~

You can't help yourself, God,
you can't help but love us:
in our hurt, you hold us;
in our turnings, you call us;
in our sinfulness, you understand us;
in our straying, you challenge us;
in our hesitation, you persuade us;
in our anger, you listen to us;
in our silence, you wait for us;
in our reluctance, you bide with us;
in our fear, you stay with us;
in our loneliness, you speak to us;
in all of life, you love us;
and you can't help yourself.

And finding no reason to do so
(other than the want, the desire, and the instinct)
you give of yourself to us and the world.
May our communities be this way, our societies, our neighbourhoods, our
    families.
And may the love that cannot help itself hold and shape this world,
cradled by, and drawn, to your Realm.

Readings

Deuteronomy 11	*The Love of God*
Psalm 23	*The Lord our Shepherd*

Prayer Activity

Choose an everyday object, or a particular colour, or an image, photograph or memory and dwell on it, look at the intricacies of it, and consider what stories from the Scriptures it reminds you of, what promise it leads to, or how God's promise was opened up through those things. Hold that throughout the day, particularly whenever you see that colour, object or image.

Marriage

Unless the Lord builds the house, its builders labour in vain.

~ Psalm 127:1 ~

Prayer for Reflection

For male and female,
for the attraction of opposites,
for the love that lets two become one ... thank you, God.

For my gender, my sexuality,
my singleness or my partner ... thank you, God.

For Jesus,
to whom neither male or female,
marriage or singularity, was an issue ... thank you, God.

For your word
that in heaven
the bonds and limitations of human loving
will be amazingly surpassed ... thank you, God.

Prayer on Today's Theme

Today, Lord,
I remember those who are soon to be married.
I ask you to fill their homes more with good qualities
        than with good things,
to enable them to discover in each other
        more than they imagine can be found.
I remember those whose marriages are strong,
and ask that the love they share with each other
may overflow for the good of others
whose lives are loveless.

And I remember those whose marriages are under strain,
asking you to help them hold the broken bits
and to discover how to be faithful
in the absence of good feelings.

Family

I kneel in prayer before the Father, from whom every family in heaven and on earth takes its name ...

~ *Ephesians 3:14–15* ~

Prayer for Reflection

With the simplicity and trust of a child,
let me love you, Lord, without holding back.

With the new encounters
and responsibilities of adulthood,
let me discover in you, Lord,
the strength and joy of my life.

With the slower pace
and limitations of increasing age, Lord,
let me find peace, serenity,
and fulfilment in your wisdom.

May all ages and stages of my family life
come together in your loving care.

Prayer on Today's Theme

Be with all, Lord,
whose families differ from the images of TV commercials;
    the lone mum or dad struggling hard to fill dual roles;
    the children whose parents fight or who have parted;
    the grandparents who feel unwanted
    or taken for granted.

Help them to remember that, whatever their situation,
    they belong to the whole human family
    and above all to the family of God.

Assure them that no-one stands alone,
all belong together,
and that you love each and every one
as if there were no-one else to love.

Jacob and Esau

Two nations are in your womb, and two peoples born of you shall be divided; one shall be stronger than the other, the elder shall serve the younger.

~ *Genesis 25:23* ~

From the time they were in the womb, there was struggle.
From the moment there were two, there was rivalry.
Right from the start there was the challenge,
Who would be first? Who was the strongest?
Who could outsmart the other?

God, today we see how even siblings whose lives begin together,
In humanity are hot on the heels of ambition and success.
Today we struggle with the thoughts that:
>Parents often take sides,
>Children can emotionally blackmail parents,
>In-laws can make life miserable for families,
>Brothers and sisters sometimes lie and deceive each other.

God, in the struggle of the story,
In the tangles of families,
In the complexities of relationships.
Help us know where real strength lies.
Help us find honest blessing in our relationships
today and always.   AMEN.

Prayer Activity

Genesis 27:38 says, 'Have you only one blessing?' As Esau asks his father this, ask yourself the same question. How many blessings do you have? Is there one you think you want so much so you are not noticing other blessings in your life?

Joseph and his Brothers (1)

But when his brothers saw that their father loved him more than all his brothers, they hated him, and could not speak peaceably to him.

~ *Genesis 37:4* ~

Creator of Love,
you know how we need to be loved.
You know that we need to feel special, nurtured and encouraged,
welcomed and one of the family.
So you gave us each other: to belong together, to connect with each other,
to be in relationships – understood and loved.

But God, you also know how complicated love gets.
How hard it is to be open and vulnerable
– love might not be mutual.
How tiring it is to keep on loving
– love might not be returned.
How painful it is to share love
– love might be lost.

And, God, you know the thin line between love and hate.

Like Joseph and his brothers, we live in families
that mix love and hate and indifference.
We often can't bring ourselves to speak peaceably to those closest to us.
Sometimes we say nothing – and our actions speak for themselves.

Forgive us, God. Teach us how to be together.
Show us a way through, with the bigger perspective
that Jesus had as people loved and hated him.
Reassure us that, if we follow Christ, one day we will know reconciliation,
    deep peace and unconditional love.

Joseph and his Brothers (2)

'What profit is there if we kill our brother and conceal his blood?
Come, let us sell him to the Ishmaelites, and not lay our hands on him,
for he is our brother, our own flesh.'

~ *Genesis 37:26–7*

God,
It's hard to know where abuse lies when there is a favourite in the family.
Favoured perhaps because of personality, intelligence, flair, the ability to
    please.

Or are they
Arrogant, scheming, egocentric individuals who like the sound and feeling
    of
Me, me, me,
Mine, mine, mine,
Getting their own way?

And the rest,
Seeking their place in the pecking order, taking turns in seeking attention.
Planning, plotting, imagining,
How much better life would be without the favourite.
Cruelty, envy and jealously creep into the heart of the human soul,
Stirring the passion of revenge
When all they really long for is for someone to notice they exist
And to show some pride in them.

God,
All of us in our way act out our longing for acceptance and worth
So when we carry the unease of our families
Remind us that in you
We are loved
We are valued
We are precious
We are of worth.

Prayer Activity

Look through some photos of your family. What memories do they hold?
Good? Bad? Try to imagine why family members behave the way that they
do and to see life from their point of view!

Rahab

*'Now then, since I have dealt kindly with you, swear to me by the Lord
that you in turn will deal kindly with my family.'*

~ *Joshua 2:12a* ~

God of righteousness, the God to whom we belong,
we give thanks for people like Rahab who, in spite of the odds, claim you as
    their own and are proud to name their place and purpose.

Lord Jesus, you, too, belonged to a family
that was imperfect and unashamedly human.
Sometimes, we confess, that family connections can be embarrassing
and relationships difficult to deal with.
When that is the case, help us to transcend the barriers of human emotion
    and prejudice
and so see your life and potential in others,
even when their lives are far removed from ours
and our values seemingly at odds with theirs.

God of mercy and understanding, Rahab, a prostitute, was able to see you
in the midst of all life brought her.
Help us, then, to recognise our need of you, not only when life goes well
but also when we find it difficult to cope with and comprehend
the dilemmas and decisions that come our way.

This we ask in the name of Christ Jesus, a relative of Rahab,
who came to bring life – life in all its fullness.

A Comment

Jesus was frequently accused by religious opponents of his day of mixing
with the 'wrong sort of people' – the woman of Samaria, tax collectors and
so on. His answer to his opponents, and to those who often saw themselves as
outside the socially acceptable norm, was always unequivocal.

'Let anyone among you who is without sin be the first to throw a stone at
her' … When they heard it, they went away, one by one, beginning with the
elders; and Jesus was left … 'Woman, where are they? Has no one condemned
you?' She said, 'No one, sir.' And Jesus said, 'Neither do I condemn you. Go
your way, and from now on do not sin again.' (John 8:7–11)

Mary, the Mother of Jesus

And Mary said, 'My soul magnifies the Lord, and my spirit rejoices in God my Saviour, for he has looked with favour on the lowliness of his servant. Surely, from now on, all generations will call me blessed.'

~ Luke 1:46–8 ~

Mother God,
nurturing your life within and around us,
we bless you and embrace your Spirit.
Help us to engage with your world,
with the earth and all its weary people,
so that, like Mary, the mother of Jesus,
we too may become Christ-bearers,
incarnating your life
and making real your love.
As children of your promises
and as members of your family,
enable us to see others anew,
as brothers and sisters,
and so live and work towards
the day when your vision is born
and your realm has come.
Blessed be you, life-giving God,
lover of the poor and lowly,
and worker of wonders.

Prayer Activity

Often on 'Mothering Sunday' church services focus on the mothering qualities that can be found in all human beings. In other words, you don't need to be 'a mother' to mother! Take a few moments to think of those people who, in your life, brought or bring mothering love and care. As you think of them, hold them in your heart and ask God's blessing on them.

Mary

She had a sister named Mary, who sat at the Lord's feet and listened to what he was saying.

~ Luke 10:39 ~

Lord, we live in a different world
from the one that you knew.
No longer do families meet
and spend long hours together
talking and sharing.

The hustle and bustle of daily life,
new technologies and communications
mean that for many children living in today's world
a conversation is only as long as a text message or e-mail.

We have lost the art of talking and listening to long stories or debates.
We want everything in bytes, short and sweet –
preferably lasting less than sixty seconds.

O that we could spend an hour in your presence,
talking and sharing with you –
our worries
for this day,
for our families
and for the wider world.

Prayer Activity

Is there something you want to ask Jesus? Close your eyes and try to imagine yourself at Jesus' feet. As you look up at him is he looking down at you? He says 'do you have a question for me?' Tell him your question and sit quietly and listen for his answer.

Settling Down

These are the words of the Lord of hosts ... build houses and live in them; plant gardens and eat the produce.

~ Jeremiah 29:4–5 ~

Prayer for Reflection

My butterfly nature makes it hard for me to settle down;
there are always distractions.
Stressful times make many demands on me –
> to do this,
> to finish that,
> to give time to my family,
> to make time for the church,
> to take time to be with you, Lord.

Help me, O God, to get my priorities right.

Prayer on Today's Theme

Father,
be with all who need to settle down:
> those newly married and in their new home;
> those with a new baby,
> whose time is no longer their own;
> those who have started a new job,
> and are feeling uncertain;
> those who have moved to a new area,
> and don't know a soul.

Be with those who need to settle down in themselves:
> to rid themselves of some habit that holds them back,
> to take time for themselves instead of yielding to others' demands,
> to make time to be with God, and to find his way forward for them.

Settle them, Lord,
> that amidst the strife and uncertainty of the world
> they may know something of your peace,
> today, and always.

May the road rise to meet you.
May the wind be always at your back.
May the sun shine warm upon your face.
May the rains fall softly upon your fields until we meet again.
May God hold you in the hollow of his hand.

~ Gaelic Blessing ~

Nazareth

They returned to Galilee, to their own town of Nazareth ...

~ Luke 2:39 ~

Lord of the home,
what memories come to mind
when we think of the place where we grew up –
The place that nurtured us in the days of our youth, as Jesus had his
　　Nazareth?

We pray for the homes where love and faith are modelled daily
And for homes where hurt and fear too often make their mark.
We pray for homes where Christ is honoured and daily meals are blessed
　　with prayer
And for homes where Christ is never mentioned and snatched or solitary
　　meals become the norm.
We pray for homes where families talk, and problems are ironed out
with love and understanding and respect –
And for homes where frosty silence marks the lack of trust,
or angry shouts and rows are the only communication.
We pray for homes where single people live,
alone but embedded in the wider family of friends and work and church –
And for homes where nothing punctuates the long and empty silence, except
　　the sob for friendship.

Lord of the home,
bless all our homes today
with the comfort of your presence
and the light and peace of your love.　AMEN.

Prayer Activity

Choose the place that feels home for you today. Be there, literally, or in your
imagination, and reflect on the good things and the hard things about this
home. Affirm the good, let go of the hard into God's love. Feel a sense of
release, of handing over and of laying down a burden.

No longer do I call you servants ... I have called you friends ...

Prayer for Reflection

You bless me with many friends along the way, Lord,
with whom I laugh and play as a child,
with whom I argue and learn in my youth,
staunch friends with whom I share
    both joy and tears without criticism.

Thank you Lord, for being the best friend of all.

Prayer on Today's Theme

Be with all, Lord,
who believe themselves to be friendless and unloved:
    those who are homeless,
      the disadvantaged,
    those who are sick,
      the disabled,
    and all who feel utterly alone.

Help them to know
    that no-one is unloved
    and unlovable in your sight,
nor should be in ours either.

My Companions

I do not call you servants any longer ... but I have called you friends.

~ *John 15:15* ~

Prayer for Ourselves

Lord,
your first friends were quite a bunch,
a pretty mixed bag:
working men, tenacious women –
one full of zeal,
a few forever arguing,
one man who eventually betrayed your friendship,
a woman who tended to your needs;
and was there really one
whom you loved better than the rest?
I recognise them, Lord,
among my own friends,
and, in humility, I even see myself
as one of yours.

Lord,
have I as much faith in my friends
as you have in me?

Prayer for Others

God the Father, Son and Holy Spirit,
community of love,
embrace in your company
those whom I commend to you:
friends I have walked with along life's way,
some for only a short time,
others who have been with me for years;
those with whom I have shared brief encounters,
who will never know how much their conversation and their company
  meant to me;
those from whom I have parted at a fork in life's road,
whom I have loved dearly,
and with whom I have shared so much.

My Relationships

No one has greater love than this, to lay down one's life for one's friends.

~ *John 15:13* ~

Prayer for Ourselves

I suppose, Lord,
I *would* do anything for my friends
– well, almost anything –
for those I like most.
And for those who like me
I bend over backwards
to accommodate their strange foibles
and peculiar habits.

Yet, Lord,
you showed us that it is not enough
simply to like those who like us,
or thole those who irritate us,
but to love with a love
      that lays down no conditions.

Lord,
you may not ask me to die for my friends,
but I need your help to learn how to live for them.

Prayer for Others

God give us strength
to love one another as you commanded.
May our relationships grow in honesty and truth,
may our meetings be creative rather than threatening;
may we be gentle in the way we treat colleagues and employees;
may we show respect to those whose lives are hard;
may we be generous in time with our friends;
may we learn greater patience with our families;
may we be more trusting of you
and of your love for us,
for it is on this that all our love depends.

False Friends

A friend means well, even when she hurts you. But watch out when an enemy puts an arm on your shoulder.

~ Proverbs 27:6 ~

Prayer for Reflection

I hope you have offended me, Lord.

I hope you have upset me, argued with me, stretched me to the limits.
I hope you have persuaded me to change my mind.
I hope this, because all my best friends have done this much.

That is why we are best friends.
That is why I want you to be best of all.

Prayer for Reflection

You have blessed me with good companions, Lord.

Let me name them and value them,
the ones who love me for what I am
not for what I have to offer.
Let me honour them
by being supportive and helpful,
and being slow to take offence.
Let me honour them
by refusing to be enticed
by the flattering of silky tongues,
or the shallow friendship of opportunists
who pretend they know me well
and ignore those who have shaped me.

Journeys

Be on your way; behold, I am sending you like lambs among wolves.

~ Luke 10:3 ~

Prayer for Reflection

Leaving home, Lord, is always exciting.
But sometimes the excitement is too much.
What will happen to me along the way?
Will I arrive safely?
Sometimes the adventure is just too adventurous!
Holiday trips and excursions are one thing;
journeys to hospitals can be frightening or wearying
whether on my own behalf or for those I love.

Help me to remember that, wherever I go,
you are beside me, even on the last journey of life.

Prayer on Today's Theme

Lord,
be with all who travel today.
Share in the happiness of holiday-makers,
in the hopes of business travellers,
in the helpfulness of pilots, drivers, and guides.
Help those who feel they must stay at home,
who are insecure and fearful unless the doors are locked.

Give courage and hope to all who journey
    blindly into the unknown.
May they feel the protection
    of your covering wings around them.

Be thou a bright flame before me,
be thou a guiding star above me,
be thou a smooth path below me,
be thou a kindly shepherd behind me
today, tonight, and for ever.

~ St Columba ~

Storm

Soon I would find myself a shelter from the raging wind and tempest.

~ Psalm 55:8 ~

Prayer for Reflection

I know that it is unreasonable of me, Lord,
but somehow I expect life
to be always smooth and tranquil.
I feel angry and upset, indignant even,
when troubles assail me.

Help me to know that difficulties and pains
      can help me reach maturity.
Help me to remember that without the irritation
      the oyster cannot produce a pearl.
Help me to remember that you will not leave me
      to face the storms of life alone.

Prayer on Today's Theme

Be close to those
who are buffeted and blown about by misfortune;
may they know your strength and encouragement until the sun shines again.
Help all who feel that their sufferings
are unjust and undeserved;
let them remember your pains on the cross.

Thank you for all who,
      without carping or criticism,
      without crowing 'I told you so',
are ready with a kindly eye,
      an open ear,
      a warm hand,
and a friendly smile for all in trouble or misery.

Calm

The storm sank to a murmur and the waves of the sea were stilled.

~ Psalm 107:29 ~

Prayer for Reflection

Moments of bright joy,
precious gems of peace and tranquillity,
these are threaded through my life
like pearls on a necklace.

Thank you for those blessed times, Lord;
they are your precious gift.
In treasuring them,
may I not overlook your gifts for today.

If things go wrong today, Lord,
help me to trust you,
to keep a calm sough,
and not to give way to panic.

Prayer on Today's Theme

For all who
    in their happiness and success,
    have patted themselves on the back
    and have forgotten you,
your pardon, Lord.
For all who
      in their anxiety, fear, and worry
      have screamed at you in anger,
your forbearance and peace, Lord.
For all who
cannot enjoy the good time
for worrying about the bad,
your wisdom, Lord.

Let us never forget that you are our friend,
sorrowing with us when we are sad,
rejoicing with us when we are glad.

A Calm Mind

Peace of mind makes the body healthy, but jealousy is like a cancer.

~ Proverbs 14:30 ~

Prayer for Reflection

A prayer for a calm sough
for me, please, Lord;

for me when I fret, and worry, and imagine the worst;
for me when I think the birds have it easy
and forget that He who sees the sparrows is also watching me.

My care at your feet,
my stress on your yoke,
my mind stayed on Jesus.

Prayer on Today's Theme

In a society
where we envy what we don't have,
and encourage each other's jealousy
until, in body or mind,
we drop like flies;
in such a society,
we need your maladjustment, Jesus.

Tread the path of simplicity
through our complicated lives,
until we see and cherish
the peace
at the centre of the storm.

Listening

You have ears, so hear what the Spirit says to the churches!

~ Revelation 3:6 ~

Prayer for Reflection

She said, 'I told you so!' – but I was paying no heed.
How often I listen, Lord, but don't hear.
Sometimes I'm deaf, Lord,
because I don't want to hear what others are saying.
I treat you the same way, Lord;
when you speak, I listen but don't hear.
I don't want to hear what you are saying.

But, Lord, how I enjoy telling you what I want,
what I want you to do now, for me, for others,
the problems I want solved right now,
the worries I want taken off my back.

I realise I always expect you to use your ears.
But I have ears too:
help me to use them to hear what you are saying
to the churches and to me.

Prayer on Today's Theme

Lord, you are never too busy to hear us.
Help us
     to have time to listen to our children
     with their endless prattle;
     to have time for our old folk
     with their repetitive reminiscences;
     to have time for our demanding friends
     with their boring tales;
     to have time for disabled companions
     whose speech is slow or indistinct.

Help us to make time to hear them all,
and in hearing them to listen to you.

Learning

It is the Lord who bestows wisdom and teaches knowledge and understanding.

~ Proverbs 2:6 ~

Prayer for Reflection

Learning is hard work,
for the young, the old, and those in between.
Learning is something that starts at the cradle
and continues to the grave.

Learning is knowing
not just what to think, but how to think,
not just cramming in, but teasing out,
not just information,
but knowing where to look for the answers.

And because learning finds its focus and fulfilment in you,
help us to catch your wisdom in the words of the Bible
and to walk with you each day.

Prayer on Today's Theme

Thank you for those
who have taken time to teach us,
who by their patience and skill
have shown us how not to make the same mistakes twice:
    parents and friends,
    teachers and lecturers,
    ministers and Sunday School staff,
    our colleagues and our children,
    those who have walked the way before us.

Exploration

Ask, and you will receive; seek, and you will find; knock, and the door will be opened to you.

~ *Matthew 7:7* ~

Prayer for Reflection

Jesus of Nazareth,
you always encouraged children,
delighting in their exuberance
and their boisterous enthusiasm.
You loved their fresh-eyed view of life.

Help me, too, not to be trauchled by their restless quests.
Let me always aspire
    to childhood's curiosity, excitement, and delight.
Let my joy of living, and my quest for newness of life,
be refreshed in you every morning.

Prayer on Today's Theme

Save older people from believing
that their zest for life and their usefulness is over.
Help all young people from believing
that older generations have nothing to offer.
May all come to see that, aged nine or ninety,
    new life,
    new experiences,
    lie all around
    waiting to be discovered.

Work

The word of the Lord holds true, and all his work endures.

~ Psalm 33:4 ~

Prayer for Reflection

With the eye of an artist,
the perspective of an architect,
    the skill of a weaver,
    the timing of a gardener,
    the faith of a sower,
    the strength of a smith,
you, Lord,
created this world in all its firmness and fragility.

Granite and gossamer,
tree trunk and butterfly's wing,
ocean and snowflake
all exhibit your design,
all are part of your intention.

O Lord my God,
how marvellous are your works in all the earth!

Prayer on Today's Theme

Protect, good Lord,
our industries from obsession with profit
    and from practices which dehumanise workers.
Provide us
with managements and unions
which measure success in job fulfilment
    rather than in points scored.
Prevent us
from overtime which undermines family life
and from unmerited redundancy.

And may the jobless be judged
according to the worth of their lives
    rather than their lack of employment.
If, in the future, there will not be
full-time work for all,
let all have some share in the dignity of labour.

Working for a Living

The ploughman should plough ... in hope of sharing the produce.

~ 1 Corinthians 9:10 ~

Prayer for Reflection

If I have criticised someone
    when they are only doing their job,
your pardon, Lord.

If I have grudged someone
    due reward for their labour,
your pardon, Lord.

If I have labelled someone workshy
    without knowing the facts,
your pardon, Lord.

When I have become so engrossed
    in the immediate demands of my job
    or in my day to day duties
that I have forgotten the purpose of it all,
your pardon, Lord.

Prayer on Today's Theme

Today, Lord, I remember
those for whom there is no work,
    who feel they cannot care for those they love,
    who feel stigmatised by society;
those who work for small reward
    so that prices can be kept down for me;
those whose work is less valued by society
    but without whom
    the world would be a poorer place.

Carpenter of Nazareth,
    preacher of Galilee,
    saviour of the world,
work your work of salvation over the whole earth.

It is God's gift that all should eat and drink and take pleasure in all their toil.

~ Ecclesiastes 3:13 ~

Prayer for Ourselves

Lord,
you were a carpenter's son,
and I am certain
you must have crafted an item or two,
your skills developing
under Joseph's watchful eye
as he placed his hand on yours to guide the plane,
his eye and yours
focusing as one on the straight edge.

Lord,
I think of those who have taught me
and nurtured my skills;
those whose hands clasped mine,
guiding me by their wisdom
and with the experience of years.
May I do my best,
not only for my personal satisfaction,
but because I realise
that creativity is no one's possession
but a gift to glorify your name.

Prayer for Others

Creator God,
be the wisdom of those who manage
in commerce, and business, and politics;
be the creative force in those who design and make and mend;
be the guiding hand upon those who teach, and train, and employ.

Let us remember those who mismanage:
when children and adults are treated as slaves;
when poor wages keep some in poverty,
and drive others to despair.
Be with those who underachieve,
and those who refuse to pass on their knowledge
as though it were their personal treasure.

Industry

A hard working farmer has plenty to eat, but it is stupid to waste time on useless projects.

~ *Proverbs 12:11* ~

Prayer for Reflection

My God,
my days are numbered,
and you have counted them all,
and know how long I have to redeem the time.
So, help me to avoid evaporating my spirit through busyness,
and make me able to stand and stare, guiltlessly;
for then I may offer you my wonder
at your world, and might discover my life
in a wider perspective.

Prayer on Today's Theme

On those who cannot work
because of self-doubt or despair,
        your mercy, Lord.
On those who cannot work
because their skills are unwanted,
        your mercy, Lord.
On those who now, in retirement,
feel unused and unvalued,
        your mercy, Lord.
On those who need to know
how and when to stop working excessively,
        your mercy, Lord.

Resting

Come to me ... I will give you rest.

~ St Matthew 11:28 ~

Prayer for Reflection

Sometimes I haven't time to rest.
I have my work, the garden, the children;
my friends, my neighbours, and my pets.
Perhaps
    when I am older,
    or not too busy,
I might just rest then.

Resting is such a good thing.
Even you, God, rested on the seventh day,
    busy though you were with all your concerns.
And one of your commandments tells me to rest.

Help me not to feel guilty when I rest,
but to be grateful that there is a season for everything,
a time to rest and a time to work.

Prayer on Today's Theme

We pray for those who must rest, and find it irksome:
    those who are ill and who find life wearying;
    those who have lost their job and who cannot find new work;
    those who have retired and who find time heavy on their hands;
    those who have completed their training or studies,
    yet can find no opening for their new-found skills.

We pray for those who never rest, who are always on the go:
    parents with young children,
    those with elderly parents;
    people whose work is so demanding
    that their feet never seem to touch the ground;
    people who think they are indispensable
    and who never let themselves off the hook.

May those who rest and those who rush
find their perfect rest in you,
their strength and their sustainer.

The Nation

It was not our fathers' swords that won them the land, but your right hand and your arm and the light of your presence.

~ *Psalm 44:3* ~

Prayer for Reflection

For this nation and its people,
its rich culture,
and its history ... thank you, God.

For this land
and its produce,
its rugged beauty
and its spirit ... thank you, God.

For my place
in its society
and in its future ... thank you, God.

Prayer on Today's Theme

God of all nations,
if it was indeed your purpose
to differentiate lands and people
by uniqueness in language, dress,
food, and philosophy,
your purpose has borne fruit.

And if it be your will
that our uniquenesses be retained,
enable those who shape opinion in our land
to distinguish genuine patriotism from narrow nationalism.
Let us pass on to our children's children
a heritage worthy of our best yesterdays
and welcoming to the good things of tomorrow.

The Government

Happy is the nation whose God is the Lord, the people he has chosen for his own.

~ Psalm 33:12 ~

Prayer for Reflection

Lord God,
you have always been at odds
with those who misuse power
or set loyalty to the state
above loyalty to their Maker.

Perhaps that is why, in scripture,
you ask that prayers be made for those who rule.
Perhaps that is why I need reminding
that politics should always be embraced by prayer,
never prayer embraced by politics.

Prayer on Today's Theme

Today, I pray
for those in authority in this land:
for the queen and the royal household,
    the prime minister and cabinet,
    the party of government
    and the parties of opposition.

May they all cherish the democracy of this country,
ensure the welfare of its people
    establish its good standing in the world,
    preserve its peace
    and safeguard its courts of justice.
And may they never be above the criticism of its citizens
    or beneath their prayers.

Politics

Unless the Lord builds the house, those who build it labour in vain.
Unless the Lord watches over the city, the watchman stays awake in
vain.

~ *Psalm 127:1* ~

Blessed are you who came in the name of the Lord:
    fulfilling ancient prophecy,
    declaring in acted parable your kingship,
    coming not on some warhorse, but on a colt,
    proclaiming quietly, amid the tumult, peace,
    challenging the city of Jerusalem,
    upsetting the powers that be with another power.

Blessed are you who comes in the name of the Lord:
    God in Man and for Man.
    'Hosanna!' we echo the ancient cry.
    A word of real praise
    and a word of real prayer.
    'Hosanna!' Save us.
    Save us now and save us ever.
    Save us from acclaiming you on Sundays
        but forgetting you on Mondays.

Blessed are you who ever comes in the name of the Lord.
    Ride into our turbulent towns and cities:
        brighten their dark streets
        quelling every ugly passion.
    Enter the places of government
        disturb our leaders with your power
        reminding them of your peaceful programme.

Blessed are you who will come in the name of the Lord,
    Enable the Church, looking to the eternal city,
  to strive for your Kingdom on earth
  to be a citadel of hope on the edge of despair
  to work for the things that are of God as well as those of Caesar
  to pray for the peace of Jerusalem –
        a vision in every parliament;
        integrity among all politicians;
        justice more than law in our courts;
        honest enterprise in all public life;
and you our Redeemer King given the glory.   AMEN.

False Pride

Prayer for Reflection

I believe, Lord,
that you intended me to like myself,
even to love myself.

Otherwise how could I expect others
to love the 'me' I refuse to cherish?

And, in any case, filled with self-loathing,
what goodness could I share
in your name?

But pride – that's something else when it prevents me from seeing
    anyone else but me,
when it presumes a perfection
    I have never achieved.

For self respect, prepare me;
from false pride, protect me.

Prayer on Today's Theme

Today, Lord,
I remember those whose position of authority
might tempt their pride:
    politicians, civil servants,
    lawyers, accountants,
    and all confidants
    and keepers of secrets.

Prevent them from abusing
    the trust their position affords them;
and should the heights of responsibility
    distort their vision,
help them, like you,
to become human.

Old Age

*Planted in the house of the Lord, the righteous still bear fruit in old
age.*

~ *Psalm 92:13* ~

Prayer for Reflection

God of all ages,
my birth day is no secret to you,
nor are my years.

You watch, unruffled,
as from the first moment of life
I grow older.
I change
and thus show that I am alive.
So you have made me.
So you have meant me to be.

Let me have no fear of the passing years,
but learn through each of them,
and thus have something to take with me
to heaven.

Prayer on Today's Theme

Those the Church calls an 'ageing congregation'
        you call your children.
Those the State calls 'senior citizens',
        you call the midwives of a new age.
Those whom families call 'a burden',
        you call an asset.
Those whose names none remember,
        you greet with affection.

Old age is our problem, Lord,
not yours.
But on your help we call
for the patience and imagination
needed to ensure that all who live long
might find some glory in the grey.

Simeon and Anna

*Guided by the Spirit, Simeon came into the temple ... There was also
a prophet, Anna ...*

~ *Luke 2:27a, 36a* ~

Lord, open my awareness to the spirituality of the elderly people in my life.
May I, may the church, may our society,
find ways to cherish the gift of old age in our midst:
years of devotion,
a perspective of reflection that is unique for each generation holding
    together then and now,
seeing the invisible more clearly for our time.

Lord, help me to recognise your presence in other people.
Open my eyes to see beyond the surface,
to see depths and wonder.
Give me wisdom to encourage others,
to help them find their vocation in life,
to draw attention to your purpose for them.

Thank you for the people who have helped me to see 'me'
beyond my family labelling,
beyond my human skills and talents.
Thank you for all who have seen the Holy Spirit in me
and pointed me to my vocation, my unique purpose.

Like Anna, like Simeon, may I listen for the Holy Spirit.
May I be prepared to wait and pray for God to be revealed.
May I look forward to the transforming and the redemption
of our land and know I am part of that.

Prayer Activity

Hold the thought, 'I have a purpose', or repeat to yourself, 'My life has
purpose', or a similar phrase. Continue this and allow divine wisdom to speak
to you, giving you perspective on your purpose for today.

Death

Prayer for Reflection

I will do it only once,
though my whole life moves towards it.
So I pray for a good death
when the time is right.
when I have finished my business,
when I have come to terms with my mortality.

Before then,
in the small and large losses of life,
in the giving away of fond possessions,
in the parting from close friends,
in the changes of job, house or church,
may I sense a meaning in loss
and have a foretaste of resurrection.

Prayer on Today's Theme

Today, Lord,
let me remember before you
those whose lives are coming to a close.
May the unknown road ahead of them
        be tinged with light.
Grant them a peaceful death, even a welcome death.
Comfort those who try to cope with deep grief
        caused by sudden death;
forgive those whose bereavement brings with it
        guilt hitherto neglected;
and give words and silence in the right proportion
        to all who tend to those who mourn.

And let me remember with you
those I loved here but see no longer,
who now serve and sit with you.
Tell them I love them
and, if it is your will,
may they be among the first to welcome me into heaven.

Dying

For since it was a man who brought death into the world, a man also brought resurrection of the dead.

~ *1 Corinthians 15:21* ~

Prayer for Reflection

Death is the only certainty in life.
Whether looked for or unexpected,
it always seems sudden, final.

I know my days are numbered,
and only you know, O God, when you will call me home.
Help me to make good use of the time I have,
for I never know how long or how short my life might be.

Prayer on Today's Theme

O God,
be with those who must face death;
those whose life will end soon, but do not know it;
those who long to die, but death won't come;
those who are afraid to die, for they fear oblivion;
those who do not fear death,
but fear the process of dying.

We remember those whose loved one will die soon;
those who must decide
when to switch off the life-support machine;
those who watch a loved one die slowly;
those who this day cope with sudden death.
And when we come at last to our departing,
bring us home with you for ever,
the family of God complete.

The Treasury

Where your treasure is, there will your heart be also.

~ Matthew 6:21 ~

Prayer for Reflection

God of the biggest bank
    and smallest coin;
God of the costliest treasure
    and cheapest trinket;
God of the highest ambition
    and daftest notion;
nothing is beyond you
nothing beneath you,
for you are the source and centre of everything.

Fix then my heart,
    my mind,
    my longings on you,
that discovering the truth at the centre,
I might see and deal with other things
in their proper perspective.

Prayer on Today's Theme

In confidence,
I examine before you my use of money.

You are both Lord of what I give away
and Lord of all I retain,
    spend on myself,
        on my home and family,
        on less important things.

I do not want to feel guilty about money,
certainly not since Christ handled currency
and spoke about it without embarrassment.

I want to be open and accountable to you
for my use of it.

So let me discuss it with you ...

Needless Anxiety

Do not be anxious about food and drink to keep you alive and about clothes to cover your body.

~ *Matthew 6:25* ~

Prayer for Reflection

Today,
I will be grateful for changing things:
    for cloud patterns
    and seasonal landscapes;
    for the restless sea
    and multi-coloured earth;
    for branch and leaf
    and fruit and flower;
    for rocks, weather carved,
    like an old face which could tell stories;
    for wind and water
    and all that was never meant to stand still.

This is your fashion-show, Lord,
better than anything humanity could ever put on.
There is no competition.

Prayer on Today's Theme

Here is a gaping sore, Lord:
    half the world diets,
        the other half hungers;
    half the world is housed,
        the other half homeless;
    half the world pursues profit,
        the other half senses loss.

Set up your cross
in the market places of our world
to remind us of your love for the lost,
and of the maliciousness of human avarice.

Redeem our souls,
redeem our peoples,
redeem our times.

Accepting Failure

Some people ruin themselves by their own stupid actions, and then blame it on the Lord.

~ *Proverbs 19:3* ~

Prayer for Reflection

Whose fault was it, Lord,
when I lost my temper and lashed out with my tongue,
and saw tears start in frightened eyes?

Whose fault is it if half the world is hungry,
or so many are homeless, and so many are jobless?

Whose fault is it if the Church is caricatured as irrelevant?

To whom can I point my finger?

Or should I bite my finger and hold my tongue
and share the blame I want to avoid?

Prayer on Today's Theme

Come to us in the morning,
come to us in the evening,
dirty and with holes in your hands.
Startle our polite meetings with your earnest insights;
upset our vague generalities with your concrete concern;
embarrass our keenness to apportion blame
by your willingness to take it all the way to hell
so that we can see the path to heaven.

Holy God, loving Father, of the word everlasting,
grant me to have of thee this living prayer:
lighten my understanding, kindle my will,
begin my doing, incite my love,
strengthen my weakness, enfold my desire,
cleanse my heart, make holy my soul,
keep safe my mind and surround my body.

As I utter my prayer from my mouth,
in my own heart may I feel thy presence.

~ *Gaelic Traditional* ~

Laughing

... a time to weep, and a time to laugh.

~ Ecclesiastes 3:4 ~

Prayer for Reflection

There are times when I feel happy:
just being with friends can make me laugh in pure joy;
thank you, God, for the blessing of shared laughter.
It is your gift too that I can laugh at myself,
at my quaint and quirky ways,
at the daft things I say and do.

Prayer for Today

Thank you, God,
for those who are the life and soul of the party,
for those whose sense of humour is infectious,
for those who are just a good laugh,
for laughter's cleansing power.

Thank you, God,
for laughing at us,
for poking fun at our pomposity,
for bursting the balloon of the unco guid.

Lord,
you give us the gift of laughter;
help us to share our laughter with others,
to lighten their lives as well as our own.

Joy

Prayer for Reflection

Why is it so disconcerting
    to find joy in a list of Christian duties?
Am I so convinced that being a Christian consists
    in a number of unwelcome responsibilities?
Surely joy is for off-duty moments
    when we lay aside our hair shirts
    and let our hair down!

Yet, Lord, perhaps the quality of my joy
is the real test of Christian seriousness.
Is not joy the emotion which comes
    when body, mind and spirit
    all fall into place,
    each nourishing the other?

Help me, Lord, to tell the difference
between the superficial joyousness
that fades when trouble comes
and true Christian joy
which bubbles up through suffering
and relives the triumph of Easter.

Prayer on Today's Theme

Risen Christ,
visit those whose eyes are haunted with suffering
and help them laugh again;
challenge those who laugh at others' expense,
and help them face their own pain;

stir those who cannot let themselves go
and release in them the joy that lies confined;

give to your Church new songs and fresh voices
that its joy in you may sound throughout the earth.

Joy and Laughter

Then our mouth was filled with laughter, and our tongue with shouts of joy; then it was said among the nations, 'The Lord has done great things for them'.

~ Psalm 126:2 ~

What kind of laughter have you made, God?
People laugh in disgust, to scoff,
we laugh when the tension is just too much.
Some laugh at their schemes and plans, excited by their cunning.
And we laugh in the face of criticism to show we don't take it seriously.
But it is the best medicine.
We enjoy a good laugh with family and friends.
Some things are so funny, we are amused, we can't help it.
We love to laugh after feeling low –
it lifts us up, we feel better.
Surely God, this is what you made laughter for
– excitement at good news,
– delight in company and shared experience,
– joy at the unexpected; the kind of joy that Mary felt as her world turned
upside down that first Easter morning,
    the kind of joy a baby can bring,
    the kind of joy that love brings beyond pain:
– joy that can't be contained, that just bursts out
like laughter.

So today God,
may I not take myself too seriously,
may I see the funny side,
and may I make someone smile, even laugh, for your sake.   AMEN.

Prayer Activity

Think about someone or something that makes you laugh or think of some good news you have recently heard. Smile to God as a prayer and give thanks for God's uplifting spirit.

Rejoicing

Rejoice in the Lord always; again I will say, Rejoice.

~ Philippians 4:4 ~

Prayer for Ourselves

Never a day goes by
    but something brings me happiness:
    a cheery word,
    a good result,
    a joke shared,
    a child's laughter,
    an exam passed,
    a loving look,
    a piece of good news,
    a hand held.

Prayer for Others

Yet I know, as I rejoice,
that there are others who cannot:
those who do not enjoy good health,
those who are worried and anxious about loved ones,
those who are discouraged,
those who feel life is a struggle and not worth living.
There are those also who do not know you,
    and so cannot rejoice in you
    and know life in all its fullness.

The Happy Life

Happy are those ...
~ Psalm 1:1 ~

Lord! What a beautiful way to start
a book of songs: 'Happy is the one.'
We often start with negative-sounding words: sinner, duty, effort, rules,
so we struggle long for a happy ending.

God! What an exuberant image of life:
'A tree planted by water channels;
It yields its fruit in season
And its foliage never fails.'
I can picture it: leafy, fruit-bearing, a seasonal life.

Lord, who are the wicked you have in mind?
Foes who endanger life? Enemies within? Pride, greed, lust, fear?
When these threaten life, help me to see them in *your* perspective –
'like chaff driven by the wind'.

Lord, let my life have the powerful focus of delight in all that is good,
your 'Law' no duty imposed but a happiness within.   AMEN.

Readings

Psalm 1; Psalm 19; John 15:1–17; Romans 13:10; Galatians 5:14

Prayer Activity

Think of your life as a tree and draw a picture of it. Place around its roots the
things that promote life and happiness, e.g. faith, friends, a book, a musical
instrument, whatever is life enhancing to you. Explore the significance for
you, today, of this image.

Blessing

Turn the wandering desires of your heart to God,
feed the roots of your life with love,
fill your soul with happiness.
And so, let your tree of life bear much fruit,
in God, in Christ, in Spirit.   AMEN.

*We are disciplined to renounce godless ways ... looking forward to
the happy fulfilment of our hope.*

~ Titus 2:12–13 ~

Prayer for Reflection

It will come anyhow –
the time when you bring all things
    to a magnificent finale.
But you have not called me
    to hang around till it happens,
    to wait in the wings,
    and to appear on cue.
I am to help accustom those I live amongst –
    to begin to move with your step,
    and to mouth the words all will later sing.

But, Lord, for others to be convinced I must practise,
so that I know the steps and have the song by heart.

Help me to be disciplined and to learn, from Scripture, from prayer,
and by listening to fellow Christians,
what we shall become when all things are fulfilled
and you are Lord of all.

Prayer on Today's Theme

I pray for the Church, when we feel our grasp is adequate
    but really we are relying on rusty memories
    of what we once learned in Sunday School;
when we feel we do not need to search Scripture,
    study those who have wrestled with the faith,
    learn from the giants of prayer in our tradition,
    or listen to the voices of today.

Help us all to discipline ourselves,
assessing how we fall short,
giving account to each other of our faith,
    our prayer,
    and how we live our lives,
that when people ask about the Kingdom of God
we can point to the quality of our life together.

False Prophets

Now therefore have all Israel assemble for me at Mount Carmel,
with the four hundred and fifty prophets of Baal and the four hundred
prophets of Asherah, who eat at Jezebel's table.

~ *1 Kings 18:19* ~

When I read this story, it wakes me up to how great was the revolution you
    brought, O Christ.
Like Elijah you listened to God and obeyed,
but hundreds and thousands of people were not killed in the name of God.

You pointed us to the battles within our own hearts.
You indicated that this is where to put our fighting energies, conquering our
    inner violence,
learning the skilful difficult way of loving our enemies ... and ourselves.
What a radical shift of perspective.

As Elijah was given Elisha as companion
as the one who continued the prophetic line,
you give us your living Holy Spirit to continue your living presence here
    and now.
We are your hands and feet and mind.

So help us now in the name of God to know how to stand against people
    who stand against our faith.
Grant us deep wisdom to be warriors for peace.
Listening for your living voice,
guiding us to your ways for now,
we trust that in Christ's name
we can leave behind choices of magic and bloodshed.

Prayer Activity

All of us have the potential to be violent. Name now before Christ an area of
your inner world where you experience violent feelings, angry feelings, or
conflicts or confusions. Have the courage to ask the Holy Spirit to help you
look at these more deeply. Notice particularly how these affect your body –
usually bringing physical tension. Notice where in your body. Ask Christ for
healing both of the origins and of the effects in your body.

True Prophets

Before I formed you in the womb I knew you, and before you were born I consecrated you; I appointed you a prophet to the nations.

~ *Jeremiah 1:5* ~

God of life and upheaval,
God of the devastating Word and the appalling vision:

I thank you today for true prophets,
for those who were not at home in the world as it was in their own day
but who lived passionately for a world that was yet to be born.

I thank you today for those who would not keep quiet
and who, regardless of the consequences,
refused to keep the vision locked away within their own hearts.

I thank you today for those who look out upon the world
with the double vision of the prophet:
who see the world in all its pain and mess and yet also see it as you would
    have it be.
Lord, teach me to see as you do. Open my eyes.   AMEN.

Readings

Jeremiah 1:1–10	*The calling of a prophet*
Matthew 4:12–17	*Prophecy fulfilled in Jesus*
Jeremiah 31:31–4	*A new Covenant prophesied*
Luke 19:41–4	*Jesus laments what might have been*
Amos 2:4–8	*The prophet denounces social injustice*
Matthew 12:33–7	*Judge them by their fruit*

Abigail

*(Nabal) is so ill-natured that no-one can speak to him … David said
to Abigail, 'Blessed be your good sense.'*

~ *1 Samuel 25:17 and 32–3* ~

Dear Lord, where would we be without 'good sense'?
In a world with so much tit for tat,
studied aggression and considered revenge,
praise be for the good sense that breaks the spiral of enmity.

We thank you for Abigail's example of risk-taking for peace –
'Upon me alone, my Lord, be guilt'.
I see a Christ figure here,
the innocent freely and willingly bearing the sin of the guilty.

Lord, it is a tough call to see 'Abigail' opportunities and to act upon them.
What a life Abigail had to endure!
married to a man 'so ill natured that no-one would speak to him'.
Nabal: a fool of a man, 'surly and mean', given to rage and drunkenness.
Abigail is 'clever and beautiful'.
What attracted her to Nabal?
Was it an arranged or forced marriage?
Lord, help those trapped in hurtful, violent and exploitative relationships.
Give them the courage and wisdom of Abigail to open the doors of
  deliverance. AMEN.

Prayer Activity

Sit quietly and relax by breathing out and in gently. Bring your needs to Jesus
as the one who has risen from the 'trappedness' of the tomb, has broken the
binding chains of death. He is present with you to bring freedom. It may
be that you need his healing for hurt, or his strength to stay with a difficult
relationship. Or it may be that you need wisdom and courage to leave an
abusive relationship. Take time to bring these personal needs to the Lord.
Remember that he is a loving, healing, encouraging and guiding presence.

David and Jonathan

...the soul of Jonathan was bound to the soul of David, and Jonathan loved him as his own soul. Then Jonathan made a covenant with David, because he loved him as his own soul.

~ *1 Samuel 18:1, 3* ~

O Lord my God, I will give you thanks for ever that my heart sings for my
    beloved
My deepest soul friend in whom my spirit delights

Formed in a covenant of love
A touching closeness not fuelled by lust or desire
But treasured with deep tenderness in union, in communion
With God and each other.

O Lord my God, I will give you thanks for ever that my heart sings for my
    beloved
My deepest soul friend
In whom my spirit delights.

When the years are silent
Separated by time and space
Meeting again seems only like yesterday
For in you I am more fully alive
More fully human
More me.

O Lord my God, I will give you thanks for ever that my heart sings for my
    beloved
My deepest soul friend in whom my spirit delights.

A love unspoken which when death parts
Comforts the mourning family
But speaks not to the aching grief in the closeness of friends.

O Lord my God, I will give you thanks for ever that my heart sings for my
    beloved
My deepest soul friend in whom my spirit delights.

Prayer Activity

Think of your friends and list the attributes you like best about them. Give
God thanks for friends and think about what it is that you give to them.

Deborah

'I will surely go with you; nevertheless, the road on which you are going will not lead to your glory, for the Lord will sell Sisera into the hand of a woman.'

~ Judges 4:9 ~

Loving God,
you create us to achieve our full potential,
you long for us to be our true selves and so worship you rightly,
you want us to feel fulfilled, complete, whole.
Help us to admit that we have not been all that we could be.
Let us see how we have conformed, made do, sacrificed the wrong things.
Show us how to get out of the habits we have formed and lazily stuck to.
God, release us, free us,
even when society puts obstacles in our way.
God release us, free us,
even when our parents and peers seem to want us to behave this way and
   that.
God release us, free us, even from ourselves,
from all we try to be and don't need to be.
Encourage us to dream, to scheme and pave the way.
From now on, help us see ourselves as you see us,
help us live the lives that you give us.   Amen.

Readings

Judges 4:4–10; Judges 5:1–31; Luke 7:36–50

Prayer Activity

Take a few steps, physically or in your mind. With a sense of your potential, realise who you are to God and be encouraged to live today with that knowledge.

Esther

Now Esther was admired by all who saw her.

~ Esther 2:15 ~

We thank you, mothering, fathering God,
for women like Esther:
for the protection we receive from them,
for their care and compassion,
their clear minds in our time of need,
their sacrifice so that others might hope.

We pray for the women of the world:
the mothers, wives, sisters, daughters, aunts, grandmothers, partners,
   friends.
We thank you for the contribution they make
to the worlds of politics, commerce, law and church,
to the worlds of education, medicine, science and industry.
We thank you for the home-makers,
the givers of comfort and kindness,
the speakers of soft words and tender understanding,
the wisdom-speakers,
the honest commentators, the faith-givers who have shaped our
   lives. AMEN.

Prayer Activity

Think of the women who, by their love, kindness, acceptance and honesty
with you, have in some way enriched your life. Think of what they did and
what they said that made all the difference in the world to you. What have you
learned from their example? Ask God to help you use what you have learned
from these women to help you help others.

Mary Magdalene

But Jesus said, 'Let her alone; why do you trouble her? She has performed a good service for me.'

~ Mark 14:6 ~

Who am I?
It matters not to me if you think of me as a wild, passionate, wicked woman,
    that you call me prostitute or harlot.

What matters is that I know my Lord loves me.

What matters is that I recognised what was about to happen to him –
that I was able to give some human 'compassion and affirmation to the one
    I loved.
What matters is that he recognised me as a prophetess.
What matters is that all people facing suffering and pain and the extremes of
    human life know what I did,
and Jesus knew this would be 'recounted – in memory of me.
May they, too, feel the perfume, sense the fragrance.
What matters is that I recognised his call to death.
What matters is that he knew that another human being understood his
    vocation at that precious moment.
What matters is our souls touched.

It matters not that you choose to play down
that we women were the first witnesses of the resurrection.
It matters not that you sweep our role in the leadership of the early church
    under the carpet of history.
What matters is that we dance the dance of life,
that we weep, and cherish and recognise divinity in those we love –
Christ in us, Christ in you –
and keep on announcing that –
in a church which so often chooses not to listen
to the wisdom Christ recognised in women.

Prayer Activity

John and Paul both ascribe to Jesus the titles 'Word of God' and the 'Wisdom of God'. The latter is personified as female in the book of Proverbs where one of the famous texts is of Wisdom inviting all nations to her table. In a similar vein, Jesus invites all kinds of people to eat with him. Here and now invite Jesus to the table within you, with all the different expressions of yourself. As he did, allow them all a place, a voice.

Bartimaeus

Then Jesus said to him, 'What do you want me to do for you?' The blind man said to him, 'My teacher, let me see again'.

~ *Mark 10:51* ~

Before I knew you
there was darkness everywhere
and life was meaningless.
Months and years passed in a blur –
the drudge of daily life seemed pointless.

The day we met for the first time
it felt like the scales had fallen from my eyes
and I could really see for the first time.

Colour filled my sight
and life took on a whole new meaning.
Suddenly, every day became precious;
I looked at the world with new eyes,
your eyes, Lord.

Thank you for making a beautiful world,
thank you for letting me share in it.
Use my eyes, ears, mouth and hands
to make this world a better place –
where we can all enjoy your creation.

Prayer Activity

Close your eyes, and as you sit quietly for a few minutes imagine how you would cope if you were blind. Think about how you would go about your daily life: washing, dressing, cooking, working, etc. Give thanks for people learning to live with a disability.

Zaccheus and Jesus

When Jesus came to the place, he looked up and said to him, 'Zacchaeus, hurry and come down; for I must stay at your house today.'

~ Luke 19:5 ~

When we feel we are unimportant and not noticed
You see in us the potential and possibility we fear to live up to.
You surprise us with an unexpected,
'I choose you.'

When our wealthy lives are lived out at the expense of the poor
You encourage us to be uncomfortable with our extravagance.
You challenge us with an unexpected,
'I choose you.'

When we worry that our bodies may be too fat or too small
You see that which is deep within us and beyond the external.
You affirm us with an unexpected,
'I choose you.'

When the lives we lead or decisions we take make us unpopular
You demand we seek justice and act with mercy.
You change us with an unexpected,
'I choose you.'

So come amongst
the lonely, the small, the wealthy, the unloved, the unpopular.

Come
and be the guest of a sinner that by choosing us,
meeting us, being amongst us,
we may live out our lives
Challenging and changing
Challenged and changed.

Prayer Activity

Invite someone new round to your house or take them out for a coffee. Enjoy the conversation and time spent getting to know each other.

Lydia

... a worshipper of God ... a dealer in purple cloth.

~ Acts 16:14 ~

Dear God,
there is so much here to reflect upon!
Lydia was a worshipper of God. But which God?
Was Lydia a Gentile, attracted to the one God of Judaism (but even more
drawn to Paul's message of Jew and Gentile together being God's
children)?

Where was the 'place of prayer' where the women gathered?
By a river bank, in a home or at a synagogue?
'The Lord opened her heart'.
What does that say to us about our frantic efforts to save the Church?
Are we expectant that the Holy Spirit will open our hearts?

A business woman.
Was she single or a widow?
Lydia combines piety and business, faith and profit, wealth and hospitality.
Capitalism has moved on:
today it is global, multi-national, largely free from constraint of
government, often unchecked by Christian conscience.
And Christendom, what of it?
Only tokens remain:
a national church, parish ministers and Victorian buildings.
There must be some way to combine a business brain and a prayerful heart,
a worshipping mind and entrepreneurial talent.
Lord, who are the Lydias today?

Prayer Activity

Make the advice of John Wesley to early Methodists a spiritual challenge to
ponder! 'Earn all you can; save all you can; give all you can.'

Hope, Comfort
and Guidance

'I am the Light of the World'

~ *John 8:12* ~

Prayer for Reflection

Help me not to fear the light,
    especially if I avoid mirrors
    because they reflect the me
    I pretend is not there.

Help me not to fear the light,
    especially if I avoid argument
    in case I am proved wrong
    and have to lose my prejudices.

Help me not to fear the light,
    especially if I only read Psalm 23
    because Psalm 22 is too disturbing.

Help me not to fear the light,
    especially when in you
    there is no darkness.

Prayer on Today's Theme

God bless the white sticks
    and guide dogs
    of those who cannot see.

God bless the sign language
    and lip reading
    of those who cannot hear.

God bless the minders
    and advocates
    of those who cannot speak.

God bless the skill of those
    who plot paths to the future
    in medicine, science and technology.

May they always know themselves
    to be higher than the beasts of the field
    but lower than the angels.

Light and Darkness

Consider whether the light in you is not darkness.

~ Luke 11:35 ~

Lord,
my world is flooded with bright lights,
offering me entertainment,
persuading me to buy,
putting a shine on bad news,
claiming to show me 'reality'.
Why does it all seem so staged?

And what of the light within me?
Does it not glow and fade as the dark silhouettes of greed or envy,
bitterness, arrogance or self hatred chase across its surface?

Help me to recognise when things seem clear only because of my driving
    ambition,
when things seem so obvious only because I am not taking others into
    account,
when my light is merely darkness dressed up.
Illuminate me from within with your Word.
Make me a lantern that shows others the way:
with a generosity which spills into darkest corners,
with a level of understanding which reveals what is true,
with a strength of love which glows mid distrust and fear.

Readings

2 Samuel 22:26–30	*You are my lamp, O Lord*
Proverbs 4:18–19	*The path of the righteous is like the light of dawn*
Luke 11:33–6	*Putting the lamp on the lampstand*
John 3:18–21	*People loved darkness rather than light*
Colossians 1:11–14	*He has rescued us from the power of darkness*
2 Peter 1:19	*A lamp shining in a dark place*

Prayer Activity

Darkness does not possess the ability to remove light, but light forces darkness
to scatter. Find a dark place and sit for a spell. Feel for the match and light
the candle. Watch the flame grow in strength. Follow the light out to the
periphery, and see how far that little light can stretch. Now kindle Christ's
light in you. Imagine it permeating your whole body and mind, and watch it
reaching out to the people and community among whom you live.

Vision

> *The man looked up and said, 'I can see people, but they look like trees, walking'.*
>
> ~ Mark 8:24 ~

Lord,
to us you say, 'Can you see *anything*?'
For too often we stumble around as those who have but little vision.

We live as in a world of fuzzy shapes and muddy greys
compared with the clarity of vision
and concentrated focus which you would give us.
Truly, in your light we see light.

Yet perhaps we prefer the grey to the glory.
Too much light hurts our eyes
and we are cosier in the shadows.

Yet, Lord, we need vision, for without it we perish;
we need visionaries,
those who would initiate us into a new way of seeing.

Today I pray for preachers and poets,
potters and painters,
prophets and playwrights,
for all disturb us, who shake us, who say to us,
'Can you see anything?'

Readings

Exodus 3:1–6	*When the extraordinary breaks into the ordinary*
Jeremiah 1:11–19	*The prophet as one who sees*
John 9:1–12	*From blindness to sight*
2 Corinthians 3:12–18	*Reflecting the glory of the Lord*
Revelation 1:12–16	*A vision of Christ*

Prayer Activity

Build a collection of photographs cut from magazines/newspapers. Look for disturbing/challenging/inspiring images. Give attention to one of these images. Let it speak to you and flow into prayer.

Hebrew Ancestors

Again Jesus spoke to them, saying, 'I am the light of the world. Whoever follows me will never walk in darkness but will have the light of life.'

~ *John 8:12* ~

God of Abraham and Isaac and Jacob,
God of Columba and Queen Margaret and John Knox,
thank you for our heritage, for our connection with those who have gone
    before,
who have blazed the trail for us and made us aware
that there is a Living Presence to follow, here in our land, on these shores.

Help us to learn from the way the Hebrews looked at time.
For them, the past was ahead of them, drawing them onwards, inspiring,
    stories to guide
and always a shining light in their ancestors, glowing through them,
a consciousness that was bigger than one person, a light that shone,
a glorious radiance that their forefathers and foremothers embodied
but was bigger than any one person ...

Like a desert caravan, following the one in front,
we are indeed part of a journey so much bigger than we can understand.
The caravan moves, but the whole earth is moving also.
We join with the caravan itself, drawn by forces beyond our conception.

Enable us to be people who see the Christ light
in the people of faith who have gone before
and with whom we feel a resonance across space and time.
Entrust us to have courage that our vision is part of their vision.
Keep us faithful to that light.

Prayer Activity

Imagine a light shining through your heart connecting you to parents and grandparents and beyond. Follow that light within you in your imagination – see where it takes you or what it brings to light for you.

Hope (1)

You are my Lord: I have no good apart from you.

~ Psalm 16:2 ~

Lord, all my life and aspirations are pinned on you,
my present and my future hopes.
Even in the face of uncertainty, illness, death,
I want to hold you firm.
Then you dazzle me with the truth
that it is you who have hold of *me*, with love.
I can only thank you for the security that gives
for any situation I may know today.

Nothing will be outwith the reach of your embrace
or diminish the wealth of your resources.
That is hope for me in life and through death.
Lord, please keep me in that place of trust
and true hope, through Jesus Christ.   AMEN.

Readings

Genesis 45:4–8; Psalm 16; John 16:25–33; Philippians 1:12–26;
John 14:1–7

Prayer Activity

The path of life. As you walk today, allow a text or hymn to come to your mind. Let the words find a rhythm in tune with your walking and your breath. Allow your walking to bring you life. The Psalms were often walked and sung on pilgrimage. You are finding your own way to join this ancient way of worship, of embodying God's love in you as you move and breathe.

The Lord's Prayer

Blessing

Hope for today be yours;
hope for the way be yours;
hope without end
through Christ, your friend.

Hope (2)

For in hope we were saved. Now hope that is seen is not hope ... But if we hope for what we do not see, we wait for it with patience.

~ Romans 8:24–5 ~

Lord,
as we look around at our world today we see people everywhere who have
  lost hope.

Lord, restore our hope;
remind us that our hope is in Jesus, in his death and resurrection.

Lord, we are blind;
in every town and city people are groping around in darkness.

Lord, help us to see the light.
May the light of hope shine out from us that others may see and desire it for
  themselves.

Lord, we are impatient.
We live in a world of quick fixes; people want it now – '24/7'.

Lord, give us patience.
Grant us excited anticipation
as we wait for the fulfilment of our hope.

Readings

	Psalm 33	*The greatness and goodness of God*
	Psalm 62	*Song of trust in God alone*
Matthew 12:15–21		*God's chosen servant*
Romans 8:18–31		*Future glory*

Prayer Activity

Sit quietly and reflect for a few moments on the deepest hopes and desires of
your heart; as you think of each, share it with God and ask him to show you
how to bring it to fulfilment, if it be his will.

Jesus and the Rich Young Man

But when he heard this, he became sad; for he was very rich.

~ Luke 18:23 ~

When we make poor choices,
When we get caught up in unhealthy patterns,
When we yearn and pine for all that glitters …
God, help us see why that is not good.

When we feel sure we are right,
When we are self sufficient and self righteous,
When we are confident in health and wealth …
God, help us know that we are not God.

God inspire in us today:
Faith beyond pat answers, motivation beyond self promotion,
Love beyond words.
Give us this day the courage to move beyond our backgrounds and
   conditioning,
Our sadness and our unwillingness to find costly but rich
Adventures with you.

Prayer Activity

Hold in one hand the thought of all things of great wealth and importance
to you and in the other hand hold faith, family and friends. Reflect on the
balance between your two hands, what hand is easiest to open?

Blessing

> God beyond answers,
> Lord beyond words,
> Spirit beyond imagining,
> Move us today.

Darkness

Even though I walk through the darkest valley, I will fear no evil: for you are with me.

~ *Psalm 23:4* ~

In the dark I lie.

No light shines through the curtain, no dim image can be seen.
No height, no depth, no breadth.
And yet so claustrophobic.
No one but me and I am scared.

Because the darkness is all around.
Like solitary confinement,
I imagine what I cannot see.
What lurks, what might I touch if I move
And what might touch me?

The darkness feels like no way out – no way
And I am lost.

Now I understand the Psalmists song, God.
Words from the struggle, cries from the depths.
And I long to know that the darkness is not emptiness,
That it is filled with your presence, for you are with me.

Lord, hear my prayer that the darkness will not overcome;
And when the faintest of light is seen again
Let all my soul shout out in appreciation
for life and light that darkness can never put out.
In our struggle, in our loneliness, in our shame,
Christ be our light today.

Readings

Psalm 23	*Shepherding comfort*
Ezekiel 37:1–14	*Valley of dry bones*
1 John 1:5–10	*God is light*

Flowering

He brought us into this place and gave us this land, a land flowing with milk and honey

~ *Deuteronomy 26:9* ~

There is a hint of promise, O God, in every wilderness;
a drop of water in every desert,
a river that flows between all rock,
a loving word in the hollowest silence,
a field of flowers where once the dust blew, resurrection among the
    tombstones,

and it comes to those who wait:
a lifetime for some, fed-up with wilderness,
as the ancient Israelites were.
Yet the word came, the promise unfolded, and a banquet of milk and honey
    was shared.

Creator, for those who endlessly wait for good news:
for healing, for peace, for love,
I pray;

and may my own prayer echo for them,
the promise they can no longer hear.
Let it voice in heaven the hope they long for,
carried on the scent of a meadowful of flowers.

Readings

Exodus 3:16–20	*God reveals the plan*
Isaiah 40:1–10	*Reshaping the wilderness*
Deuteronomy 27:1–8	*A place of rejoicing*
Isaiah 48:12–22	*Living like water from rock*

Prayer Activity

Reflect on some flowers you have in the house or in the garden or a picture in a magazine. Think about what the earth would be like without those flowers, how dull it may be, how unfulfilled it may look, what potential lay unused. Now pray for someone, someone who is having difficulty of some kind, a neighbour, a family member, a prisoner of conscience. May you see your prayer in the same way the earth sees her flowers.

Therefore from one person, and this one as good as dead, descendants were born 'as many as the stars of heaven and as the innumerable grains of sand by the seashore'.

~ Hebrews 11:12 ~

Wilderness – a place of wonder, of expansion, of terror, of desolation;
Wilderness – a state that allows great potential to be born within us, yet
often through utterly rigorous testing
That we truly question whether we will get through it;
Wilderness – a condition that calls out deep prayer from within us.

Wilderness – a place of un-ending-ness;
No clear end in sight;
Goals missing or never materialising;
Monotony of every day;
Slow, plodding, getting nowhere.
How many of our days are like this?

Sand, sand and more sand;
Barrenness, no purpose, no meaning.
And God said 'I will indeed bless you, and I will make your offspring as
numerous as the stars of heaven and as the sand that is on the seashore.'
God speaks poetry and inspiration into the very fabric of the wilderness.
God places a treasure, which invites a change of perspective that transforms
unending desert into infinite potential – from lack and distress to hope and
promise,
Even when I cannot see the promise fulfilled – yet.

Help me see the treasure in the 'sand' of my life;
Heal me, free me, turn me around to see the wonder in the tired, weary,
monotonous aspects of my life now;
Expand my limited way of looking, my restricted feeling of myself,
And do this for others, too, who I now name and ask that they know your
blessing.   AMEN.

Prayer Activity

As if in one hand, 'hold' the aspects of your life that feel like a wilderness in a negative way. In the other hand, 'hold' abundant aspects of your life. Let each aspect speak their truth: allow dialogue, both with each other and with Jesus. Allow words of prayer to arise: of longing, of intention and of hope.

Wandering

Sarah saw the son of Hagar the Egyptian, whom she had borne to Abraham, playing with her son Isaac. So she said to Abraham, 'Cast out this slave woman with her son; for the son of this slave woman shall not inherit along with my son Isaac.'

~ *Genesis 21:9–10* ~

Pilgrim God:

Ishmael was the son
Of Abram's impatience,
The hapless child
Of his unwillingness
To wait in the howling wilderness
Of the not-yet fulfilled promise.

Ishmael and his mother were the victims,
The collateral damage
Of a botched attempt
To accelerate the pace
Of your unfolding purposes.

Help me to see, Lord,
That there are times
When to act is to be disobedient,
That there are times
When to run ahead
Is to fall hopelessly behind.

Today, I remember all those who must
Learn the way of patient obedience;
Who find themselves stranded
In the featureless desert,
In the twilight world, the 'not yet'
Of your covenant promise.   AMEN.

Prayer Activity

In Biblical terms, the 'desert' is the place of prayer, the hidden place of being behind the busy place of doing. We can see this pattern clearly in Jesus' ministry. A Russian word, 'poustinia' (meaning 'desert') refers to the place of quiet, of withdrawal, of prayer. Set apart somewhere in your house or garden as a 'poustinia'. Place there some objects as a focus for prayer – an open Bible, a cross, or perhaps some photographs of people you pray for.

Loneliness

Turn to me and be gracious to me, for I am lonely and afflicted.

~ Psalm 25:16 ~

So many people
So much loneliness
What a mystery.

When we cross the street to avoid someone, help us to listen to our aversion;
Going deeper
Meditating on our reaction – is it prejudice?
What are we scared of – is it anything to do with them?
Is our avoidance a protection – and if so from what?
God, may thus our meeting again become healthier, more open, that I could
    be more honest with myself and with you.

God, may I now face my deep loneliness, the leper within me,
The parts of myself I reject, that I do not want others to see, even you:
Is it so bad?
How can I befriend my own feelings of inadequacy,
The parts of myself I allow to get lonely and abandoned, so feeding my
    fears
Circling around in a downward spiral?

May I let you confront the parts of me that feel abandoned and check their
    reality
What I can change,
What I cannot change.
And may I have the wisdom to know the difference,
And the prayerfulness to dare to know myself,
Accept myself, open myself
Naked to your enfolding love,

Trusting you to bring the comfort that I need – and the challenge.   AMEN.

Prayer Activity

Most of the miracle stories of Jesus include some healing of emotions and
bring social inclusion to people who were outcast. Think of any situation in
which you feel lost, lonely, isolated, inadequate or misunderstood. Ask Christ
to bring to your mind one of the miracle stories as 'medicine' for the situation
you have thought about – and ponder – let Jesus' healing flow into you.

Patience

I waited patiently for the Lord; he inclined to me and heard my cry.

~ Psalm 40:12 ~

Lord,
we find it so hard to be patient in our world.
We want everything immediately:
instant credit, instant meals, instant entertainment, instant relationships,
    even.

No, we don't want to wait; we want it NOW!

Yet the Scriptures are full of people waiting –
in stillness, in hope, in longing,
waiting for your promises to become reality,
waiting for the dawn of your Kingdom,
waiting for you to act ...

You would remind us that the waiting time,
the time of 'Yes ... but not yet ...'
is the learning and growing time.

You would call us to action in waiting,
being active in your service,
being busy about our Father's business as we await your Kingdom's
    dawning ...

Today I remember all who wait –
the oppressed, the exploited, the anxious, the grieving.
May they find you in their waiting time.

Prayer Activity

Mental relaxation in God's presence can be a form of patient prayer. The discipline is one of relaxing the mind and waiting. Practise this kind of praying. Allow yourself to relax and to enter into the experience. Taking time simply 'to be' can sometimes help us to become more aware of the wonder and vitality of life's gifts.

Understanding and Reason

For now we see in a mirror dimly, but then we will see face to face.

~ 1 Corinthians 13:12 ~

Eternal God, whom no one has ever seen nor can see,
we admit that you are beyond our highest thought of you:
    our best language often mere babble,
    our understanding only partial,
    our very reasoning sometimes unreasonable.
But we bless you that we can reason and understand.
We rejoice that limited though we are,
we can yet appreciate that you make sense,
    and often the only sense.
We rejoice that you reveal yourself in many ways:
in nature, in Scripture, and supremely in Jesus your Son
who bids us call you 'Father' – a god, the God,
to be reached and realised in humble love,
as we respond to that down-to-earth love that first loved us.

As we thank you for your unreasonable mercy and love
    that can pardon and empower us,
    that can spare and save us,
deliver us from futile reasoning and the closed mind.
By the Holy Spirit,
open our eyes to see wonders in your world and in your law,
unstop our ears to hear your word in scripture and in Christ,
quicken our intellects to appreciate life and better to understand it.

Father of lights,
we remember those who grapple with problems and perplexities:
    seeking a way through political dilemmas,
    seeking beneficial scientific solutions,
    seeking to unravel the secrets of the universe.
Give them, and give us, that wisdom
that has its beginning in you. AMEN.

Prayer Activity

Look into a clear night sky and, like the Psalmist, ask the question: 'What is man that thou art mindful of him … ?' Move from wondering enquiry to real thought and some understanding and appreciation of the universe and your place within it – and give thanks.

Like a Child

You are my hope, Lord God, my trust since my childhood.

~ Psalm 71:5 ~

Prayer for Reflection

I cannot remember, Lord,
my first stumbling steps
as one parent held out a hand to scoop me up
and the other launched me into the first steps of life on my own.

I cannot remember, Lord,
my first fumbling words
when I was able to call my parents by name
and when words opened out my little world.

But when I think of it now
I *do* remember what it felt like
to have the trust of a child.
Adventure and excitement were the name of the game,
living in the present, living for the present,
living in the here and now.

Now that childhood has been left behind
and the pressures and demands of adulthood
        press in on me,
help me not to forget how to lay things aside
and to place my confidence in you.

Prayer on Today's Theme

Bless today
those who need to cry
but are afraid of seeming childish.

Bless today those who need to trust you more
but who feel adults ought to be able
to stand on their own feet.

Bless today those who take themselves too seriously
and have forgotten how to be spontaneous.

Help them all, O Lord,
to recover the ways of the child
and become more fit for the Kingdom of Heaven.

Jeremiah

*Now the word of the Lord came to me saying, 'Before I formed you in
the womb I knew you, and before you were born I consecrated you; I
appointed you a prophet to the nations'.*

~ Jeremiah 1:4–5 ~

Gracious God,
they called Jeremiah the weeping prophet, did they not?
For surely he lived with the agony of double vision:
    the cold reality of life as he saw it around him,
    the injustice, the heartlessness
    and the idolatry of his times.
Yet at the same time he saw a different reality:
    society re-fashioned in righteousness and justice,
    grounded in your steadfast love and mercy.

Jeremiah saw your future, grasped the vision,
and brought it into conflict
with the fragmented realities of his day.

Lord, save us from an escapist religion.
Help us to face up to things as they are;
but, like Jeremiah,
help us seek to live towards the vision,
even in the harsh realities of the times.

Prayer Activity

Quieten yourself. Focus on an aspect of your community or church where
there is discord, division or injustice. Reflect on the cold reality of things
as they are. Then reflect on what God wants to do in that situation. Picture
the changes that God would bring about. Now – commit yourself to living
towards that vision.

Betrayal and Trust

Cast your burden on the Lord, and he will sustain you.

~ Psalm 55:22 ~

Lord, I need a sanctuary to fly to,
where I may be still.
My life is too often a battleground:
angry voices, harshness, brutal and unforgiving.
Each day, too, often brings another bruising encounter
in the home or in the work place.
Words like weapons cut and tear and I am left scarred and sore.
Find me a safe place, Lord,
where I may speak with you,
a place where my trust may grow again,
even out of the brokenness of betrayal and pain;
a place where I may find shelter for a while,
then return strong again to face the world;
a place where I may call to you in my hurt,
and find myself soothed and comforted and healed.
A trusting place.

I pray for all today who need such places:
the harassed mother, the exhausted father, the frightened child, the bullied
    teenager,
the lonely, the frail, the sick, the troubled.
May each one find that oasis of calm, that safe haven of hope,
that trusting place where you will come
and bless them with your gentle love.   AMEN.

Readings

Psalm 55; Isaiah 35; Zephaniah 3:14–20; Matthew 14:22–7; Luke 19:1–10

Silence

Prayer Activity

People do let us down. Sometimes it is intentional, sometimes it is without
realising. It is a fact of life we have to come to terms with. How do you rely
on God in such circumstances? How can you keep yourself from bitterness
and from wanting to pay the other person back? Can you hand your bitterness
over to God as the psalm does? Remember a betrayal which is current for you
or a memory that still bothers you, however dimly. Ask God to help you, and
show you new ways to deal with the feeling of being betrayed.

Security

I have called you by name, you are mine.

~ Isaiah 43:1 ~

Prayer for Ourselves

I'm such a worrier, Lord.
Sometimes my worries are real enough,
weighing inside me like boulders.
I worry about having enough money.
I worry about my health.
I worry about people not liking me.
Other times I worry needlessly.
Sometimes I expend so much energy
    just being anxious!

Yet even when my worst fears come true,
help me to remember that you are always there
and will hold my hand tightly.

Prayer for Others

I pray for those who have good cause to worry.

When landmarks have been removed,
and life does not make sense any more,
Lord, bring a sign that all is well.
When familiar faces no longer surround
and all seems strange and threatening,
Lord, call such people by name.
When some have lost confidence in themselves,
Lord, be their Rock.
When powerful waters threaten to engulf,
Lord, be a foothold and a haven.

Comfort

Even though I walk through the darkest valley, I fear no evil.

~ Psalm 23:4 ~

Prayer for Ourselves

By the word of a neighbour
　　you comfort me;
through a letter from a friend
　　you comfort me;
in the kindness of a stranger
　　you comfort me;
in many and unexpected ways
　　you comfort me each day
and give me strength to face the way ahead.

Prayer for Others

Lord, help me be a comforter to others,
　　to listen and not always to speak,
　　to understand more and judge less,
　　to build up and not put down.
May the church, in Jesus' name,
offer healing and comfort,
consolation and peace,
and fresh hope for tomorrow,
to all who are lonely:
those cut off from others because of their success,
those isolated through rumours and gossip,
those separated because of their high office,
those disregarded because they have little,
those who espouse an unpopular cause.
May all find strength in your divine friendship.

Comforting

Your shepherd's staff and crook afford me comfort.

~ Psalm 23:4 ~

Prayer for Reflection

As I hear the key in the door and a loved one returns,
    I am comforted.
As I relish a good meal and congenial company,
    I am comforted.
As I enjoy a hot bath before bed,
    I am comforted.
But I can be so busy looking after my own comforts
    that I forget others and their need for comfort,
especially those deprived of home,
    or family life, or secure routine,
    either by natural disasters,
    by the cruelty and selfishness of others,
    by illness,
    or by human failing.

Prayer on Today's Theme

Lord, may we try to bring comfort in your name, by being there –
    with the touch of a hand,
    an arm round the shoulder,
    the hug of sympathy and love.
Help us to reach out to those who are hurt and sore,
    by being open to their feelings,
    by putting their needs before our comfort,
    by seeking help for them
    when we ourselves cannot give it.
May we never criticise others,
    until we have put on their shoes
    and walked where they have walked.

Encouragement

For whatever was written in former days was written for our instruction, so that by steadfastness and by encouragement of the scriptures we might have hope.

~ *Romans 15:4* ~

Sometimes we get so discouraged;
life is an ever-constant struggle,
even our faith fades and falters.
In the midst of this remind us
that you encourage us still.

Triune God, Parent, Son and Spirit,
refresh us daily
with words of encouragement.

We are week and feeble,
constantly needing and seeking
your attention and approval.

Yet why do we find it easier to put others down
and look for the negative in every situation
instead of giving a word of encouragement
or even a smile to people we meet?

Lord, as you encourage us by your presence and your word,
may we seek to find ways of encouraging
all those we meet today and every day.

Prayer Activity

Reflect on any chance meetings or activities you have taken part in during the last twenty-four hours. Were there times when you chose to criticise rather than encourage? Think ahead to encounters you are to have today, tomorrow. What difference could your encouragement make?

Valley of Dry Bones

O dry bones, hear the word of the Lord ...
~ Ezekiel 37:4 ~

Spirit of God, when all seems brittle and dead
you come with breath and life
to move across the dry bones of our lives
and help us find the spring of new life.
Each new day you come to us,
and as the sleep falls from our eyes
once more, again, we start afresh
to laugh, and work and live
and be ourselves the new creation born from above.

Into the brittle, breaking world
breathe life.
Into the clamorous, edgy world
breathe peace.
Into the dull and dreamless world
breathe vision.
Into my world, which is your world,
breathe the faith, hope and love that makes all life worth the living.
    Come, Holy Spirit, come.   Amen.

Prayer Activity

Thank God for your bones and flesh and breath. Become aware of your breathing. This is a good way to pray if you are feeling dry or dead – for you get in touch with the fact that you are truly alive. After you have simply felt and observed your breath for several minutes, pause. Before you do anything else, reflect on your experience.

Blessing

May the Spirit of Christ bring you life.
May the Spirit of Christ bring you peace.
May the Spirit of Christ bring you vision.
Today and every day.   AMEN.

Refuge

... my refuge and my fortress; my God in whom I trust.

~ Psalm 91:2 ~

Lord, this a psalm for the dark time, a song for the down time.
a hymn for the frightening time.

It is a psalm that comes to us with the reassuring voice of a mother
driving away the spectres of night:

'It's all right, don't be afraid. I'm here, right beside you.'

It is a psalm that comes to us with the strong tones of a father
pulling back the curtain of fear:

'Don't worry – you are mine. I won't let you go. Be at peace. All is well.'

This psalm, is a retelling of all you are to us
and of all that we are to be
to your world as to your Church:

a welcoming shelter from the storm,
a warm place of refuge and acceptance,
a homely inn on the road,
with bread and wine for weary travellers.   AMEN.

Readings

2 Kings 6:8–19; Psalm 46; Psalm 91; Matthew 23:37–9; Romans 8:31–9;
Revelation 21:1–4

Silence

Prayer Activity

'The Lord is my safe retreat.' Create a picture of a place of safety or security
for yourself, either real or imaginary. Be there. Get in touch with your feelings
and the sensations in your body. Meet with Jesus and talk of whatever comes
to the surface for you.

My Companion Darkness

... for my soul is full of troubles.

~ *Psalm 88:3* ~

Lord,
– why me? why this? why now?
I see the bad times coming – I pray.
The bad times come – I pray.
The bad times get worse – I pray:
and what feels like nothing happens.
Where are you, God, when I need you?
Is it something I have said, is it something I have done?
What do I have to say, what do I have to do
so that I can hear your voice and know you are with me?
Day and night – and nothing!

If only I knew the secret formula of words and actions
that unlocks your heart and prompts you to act.

Lord,
there are times when prayer is hard work,
and times when I wonder why I persevere with it.
My own needs empty my resources for living.
The needs of others drain my treasury of life.
I am left, emptied and drained, and I don't know what to do.
The lights go out, one by one, and darkness is my only companion.
Yet still I pray,
sometimes beyond reason, sometimes beyond hope,
asking again and again,
laying bare my soul,
stretching out my hands,
and believing even in this darkness
that you will hear and you will come.
Come, Lord, come!   AMEN.

Prayer Activity

New life is born out of darkness, for example, from the womb. What part of
your life 'feels dead'? Every time you feel hopeless, alone, in darkness, make
a gesture of faith – remembering a favourite verse, Bible passage, saying a
prayer, lighting a candle, playing music, recalling the faithfulness of God in
the past. Start now with a present situation or a memory which is still hard
to bear.

Sodom and Gomorrah

*So it was that, when God destroyed the cities of the Plain, God
remembered Abraham, and sent Lot out of the midst of the overthrow,
when he overthrew the cities in which Lot had settled.*

~ *Genesis 19:29* ~

Loving God,
I bring before you this day all the places I don't feel safe –
places where I fear something lurks in the dark, blind alleys where I avoid
  walking,
areas where I feel at risk of crime and violence.

Sodom and Gomorrah seem like extreme other worlds to me, but their story
  reminds me of places I've heard of and seen glimpses of, where depravity
  and evil are evident.

Forgive us, God, for the times we have contributed to making our
  environments dangerous and insecure;
forgive us for tarring people from certain places with the same brush;
forgive us if at times we have run away and thought the only solution was
  destruction and obliteration.

Thank you, God, for showing us another way,
For showing us the light shining in the darkness,
for showing us good people in bad situations,
for helping us understand the reasons behind problems.

Forgiving God,
thank you for healing and restoration of humanity in Christ,
who on the cross, turned a place for criminals, a place of punishment and
  pain into hope for the world.   AMEN.

Prayer Activity

When facing darkness or destruction most of us find a reaction inside of fear,
panic, distress or despair. How do you hold on to the truth that in the midst of
your emotional response there is also present God's Holy Spirit within you?
A good way for many people is simply to repeat one of these words – God,
Jesus, or Love. It can be helpful to do this in rhythm with your heartbeat or
your breath. Practise this today, holding God's presence alive in all situations,
however dark and difficult.

Jesus Heals at Night

That evening they brought to him many who were possessed by demons ...

~ Matthew 8:16 ~

Lord of healing,
we find it hard to picture the ancient world
and how people understood sickness in all its myriad forms:
physical, mental, emotional.

However, our hearts are warmed by your response.
We see you at work late in the night, exercising a ministry of healing.

Lord of the present,
bless all involved in the work of healing:
overworked nurses, junior doctors who work, even when fatigued, late into
    the night.

Lord, you bear our infirmities and our diseases.
In the miracle of this love I rest.
Through your love, help me to respond to the stressed and distressed.
So let it be.

Readings

Genesis 35:3; Isaiah 25:4; Matthew 8:14–17; Romans 8:35

Silence

Prayer Activity

Light a candle (or imagine doing this). Notice the flame: it is both vulnerable
and powerful. Let it speak to you of the light of God in your heart, both
vulnerable and powerful. Bring into the light of God anyone for whom you
want to pray.

Lord's Prayer

Blessing

> The Father's gentle strength enfold you in your distress,
> the love of Christ bring healing to your pain;
> the Holy Spirit lift up your heart with peace
> beyond all telling.   AMEN.

Patmos

After this I looked, and there in heaven, a door stood open!

~ Revelation 4:1 ~

Lord, this is the place of vision, where heaven is opened wide to those that
    have eyes to see.
This is the place of hearing, where heaven's silence is broken for those that
    have ears to hear.
Truly to see, truly to hear, would transform us and our world.

But this is the tragedy, Lord:
that we miss the vision of glory and focus on the glittering fripperies,
that we miss the music of your holiness and hear only the dissonant chaos of
    our jangling, funfair world.
They called John the seer of Patmos, did they not, Lord?

Make of us, your church, a church of seers
of those who will not rest content with the world's glitter.
When we have seen your glory, make of us, your church, a church of
    hearers
those who will not rest content with the empty words of our time,
but who hear the Word that resonates from eternity.   AMEN.

Prayer Activity

Ask for vision. Sing several times a chorus or verse of a hymn about vision,
about glory. Or remember a Bible story where an individual describes a
vision. Ask for vision in your life.

Raising Lazarus

'Loose him; let him go.'

~ John 11:44 ~

Lord Jesus,
in face of death you wept,
but knew that tears were not enough and not the end.
The power within you reached out
and brought hope again.
the power within you banished darkness
and brought light again.
The power within you confronted death
and brought life again.

Lord of Life,
bring the miracle of life
into the dead places in our lives;
bring the miracle of light
into the dark places within us;
bring the miracle of hope
into the time when we despair.
For all who grieve
and all who hurt
and all who are burdened
and all who fear
come with your great voice to call by name
that each one might be set free
and let go once more into your world.   AMEN.

Readings

Exodus 6:1–13; Psalm 22:1–26; Lamentations 3:49–58; Mark 14:32–42;
Luke 10:25–37; John 11:1–44

Prayer Activity

Jesus wept. Distress is normal. God can meet you in your distress. Put a hand over your heart and allow your attention to rest with either your heartbeat or your breathing. Allow this to speak to you of the life which is within you every moment. Hold together this life and any distress or concern you are experiencing. Allow the natural rhythm of breath and heartbeat to help you 'hold' any distressing circumstances and unite them to the love of God.

In God's Keeping

I lift up my eyes to the hills – from where will my help come?

~ Psalm 121:1 ~

I lift up my eyes to the hills:
to their enduring solidity,
to their craggy splendour,
to their smoky blueness on an autumn afternoon.

Deep within me,
I am stirred by their grandeur,
entranced by the song of their silence,
captivated by beauty not their own.

For my help
is not in the hills,
but in the one who made them.
My hope is not in the rocks,
but in the one who shaped them.
My vision is not of the dancing light,
but of the one who dances.

You, ground of all beauty,
shape something beautiful in me.
You, artist of enduring loveliness,
craft in me the image of Jesus.
You, source of all light,
shine out from me today.   AMEN.

Prayer Activity

It can be hard to experience the truth expressed in Psalm 121 when difficult things happen. One way to help us stay close to the feeling of solidity and security we associate with mountains is to take the prayer St Patrick's Breastplate and practise experiencing 'God before me, God behind me, God beside me, God below me, God above me, God within me'. Imagine, feel and invoke God's presence around and within you. You may create your own 'dance' with your hands, with your whole body, or in your imagination, in order to deepen this prayer.

Strength

Lord,
there are times when I am worn out with grief,
with no way forward and no way back.
Surely you are supposed to hear my cries,
and have mercy and save me.
But still my pillow becomes wet from tears;
my body loses its appetite;
my mind falters;
my soul is weak to the point of exhaustion.
As trouble overwhelms me,
and panic sets in and I have nowhere to turn,
my only words are to you:
God give me strength. AMEN.

Readings

Psalm 6; Psalm 42; Psalm 63; Matthew 27:45–50

Prayer Activity

'Heal me.' The writer of the Psalm and his contemporaries understood, possibly much better than we do, that healing is to do with allowing emotions to flow. This enables a letting go that can release us into strength and new life. Look at how many of the emotions expressed here follow what we now call a 'grief process': anger, weakness, falling apart, despair, groaning, depression, sadness, loss. It is a process which leads to acceptance and onwards into new strength. Can you identify in your life where you long for release and healing? What can you do to allow your emotions to flow? Play music, ask a friend to listen to you, write or draw your emotions, use gestures to express your feelings? Experiment and experience the movement from weakness to strength.

Blessing

May God, source of strength and life,
reassure you in darkness,
restore you in sickness,
and hold you in weakness. AMEN.

Times of Trouble

Hope of Israel ... saviour in time of trouble, must you be like a stranger in the land?

~ *Jeremiah 14:8* ~

Prayer for Reflection

Father, when I look back on my life,
I tend to shut out from my mind's eye
    the shadowlands of suffering and sadness
and to see only the sunlit uplands
    of contentment and joy.

But not every day of my life
has been filled with goodness and mercy
    – when I was alone,
    – when I was afraid,
    when I feared the worst
        and you seemed a long way off;
not there when I needed you.

But these were days when you were near
    and I never realised it;
when you were my protector and provider,
    unseen, but near at hand.

Truly, you are my refuge and my strength,
    a timely help in trouble.

Prayer on Today's Theme

We give thanks with those
    whose time of trouble is past,
    and who are richer and stronger
        for their experiences
because they have found themselves,
or because they have found you.

Be with those in trouble now:
    who have lost something from their lives,
    who have an incurable illness,
    who are without friends,
    whose lives seem empty.

Strengthen those
    for whom troubles loom on the horizon.
Take from them the fear that your power can fail,
    and fill them with the hope
        that you will never grow weary.

—— Fear – a Man Released from Torment ——

He had often been fettered and chained up ...

~ Mark 5:4 ~

Lord God,
fear comes in many guises into our lives.
It is legion:
the fear of the unknown
which blights our vision,
the fear of pain
which narrows our world,
the fear of failure
which challenges our confidence.

When such fear comes, we are in fetters, we are in chains.
Fear comes to war-torn lands;
fear comes to homes where hunger stalks;
fear comes to the lonely, the frail, the dispossessed.

When such fear comes,
blotting out the sunlight hope of well-lived life,
come to our rescue
and help us through fears seen, and unseen,
that we might be set free
to walk and live and love unhindered,
acknowledging your power to cast out fear
through your perfect love for us all.   AMEN.

Readings

1 Kings 19:9–18; Isaiah 35; Isaiah 43:1–7; Matthew 14:22–7; Mark 5:1–20;
1 John 4:7–21

Silence

Prayer Activity

Feel the earth beneath your feet or feel the chair beneath you. Sense the solidity and be glad of the security. Remain with that feeling for a few minutes. Ask God to remind you of this solidity whenever you face difficulties.

Conflicting

What causes fighting and quarrels among you? Is not their origin the appetites that war in your bodies?

~ James 4:1 ~

Prayer for Reflection

Two sides awaiting the first stone to be thrown ...
Brother and sister competing for attention ...
Two negotiators at loggerheads over a contract ...

O God, I want what I cannot have;
I envy others their good fortune.
I seek the things that don't really matter –
  money and possessions;
  a good name and a good position;
  popularity and applause.

Prayer on Today's Theme

God bless
the husband and wife who once loved, but who can now only quarrel and
 fight.

God bless
colleagues at work where contention and conflict disrupt relationships.

God bless
those who feel society is ranged against them,
and that the good things in life are passing them by.

God bless
those caught up in civil war whose lives are blighted by violence and loss.

May all strive
  to love rather than hate,
  to share rather than hoard,
  to follow Christ rather than gratify self.

Suffering

He will wipe every tear from their eyes.

~ Revelation 21:4 ~

Prayer for Reflection

'Why should this happen to me?'
I say this in anger when accident or illness strikes,
when my family is divided,
  my business hopes are dashed,
  my well-laid schemes come crashing down.

But Jesus never offered me a life free from suffering;
but he did offer to carry me through it.
And that is what I have found:
whenever I am up to my neck in trouble,
you have revealed yourself to me as never before.

Prayer on Today's Theme

We pray for those who suffer today
through no fault of their own,
those who suffer as a result of genetic defect,
those who have a disability or handicap,
those whose lives seem
  an endless procession of tragedies,
those who wear the badge of self-inflicted pain,
those whose wounds have healed, but a scar remains,
those whose wounds never heal.

Lord,
your shoulder is underneath
the heavy end of all our burdens;
give us courage to carry our load in your strength.

Sorrowing

We do not want you to be uninformed ... you may not grieve as others do who have no hope.

~ *1 Thessalonians 4:13* ~

Prayer for Reflection

He was killed in a road accident,
    and only twenty years old.
She died of a brain haemorrhage,
    and was expecting her second child.
He went off to work as usual, and we never saw him again.
I weep for them all, and for those they left behind.
So many tragedies!
Lord, how did you let these things happen?

But it happened to you, Lord.
Your child was killed.
You know our grief, you weep with us.
You bring us through the darkness.

Prayer on Today's Theme

O God,
be with all who sorrow today:
    those who have lost someone
    or something they cherish dearly,
    those who will cry themselves to sleep tonight,
    those who feel you are far away,
    those who cannot accept what has happened to them
    or their loved one,
    those who cannot weep
    but can only bottle things up inside.
Help them to see that we do not stay
in the valley of tears for ever,
and that you are beside us when we walk through it,
to comfort and to lead us to the sunlight beyond.

Hagar and God

Abram said to Sarai, 'Your slave girl is in your power, do to her as you please.' Then Sarai dealt harshly with her, and she ran away from her.

~ Genesis 16:6 ~

O Holy One
Present in our despair

When relationships turn sour, become complicated, jealous or abusive.
You come close in the weeping.

When there is no one to turn to, no way out of a situation, other than to walk
away,
You come close in the weeping.

When life is dry and barren and we are lost and lonely in the desert.
You come close in the weeping.

When a parent reaches rock bottom and cannot even bear the crying sound
of their child.
You come close in the weeping.

Be a comfort and a guide
A light in our dark places.
'Do not be afraid,' you say to the cries of our distress.
Come Lord,
Come close
Come close in our weeping.

Prayer Activity

'I am sometimes more aware of God on Good Friday, than I am on Easter
Sunday.' Think of the times when you have been at your most sorrowful
– how has God's presence been revealed to you? Do you feel God close to
you? Spend some time thinking abut the people today who need to feel God's
presence is with them.

Blessing

In weeping, God is with us
In despair, God is with us
In silence, God is with us
Come close,
God be with us.

Job

The Lord blessed the latter days of Job more than his beginning.

~ *Job 42:12a* ~

In the beginning, the earth was a formless void and darkness covered the
    deep.
Out of the void, Lord, you created the world and everything in it.
You commanded the light to come forth and gave human beings life.
You gave us water, plants and animals, everything we needed to survive,
and you gave us free will.

Lord, what a mess we have made of your world.
We have plundered land and sea;
we are quickly draining the earth of her natural resources;
we have used our free will selfishly and ineffectively.
More than half of our world's population is hungry and poor,
while the rest say: we want, we need, we shall have.

Save us from the easy answers of Job's friends.
Help us to stand up against the people
who use their power to the detriment of others.
Let us use our free will to choose the right way, your way,
and give us courage to stand up
and help our brothers and sisters who are suffering.

Readings

Job 1:1–22; Job 42:10–17; Romans 8:18–30; 1 Peter 2:18–25

Prayer Activity

Our bodies use pain to alert us when something is wrong. We have all felt
pain at some time in our lives. Try to remember a time when you were in pain.
Do not dwell on the pain itself but think what your reaction was to the pain:
positive or negative? We cannot avoid pain but we have a choice about how
we react to it.

Job's Comforters

Then Job answered: 'I have heard many such things; miserable comforters are you all. Shall windy words have an end? Or what provokes you that you answer? I also could speak as you do, if you were in my place; I could join words together against you, and shake my head at you ... If I speak, my pain is not assuaged, and if I forbear, how much of it leaves me?'

~ *Job 16:1–4, 6* ~

Her reality challenges my faith
Because it will not fit it
Neatly.

His universe, where he must live,
Challenges my faith
Because it is bigger than my cosy little God.
Your pain challenges my faith
Because it is deeper than my consolations can reach.

So I turn from encounter to exhortation,
And I exhort only – and desperately
Myself. I comfort – only myself ...
If only I could listen, and forgo my own comforting speech.
If only I could bear with all that must be told,
And just sit there and hear it.

O for a ragged faith,
Torn and slashed by reality,
Frayed from embracing things as they actually are,
And not understanding!

O for an angry faith,
That searches for God in what is, and not in what I wish were there.
O for an inconsolable faith
That will settle for nothing less than God.
O for a ruthlessly honest faith
That censors nothing for consolation's sake.
Bring me, bring us, to the point of true consolation
Where truth and faith coincide.

Grief

You should not grieve like (those) who have no hope.

~ 1 Thessalonians 4:13 ~

Prayer for Reflection

When a school lost its laughter,
when a nation lost a Princess,
and India's poor lost their Mother,
I wept for them, and with them,
as together we asked, Why?

Yet I remember the Israelites going into exile in Egypt,
and Job losing all that he had,
and a new teacher from Nazareth
    meeting an ignominious end,
and the young church
    meeting a solid wall of persecution,
and I realise that, where there is God,
we haven't yet heard the end of the story.

Help me to understand
that out of great disaster
can come a greater life.

Prayer on Today's Theme

Remember those who grieve today,
and pray they would know that:
    just as sure as the mystery and miracle of birth,
    just as sure as the mystery and miracle of love,
    just as sure as the mystery and miracle of suffering,
so too is death –
for therein lies the mystery of God's love,
and the miracle of Christ's resurrection.

Those who Mourn

Blessed are the sorrowful, they shall find consolation.

~ Matthew 5:4 ~

Prayer for Reflection

What did they think, Lord,
those who watched you cry
in front of women,
    in front of other men,
    for your dead friend
    and your favourite city?

Did they admire your tenderness,
    having seen your toughness?
Were they disgusted by your tears
    and loss of self control?
Or were they drawn into your sorrow
    for the plight of the world
    and the pain of its people?

Help me to share the solidarity
    of your deep sorrow,
so that I can share the certainty
    of your deeper joy.

Prayer on Today's Theme

Where the hearse stops
    and the mourners gather,
    and the blinds get pulled,
    and choking people say 'I'm sorry' ...
be there today, Lord.

Where the hardly worn clothes are parcelled,
    and the insurances are cancelled,
    and a weary voice says,
    'She's not here any more' ...
be there today, Lord.

And where people can't cry
    or won't cry,
    or turn, raging to heaven and ask,

'Why him? Why now?' ...
be there today, Lord.

You won't have to do much.
Your presence will be everything.

Golgotha

And they brought him to the place called Golgotha (which means the place of the skull) ... and they crucified him.

~ *Mark 15:22, 24* ~

Lord Jesus Christ, few places associated with your name
remain so bleak, so dark, so empty of all hope as Golgotha.
The skull-like hill whose unseeing eyes produced no tears when you,
at last, came to the place of death,
and died.

When we are brought to the place of death,
to mourn a partner, child or friend,
be with us there.
Where chilling graves and faceless crematoria rob us of our loved ones,
and in the place of death we stand bereft,
be with us there.

Lord Jesus Christ,
in place of death and loss and grief,
come to the mourning place
and wipe away, in time, the tears
and ease, in time, the aching heart.
Give, once more, the promise of eternity
and spring, and light and peaceful days –
the place of death, the leering skull,
replaced by life and your unfailing love.   AMEN.

Prayer Activity

Can you face your pains and the things you find unbearable in a way that does not close you in on yourself but rather opens you and helps you break through to a greater reality, a bigger perspective? Watch yourself as you reflect on recent pains and notice your tendencies of avoidance and temptations to run away or be violent. Can you follow in Jesus' footsteps and face the pain, remain with it, surrender to the feelings, and trust and have faith that you will be brought through to a better place?

Climbing

I lift up my eyes to the hills. From whence does my help come? My help comes from the Lord, who made heaven and earth.

~ *Psalm 121:1, 2* ~

We recall the mountains and hills of the Old Testament:
    Ararat – where the Ark came to rest.
    Sinai – where the Commandments were given.
    Zion – on which Jerusalem is built.
    Hermon – whose dews water the Holy Land ...
Such high and holy places prompt us – to pause and wonder and give
    praise!

We recall the mountains and hills of the New Testament:
    The Mount – where Jesus spoke the Beatitudes.
    The hills – where he withdrew to pray.
    The little hill of Calvary – where he died for us
    The mountain of Galilee – where, risen, he left his disciples ...
Such high and holy places prompt us – to pause and wonder and give
    praise!

We recall the mountains and hills we have known:
    Their rugged majesty, their steadfast beauty
    The fulfilment felt as the top was reached
    A different perspective gained, another world sensed ...
Such high and holy places prompt us – to pause and wonder and give
    praise!

Today, we recall that mountain where Jesus was transfigured, give us also a
    vision of majesty eternal.
As climbers attempt a mountain because it is there,
help us to attempt the mountain of faith and know that You are there:
greater than any mountain, higher than any hill
    with your glory in Christ
whose vision can transfigure us
    and make us holy as he is holy.
So help us, God over all.   AMEN.

Prayer Activity

Take 'time out'; get away from the everyday. Climb or imagine some hill-top. Quietly commune with God. Thrill in the encounter at such a place. Then, with fresh vision and new perspective, come down again to live again.

Healing

Come let us return to the Lord. He has torn us, but he will heal us …

~ Hosea 6:1 ~

Prayer for Reflection

I bought a spray at the chemist
for cuts, burns, and insect bites.
So I sprayed it,
and it did take the pain away,
    if only for a few moments.

And there are other pains,
    anxieties of the mind,
    bitterness of the soul,
and I need to find healing for these too.

You, Lord, healed the blind man so that he could see,
and the leper so that he could live again;
you took away the shame of the fallen
and restored hope to the outcast;
you gave sinners a fresh new beginning.

Prayer on Today's Theme

Thank you, God, for all who try to relieve pain:
doctors, nurses, and dentists;
    physiotherapists, and radiographers;
    psychiatrists, and psychologists;
    researchers and medical technicians.

Thank you too for those who put a plaster on;
    or stitch up wounds,
    or give us medicines to make us better;
those who try to comfort us,
    pastors, chaplains,
    and those who hold or lay on hands;
those who kiss it better,
    and listen to our moans and groans;
those who always make time, who never take offence.

Waiting (1)

Now, Lord, what do I wait for? My hope is in you.

~ Psalm 39:7 ~

Prayer for Reflection

Some days, Lord, I am on tenterhooks
    with apprehension, anxiety ...
    small things,
like, will the bus come on time?
    will anyone notice my blouse isn't ironed?
    not so small things,
like, will my tests from the hospital be positive?
    will I be equal to today's demands?

Today, Lord, let me rather be on tiptoe,
    ready to receive new surprises,
    to field new challenges,
    make new acquaintances,
alert and expectant,
    in the small things, and the not so small.

Prayer on Today's Theme

We pray for those who weary while they wait:
those who long for a child,
who await the birth of their baby, who wait for results of examinations
    which will further their career,
for news of a member of their family,
or for the outcome of an interview.

Help them to trust in you as they wait,
to remember how much you have done for them,
what you still do for those who wait with patience,
and to look to you with confidence and hope.

Waiting (2)

I wait for the Lord with longing; I put my hope in his word.

~ Psalm 130:5 ~

Prayer for Reflection

Eternal God,
so much in life
encourages my impatience,
    my desire for quick results,
    my requirement of an instant cure.

To be still,
to move from my agenda to your timetable
is not easy ... unless I have the company of others.

Help me, therefore, to wait for the right moment
    or the right word
    or the right person;
  to wait with longing
  or, as a sign of love,
  to wait on you
  as on my dearest friend;
and to do so
in company with Hannah, David, Mary and Paul
who learned to wait on the Lord.

Prayer on Today's Theme

Today I pray for those who are the slaves of deadlines,
    quotas,
    short tempers
    and other people's demands.
I remember those who have no time for themselves,
      no time to relax
and who grow discontent when they have time on their hands.

Give them a love of quietness, Lord,
in case their passion for busyness
may lead them to disregard their friends,
    dislike themselves
    and forget you
    whom we encounter in stillness.

Patience

The Lord is merciful and gracious, slow to anger and abounding in steadfast love.

~ *Psalm 103:8* ~

Prayer for Ourselves

I've done it again, Lord!
Opened my mouth and thought afterwards,
acted on impulse without thinking things through,
thought the worst without knowing the facts.
At times I seem to live on such a short fuse.
Yet still you are patient with me, showing me where I have gone wrong,
pointing out the better way.
Teach me how to be long-suffering, and help me to grow in grace
so that my anger may arise out of love for others, not in defence of myself.

Prayer for Others

Grant us patience, Lord,
with those who are slow,
whose bones ache as we rush past.
Help us to pause with those for whom the world moves too fast.
May we remain faithful to those who cared for us when they come to need
    our care,
as we remember Jesus
who had time and patience
        with a pestering Zacchaeus,
        with a persistent Bartimaeus,
        with a trauchled Martha in the kitchen,
        with a perplexed Mary in the garden.

Rising

In his great mercy by the resurrection of Jesus Christ from the dead,
he gave us new birth into a living hope.

~ 1 Peter 1:3 ~

Prayer for Reflection

It is hard to rise from bed, Lord,
when rudely awakened by the shrill call of the alarm.
It is hard to rise from tradition, Lord,
when challenged to rise to new opportunities to serve you.
It is hard to rise from selfishness, Lord,
when commanded to love my neighbour as myself.

Prayer on Today's Theme

We remember those who cannot rise today:
bedridden at home or in hospital,
sitting in chairs in homes for the elderly
or in hospital wards;
those who cannot get beyond their front door,
    because they are too infirm,
    or afraid of going outside,
    scared about what others might say if they saw them.

God, we thank you for the rising of Jesus from the tomb,
that we may rise with him to newness of life.
We give thanks that with him
each new day is a small resurrection,
with its opportunity to live for you.

Renewal

So we do not lose heart. Even though our outer nature is wasting away, our inner nature is being renewed day by day.

~ 2 Corinthians 4:16 ~

Prayer for Ourselves

Another day
for meeting new challenges,
for encountering new faces,
for undertaking the routine tasks
with renewed energy.
Another day
in which I am being remade
into the likeness of Jesus Christ,
hour by hour inwardly renewed.
Enable me, Lord,
to embrace the new day,
and to see it as a good friend
who will lead me nearer to you.

Prayer for Others

We pray today
for those who fear renewal:
those who live in the past,
those whose lives are a dead end,
those who are locked up in yesterday,
    who fear today,
      and cannot face tomorrow.
We pray too
for those who can no longer draw
    on their normal springs of renewal:
because they have lost their homes
    through natural disaster,
because they are separated from those they love
    through the cruelty of oppressors,
because they have lost hope
    through continual disappointment,
because they are in conflict
    with those who were once their friends.
Even when they feel they have lost much,
may they never lose heart.

The Sick

And he cured many who were sick with various diseases.

~ Mark 1:34 ~

They came to you in great numbers, healing Christ, because they wanted to
    be well.
They pushed in on you and clamoured at your feet – not caring if you saw
    them touch you or not so long as they were better.

And you came to them because 'those who are well have no need of a
    physician',
reminding us that our lack of sight, our discomfort in our own skin,
our inability to move and speak are linked to our separation from God.

Christ who brought healing, wholeness and hope,
we come to you now, wanting you to see the mess of our lives,
the brokenness of our world, the fragility of our bodies.
For like the lepers we desire to be clean,
like the blind we need to see things we've missed before,
and, like the woman who touched your cloak, we humbly approach you
hoping that our faith can make us well.

Lord, as we pray for those ill at home or in hospital today, we pray too for
    ourselves as carers and prayers.
Because we believe – help our unbelief.

Prayer Activity

Sit quietly for a few moments. Listen to your breathing. Think of God as
'Holy Breath' and cherish how close God is to you. Now acknowledge that
God is also as close as that to others, and in this moment remember those who
are ill at home or in hospital.

Temptation

Do not put us to the test, but save us from the evil one.

~ *Matthew 6:13* ~

Prayer for Reflection

Sometimes, Lord,
it amazes me
how I sat examinations
in my childhood,
harder ones in my youth,
developed my proficiency,
    my skills
being tested all the time,
and aiming to succeed.

And yet despite all this effort,
and even proof of passing the test,
in the dilemmas of daily life,
experience has not bred expertise.

From the trite answer,
    the easy solution,
    the careless response
and all such allurements,
Good Lord, deliver me.

Prayer on Today's Theme

Lord Jesus Christ,
you have harried hell,
detoxified darkness,
and conquered the powers of wickedness.

Confront today
those who consort with what is evil,
    who misuse money,
    exploit the vulnerable,
    trade in malicious gossip,
    or demean their own bodies.

Shout at them,
as loudly as you shouted at Lazarus,
that they may walk away from death
and come to you for cleansing.

The Value of Wisdom

The wise get all the knowledge they can, but when fools speak, trouble is not far off.

~ *Proverbs 10:14* ~

Prayer for Reflection

Lord of the ages,
when I delude myself into thinking
that I am growing wiser with the passing years,
help me to question my assumption.

Help me to listen to younger people, and their ideas,
and not to be wearied by their enthusiasm or their endless talking
... and this, just in case they may be nearer
  your will for the world
  than I am.

Give me, Lord,
the humility to be reticent where that is needed,
and the sensitivity to speak the truth in kindness.

Prayer on Today's Theme

Loving God,
confront today those who never question
that they might be wrong;
surprise those who stumble through life in slavery to rules you never
  intended;
befriend those who believe you have the truth and are keen to find it.

Straight and Narrow

Narrow is the gate and constricted the road that leads to life, and those who find them are few.

~ *Matthew 7:14* ~

Prayer for Reflection

Sometimes,
like a blindfold woman
trying to put a tail on the donkey,
I rely on my skill
and end up wide of the mark.

And sometimes,
like a drunk man making for home,
I end up walking in circles.

… and this,
not so much to do with my sense of direction
as with the way I go astray
when it comes to faith, hope, and love.

All the time that I rely on my own skill,
I fail to lean on and learn from you, my Saviour.

God give me the grace which I lack
to find the direction my life is meant for.

Prayer on Today's Theme

A thought
for those who knowingly lead others
up the garden path …

A thought
for those who deliberately persuade others
that everybody should do what they like …

A thought
for those who intentionally tell others
that freedom should have no limits,
even if it infringes on someone else's life.
Show them your cross, Lord Christ:
ultimate freedom without limit,
but ultimately reached by a narrow road.

Eyeing up

If a man looks on a woman with a lustful eye, he has already committed adultery with her in his heart.

~ *Matthew 5:28* ~

Prayer for Reflection

The rumours were rife, Lord,
but the evidence was non existent.

You enjoyed the company of women,
and they enjoyed your company.
But there was no more –
just the kind of unthreatening love
which is all too uncommon.

Help me, like you,
always to see people as people
and never as objects of lust,
need or pleasure.

What do I pray
    for those who abuse
    the minds and bodies of others?

What do I pray
    for those haunted by the memory
    of what was once done to them?

What do I pray
    for those who sit and listen,
    trying to unravel years of torment
    or of tormenting?

Through disgust, anger,
or through confusion,
for each I pray,
'Your will be done.'

Poor in Spirit

Blessed are the poor in spirit, the kingdom of Heaven is theirs.

~ Matthew 5:3 ~

Prayer for Reflection

I know what I know,
but not what I do not know.
So, when a wiser person,
    a different opinion,
    an alternative view.
confronts me,
I can be defensive at best
and arrogant at worst.

I am afraid, Lord,
    of the insecurity of not knowing,
    not being in charge,
    having to admit my poverty.

How can such a condition be blessed?
How can I understand
    unless I risk living happily
    with my limitations?

Prayer on Today's Theme

The day will surely come
    when those bent with care will walk tall,
    and the dehumanised will dance for joy,
    and the weary will smile warmly,
    and the stigmatised will take the centre stage,
    and those wrongly accused will be liberated.
    and those who suffer in silence will laugh loudly.

Until then, Lord, bring my life into contact
with those who know their need,
that I may receive the benefit of that company
to which you have given your blessing.

Arrival

Trust in the Lord is a tower of refuge.

~ Proverbs 29:25 ~

Prayer for Reflection

O Lord,
you have been with me at the successful conclusion of many of life's
    journeys;
        passing exams,
        sitting a driving test,
        establishing a home and family,
        getting a job.

Let me never grow smug or self-satisfied.
Without your love I have no hope of success;
without you, I am nothing.

Prayer on Today's Theme

Lord,
some people are never successful in the world's eyes.
They never pass exams,
        for they have no opportunity of sitting any.
They cannot pass their driving test,
        for they have no money for lessons.
They cannot have children,
        or are overwhelmed by family problems.
They cannot get a job,
        for there is no work for them to do.

They have not failed in your eyes.
Help them to value themselves as you value them
and to feel at home and complete in you.

Fooled by Fakes

Beware of false prophets, who come to you dressed as sheep, while underneath they are savage wolves.

~ *Matthew 7:15* ~

Prayer for Reflection

Beware, my soul,
of cheap grace,
of easy religion,
of pious con-men,
of dead tradition,
    which masquerades as the truth,
of spiritual novelties
which breed a craving
    for more of the same.

Bless, my soul,
the Lord your God
who in flesh and spirit
and through wood and nails
purchased your whole salvation.

Bless, my soul,
the Lord your God;
and never forget his love.

Prayer on Today's Theme

Remembering my local church, the one about which I can both delight and
    despair, I pray for renewal:
start with the notice board,
    if the sight of it depresses you, Lord;
start with the door,
    if the welcome seems more like a warning;
start with the worship
    if it celebrates the past
    and suspects the future;
start with the leaders, the elders, the managers,
    if they rate success higher than obedience;
start with ...

start with me.

Rock Solid

Whoever hears these words of mine and acts on them is like a man who had the sense to build his house on rock.

~ *Matthew 7:24* ~

Prayer for Reflection

Let me reflect with you, Lord,
on what I have learned ...
and how I have grown ... ;
on what I have discovered about myself ...
and what I now realise about you ...

Breathe on me, breath of God.
Let me know how much I am rooted on the rock,
    whose name is Jesus,
and how much more of me
    has still to be embedded in him.

Prayer on Today's Theme

For the good government
of this land I pray,
that through the Queen or President,
through parliament,
through local councils, justice and decency in public life
may be preserved, and the earthly preconditions be laid
for that quality of life
embodied in Christ's kingdom.

Advise us when we deliberate on politics
and vote for candidates,
that we may act
not according to our latest whim,
but with your will for the world in our minds
and the needs of the world before our eyes.

Inform our judgements,
redeem our passions,
dispel our apathy;
for you made and love this land
and want it to be ruled wisely and well.

Hunger

All raise their eyes to you in hope; and you give them their food when it is due.

~ *Psalm 145:15* ~

Prayer for Reflection

You, Jesus Christ,
are the Bread of Life
and the Water of Life.
This I believe and cherish
out of conviction,
and because my stomach is full.

Perhaps I would feel differently, Lord.
if my bones showed through famine
or my stomach swelled through malnutrition.

Forgive me
for saying 'I'm starving' when I mean I have an appetite:
for saying 'I'm gasping' when I mean I feel like a drink.

Teach me to hunger and thirst for your justice;
then the appetites of all will come closer to being satisfied.

Prayer on Today's Theme

Lord Jesus,
you saw a hungry crowd and had compassion on them
so much that you did not rest until they were fed.
Yet today many of your followers dine well
without a thought for those who have little nourishment.
Strengthen, therefore, the resolve of all Aid agencies
both to feed the hungry and to stir our consciences.

End the tyrannies both of hunger
and of those who use starvation
to suppress the human spirit.
And let our tables always be open
lest one day at a greater feast
we find our place taken by one we refused to feed.

The Lord is close to those whose courage is broken; God saves those whose spirit is crushed.

~ *Psalm 34:18* ~

Prayer for Reflection

For my home,
for its familiar furniture,
> the photographs of family and friends,
> the food in the kitchen … thank you, God.

For my home,
for those who come to my door,
> who send me letters,
> who telephone me … thank you, God.

For my home,
in which – without great cost –
I can offer that hospitality
which is a sign
and hallmark of your kingdom … thank you, God.

Prayer on Today's Theme

Lord Jesus,
how can we speak of the heavenly city
to those who live in a cardboard city?
How can we speak of family values
to those for whom the family has failed?
And how much longer will soup kitchens,
> hostels for the homeless,
> and the begging hands of sorry people
be part and parcel of city living?

Through the work of voluntary agencies,
through the policies of local and national government,
and through my refusal to walk on by,
may homes be found for the homeless.

But, more than this, may the worth of those at risk be recognised
before drink, drugs, or misery
become their only companions on the street.

— 'I am Gentle and Humble-hearted' —

~ Matthew 11:29 ~

Prayer for Reflection

As clearly as those who were self-obsessed
    knew the edge of your tongue,
so those who were self-effacing
    knew the pleasure of your company.

And only you and I, Lord,
know into which category I fall,
and whether,
at this stage in my life,
I have to hear your hard words
or feel your gentle presence.

May I never avoid your anger
    which is just;
nor dismiss your humility
    which is tough and tested.

Prayer on Today's Theme

God bless today
those to whom life has been raw and rough:
    women who have been treated
    like objects;
    men who have been bred
    to be bullies;
    children who have been hardened
    through a lack of love;
… and all those whose job
    or appearance
    or temperament
makes them the butt of cruel humour.

Don't let this day end
without someone showing them
the gentleness of Jesus Christ
which comforts and converts.

'I am the Good Shepherd'

~ John 10:11 ~

Prayer for Reflection

... and you know your sheep
and you call them by name.

And if I were to be quiet enough;
if I were to silence all the words
I want to say
and if I were to forget
all the words I would put
in your mouth,
I might just hear
you calling my name
as if it were the only name.

And then I would be glad
to realise again
that the Lord is my Shepherd.

Prayer on Today's Theme

Let me remember with you, Lord,
those for whom I have a special care,
not because of my job
but because of my conscience.

I remember those whose health
    never seems to improve,
    and ask that they may learn
    and share the meaning of suffering.

I remember those whose mind
never seems to settle,
and ask that they may discover
the path to peace which evades them.

I remember those whose love
never seems to be valued,
and ask that they will know
your deep cherishing.

I remember those who care for me
and pray for me without asking.
May they always have a place in my heart and in heaven.

Spies

The Lord said to Moses, 'Send men to spy out the land of Canaan,
which I am giving to the Israelites.'

~ *Numbers 13:1* ~

Lord, how often has humankind claimed that you have told them
to take the land you have given them and to fight their enemies?

The Old Testament is full of stories where we are told: 'God says' go, take,
    fight and kill.
We recognise that, today, leaders still claim your authority for the wars
    they wage against our so-called 'enemies'.
We still send spies on secret intelligence-gathering missions;
we are still afraid to trust each other and accept that each is different.
We forget that you created all life in all its variety;
we forget that Jesus commanded us to love our enemies.
How long do we need to continue to act out of fear?
How long do we need to continue to spy on our neighbour?
How long do we need to covet our neighbour's land?
How long do we need to oppress and exploit?
Loving God, help us to wrestle with the difficult decisions that need to be
    made about intelligence and security.
Help us to see the bigger picture – without blinkers – seeing only our own
    small situation in life.
You sent Jesus to show us the way;
help us to trust in you and not to be afraid.   AMEN.

Readings

Genesis 42:1–25	*Joseph's brothers go to Egypt*
Numbers 13	*Spies report on the Promised Land*
Numbers 14	*Rebellion, intercession, disobedience*
Joshua 2	*Spies sent to Jericho*
1 Samuel 26	*David spares Saul's life*
Luke 20:20–6	*Spies sent to trap Jesus*

Disappointment

Do not disappoint my hope.

~ Psalm 119:116 ~

Prayer for Reflection

I sometimes think my expectations are too high!
I can even demand more from others than from myself.
– tidiness in the home,
– efficiency at work,
– consistency in politicians,
– reliability in church duties.

But then I sometimes wonder if I ever fulfil
other people's expectations of me!

I remember Jesus in the garden,
castigating God for not coming up to scratch,
but then realising that there was still something more
that he was expected to do.

Help me, Lord, not to disappoint you today.

Prayer on Today's Theme

I think of those whose relationships,
or creativity, or career,
have not matched their expectations.

I think of those whose self-esteem is low
because others remind them continually
how disappointing they've been.

But I think too of the father
who saw the approach of the son
    who had been such a disappointment,
and ran and embraced him,
and welcomed his lost child home.

Remind them all, and remind me,
that your love will always exceed all expectation.

Gateways

I shall restore her vineyards to her, turning the valley of Achor into a gate of hope.

~ *Hosea 2:15* ~

Prayer for Reflection

Today, Lord, I will come to many doors
    and face many gates;
some I will go through with confidence,
at others I will hesitate,
at some my heart will be in my mouth.

If behind any I find bad news,
    or rejection,
    or disappointment,
    or defeat,
give me the strength to push right through,
for you have promised that you are the door,
    and anyone who enters through your door
    shall be safe.

Prayer on Today's Theme

Today I remember
those who feel trapped,
    by the bars of a prison,
    by the responsibilities of parenthood,
    by pain and illness,
    by a disability,
    by low self-esteem,
    by being in the public eye,
    by not having enough money,
    or by having too much.
Let them see
that there are two ways of looking at a valley,
    up at its steep sides
    or ahead to the way between the mountains,
    a gateway to what lies beyond.

Improvements

A better hope is introduced, through which we draw near to God.

~ Hebrews 7:19 ~

Prayer for Reflection

It wasn't clear to everyone at the time that Jesus was a better way.
They needed a lot of persuading
to leave the old system of sacrifice and ritual,
and adopt the new way of faith.

I don't like change either.
It frightens me,
it makes me feel uncomfortable, uncertain and unsure.

Sometimes, though, I do like to learn new things
    and am grateful for what they bring;
new friends too,
after the initial worry about whether they will like me,
whether they might turn out to be boring,
or whether they are really what they seem.

Simon did not keep you to himself, Lord,
but said to Andrew, 'Come and see'.
Help me today
to bring something new to someone's life,
even introduce them to you.

Prayer on Today's Theme

Be with those who feel that new things are a threat:
the young person starting a new job
when everything is strange,
the older person at work
who cannot grasp new technologies and methods,
writers, preachers, journalists and leaders of opinion
who have fixed ideas.

Encourage those who have alternatives to offer,
newspaper columnists who challenge the popular view,
the new member of a group or company who introduces fresh ideas,
those who fearlessly proclaim the Gospel.

Give to us all the courage of Abraham,
who, at a word from God,
left the safety of all he knew,
and went on a journey.

Community

Christ Jesus our hope
~ 1 Timothy 1:1 ~

Prayer for Reflection

I know you are hope for me, Lord –
but you are also 'our' hope.
I may pray alone,
but I belong to a community,
indeed several communities:
> of family, of village, of city,
> of the body of Christ, the Church,
> the community of saints who uphold me,
> the institution I serve or belong to,
> my group at work, my friends in leisure.

Because you are 'our' hope, Lord,
help me see these people as precious to you.

Prayer on Today's Theme

I pray for those who never seem to fit in
> to the communities they are supposed to belong to:
because they feel they have nothing to give,
because they fear others will put them down,
because they are over-sensitive
> and respond with aggression,
because they are the 'wrong' sex or colour.

Lord Jesus, you often found the most difficult people
> the best company,
and in making them your friends
you showed society that they'd got it wrong.
Help those who feel cast out
to know that they have been counted in,
for you are their hope too.

My Lifestyle

I came that they might have life, and have it abundantly.

~ *John 10:10* ~

Prayer for Ourselves

I enjoy a full and active life, Lord.
Those with whom I work
    seem satisfied with my efforts,
    and have even been heard to say 'Well done'.
My friends have laughed in my company,
    and been there for me when I have needed them.
My family are always at the end of the phone
    and we have shared life's celebrations,
    as well as life's endings, over the years.
My health, all in all,
    has enabled me to run and play,
    and provided the stamina to endure.
My pocket has always contained enough spare change
    to help another in a crisis.
I have experienced
    the passion and excitement of love,
    – as well as love's struggle.
Both in giving and receiving
    life has engaged me in its mystery,
    and I am grateful, Lord.

Prayer for Others

Fill with your love, O God,
the hearts of those whose lives seem empty
of relationships that matter and jobs which satisfy.
Fill with your compassion, O God,
those who keep their fingers gripped so tightly on their money and
    belongings,
that they have forgotten how to share.
Fill with your humility, O God, those too proud to recognise
how their standard of living is obtained at the cost of another's freedom.
Fill us all with such gratitude, O God, that all may witness to the gift of life
with a life of thanksgiving and hope.

My Health

'Do you want to be made well?'

~ John 5:6 ~

Prayer for Ourselves

A centurion ran to catch you and plead for his servant;
a man cried out to you as his daughter lay dying;
a woman risked humiliation, reaching out to you through the crowd,
    that she might be healed.
Yet, the man by the pool seemed to bask in his misery,
as others stepped, and jumped, and dived into the waters of new life.
Whenever I feel sorry for myself, Lord, cajole me out of my lethargy.
When I shrink back,watching others grasp for hope,
make me rise up and plunge into your love.

Prayer for Others

Christ, healer,
by your wisdom,
guide the environmentalist,
the researcher, the scientist,
all who seek to bring us healthy surroundings in which to live.

By your grace,
teach us to value each person we encounter,
in spite of the prejudice bred within us
about disability,
particular diseases,
our misunderstandings about illness of the mind.

In your strength, Lord,
enable us all to look after ourselves,
in what we consume, what we do, how we live,
that so exercised in body, mind, and spirit,
we might be all that we can be.

My Fears

The Lord watches over all who love him.

~ Psalm 145:20 ~

Prayer for Ourselves

Lord, my greatest fear is not
when the world will end,
    nor how,
(though perhaps it should be).

The fears which haunt me are more mundane – even laughable.
I am afraid of the dark, at times,
and of spiders and snakes.
And there are some things that really scare me:
I am afraid of growing old alone;
afraid that the phone won't ring tonight,
or that it will ring,
and I won't like what I hear.
I am afraid of losing my friends.
I am afraid to make commitments.
I am afraid, as are so many,
that life will pass me by
and I will be left
thinking only what might have been.
Help me today to take the risk and put all my trust in you.

Prayer for Others

God,
you are both father and mother to us all,
watch over those who are afraid.
To those who fear the night
and the thoughts darkness brings;
to those who fear a new day
with all its anxieties;
speak your words, Lord, 'Do not be afraid'.
To those who fear that they cannot cope, who consider themselves failures,
those so distressed they consider suicide;
speak your words, Lord, 'Do not be afraid'.
To those who fear for one they love, who is ill, or dying, or left alone;
to those afraid to face up to the truth about themselves or a relationship;
speak your words, Lord, 'Do not be afraid'.

My Journey

Surely goodness and mercy shall follow me all the days of my life.

~ Psalm 23:6 ~

Prayer for Ourselves

As I look back on my life, Lord,
I see so many twists and turns,
and not a few dead ends.
At times I have had to retrace my steps and find my way again.
I recognise paths I have walked unafraid, places I have rested and been
    refreshed, occasions on which I have had fun and been invigorated,
and quiet corners in which I have lamented.

Yet I see now
you have always been there, following me all the days,
picking up the pieces, cajoling me forward,
supporting me when I have had to lean on you.

Still there is much travelling to be done
for my pilgrimage is not yet over.
Yet, the more I reflect on your abiding presence,
the greater the confidence I discover and the courage I receive,
to take the next step.

Prayer for Others

Light the path, dear Lord,
of all who journey today:
those at sea, in the air,
travelling by rail, on the road,
and those who walk,
that you might be their company and direction.

By your guiding, Lord,
lead those who travel uncertainly through life
and wonder where they are heading.
May your light
warn travellers of hazards on route,
that all may navigate a safe and true course.
Bring us all home at the last
to a safe harbour, and eternal rest
in your kingdom.

Longing

As a deer longs for flowing streams, so my soul longs for you, O God.

~ *Psalm 42:1* ~

Longing is at the centre of my life,
a hunger for food, for sex, for love.
I have a thirst to belong,
to be at home, at ease with myself, with others, with life.

I confess that I have never longed for you
in the way the writer of these religious poems has longed.
What agony! What yearning!
Yes, I recognise it, but not in such
painful depth of spirit.

> *Tears are my food day and night ...*
> *my flesh faints for you,*
> *as in a dry and weary land*
> *where there is no water.*

Lord, I have never been to these extremities:
so utterly alienated from human company,
in mortal danger from cruel enemies,
crying out for revenge, despairing of spiritual aid.

God, make haste to help those
whose misery, or harsh environment, or broken spirit makes them cry.
Come to their souls with peace. Answer their longing with belonging.
Bring them to the point where they, too, can say:

> *My soul is satisfied as with a rich feast,*
> *and my mouth praises you with joyful lips*
> *when I think of you on my bed,*
> *and meditate on you in the watches of the night;*
> *for you have been my help,*
> *and in the shadow of your wings I sing for joy.*

Readings

Psalm 42; Psalm 43; Psalm 63; Matthew 11:28; John 7:37–9;
Romans 8:18–30

Wisdom

The fear of the Lord is the beginning of knowledge; fools despise wisdom and instruction.

~ Proverbs 1:7 ~

Lord, we live in a world of information:
of websites and databases,
of satellite television and video-conferencing.
Facts and figures are at our very finger tips.
Every kind of knowledge is but a moment away.
Yet, Lord, we who know so much
have so much to learn in the halls of wisdom.
The ancients, the sages and prophets (though we might think them
   primitive)
are truly our masters and our mentors.
We who are overflowing with information
are summoned to that school which charges no fees
but from which we never graduate
this side of eternity.
I remember that reverence of you is the beginning of wisdom.
I pray for all preachers, teachers, and evangelists
as they seek to introduce people to the One who is the wellspring
and fountainhead of all wisdom and learning.

Readings

Psalm 1	*The way of life and the way of death*
Ecclesiastes 3:1–8	*A time for everything*
Matthew 7:24–9	*Hearing and doing*
1 Corinthians 2:6–10	*Wisdom is more than knowledge*
Proverbs 8:22–31	*Wisdom and creation*
Matthew 25:1–13	*The wise and the foolish*

Gethsemane

They went to a place called Gethsemane; and he said to his disciples,
'Sit here while I pray.'

~ *Mark 14:32* ~

Holy, human Jesus,
anxious, distressed, unsure of your own future,
you sought sanctuary in a garden,
sheltering underneath the twisted branches of an olive tree and far away
   from the noise of a crowded city.
Just like us, you felt the need to be alone, yet not too alone.
With friends nearby, you were able to be honest with yourself
and honest to God.

Holy, human Jesus,
when we are anxious, distressed, unsure of the future,
help us to find sanctuary for our souls and care for our bodies.
When we encounter our own Gethsemane moments,
enable us to stop ... and sit ...
and to find the strength to ask you,
'Sit here while I pray.'

Holy, human Jesus,
when our friends and loved ones avoid or abandon us –
not because they do not care
but that sometimes they don't know how to care –
reassure us of your company
and inhabit our darkness,
so rekindling your life within us.

Prayer Activity

In the good times, remember the bad; in the bad times, remember the good.
Many Christian sages have given this sound advice. Hold in one hand an
experience you describe as bad and in your other hand a good experience
for you. Notice your thoughts and feelings in each situation, look for God's
presence in each and reflect on similarities and differences. What have you
learned?

Jericho

Today salvation has come to this house.

~ Luke 19:9 ~

Sometimes, God, I feel left out.
I watch others worship and I think, 'I couldn't do that, I would get it wrong.'
I see people happy and praising and I wonder why I don't feel like that.
I look at groups of friends and want to know what makes them liked and
    confident, and never lonely.

Lord, I am lonely. Sometimes my life is a lonely place to be.

Today, I pray for a moment in my life like Zacchaeus had.
I believe I could be transformed.
If you walked down my street.
If you came to my house!
If you chose me in front of others who overlook my existence.
If you spent time with me, one to one, giving me the opportunity to tell you
    who I am and realise the areas in my life where I need redirection.

God, help me to see that you offer these things, that life, *now*.
Give me a space in this day to find my Jericho place ...
    where the walls come down,
    where I forget about the crowds and meet with you, just as I
      am. AMEN.

Readings

Joshua 6:1–5; Psalm 139; Luke 19:1–10; 1 Corinthians 13

Prayer Activity

Can you truly, truly welcome the unexpected today and expect God to be
there? Can you recognise when you are being encouraged and affirmed, and
really, really rejoice? Can you see God even in apparent disaster and respond
instantly – trusting that good will come again?

Bethany

He left them, went out of the city to Bethany, and spent the night there.

~ Matthew 21:17 ~

Heavenly Father,
most of us long for a place apart,
where acceptance and genuine welcome are assured.
Slip off the shoes, sit down, relax, listen and share stories of the day, enjoy
   the aroma of food cooking,
the laughter and seriousness of mutual understandings.

A place for silence and tears and dreams, where we may be ourselves.

In Bethany you knew such a place apart with friendship shared and pain and
   restoration.
From Bethany, you walked refreshed the dusty path to city and to destiny.
Father, thank you for Bethany homes and people along my path of life,
unconditional welcome, enjoyment and refreshment, then back into the fray,
   enriched, encouraged.
Often challenged.

My home, too, Lord Jesus, is open for you, and those you send my way,
Be known here through open friendship,
simple acceptance and hospitality shared.
For your love's sake.   AMEN.

Readings

Genesis 18:1–8; Proverbs 15:14–17; Matthew 21:14–17; Luke 19:1–10;
Romans 12:9–12

Silence

Prayer Activity

Allow yourself to remember people who, by their hospitality and loving acceptance, have enriched your life of faith. Think about them and give thanks to God for them. Consider what you can learn even now through their example. Ask God to show you the special blessings of your own particular situation, then consider if those things may in some way become blessings multiplied to others.

Gaza

Once Samson went to Gaza, where he saw a prostitute and went in to her.

~ *Judges 16:1* ~

Heavenly Father,
there is nothing new under the sun,
the old temptations and pitfalls are just as potent as ever,
and the consequences just as damaging.
Samson got away with that, but fell for the next.
Pride and folly with the catalyst of complacency.
'It could never happen to me,'
but it did,
and his lifetime's calling was destroyed.
Lead us not into temptation
and deliver us from evil,
greed, lust, pride, deceit – and more … an ugly list.
We need your help to recognise
sin in its most subtle or most blatant form
and act with strength to take the way of escape you have promised.
The world says sin doesn't really matter. Be your own person – whatever
    the cost.
An inner voice tells us that we have been bought with a price,
the precious blood of Christ,
so all is significant.
And when we fall, O loving Father, don't let us creep away
to hide in shame, but come before you,
and know the final word is yours:
'Forgive them.'   AMEN.

Prayer Activity

When you find yourself tempted, remember that, like Samson, you have choices and you have the strength of the Lord. Strength is a gift to be used appropriately. Meditate upon a symbol of strength for you, perhaps from the Samson story – a pillar, a rock, a light, a torch, a lion, a jackal, bees or honey. Ask for God's help to remember this when you are tempted, and choose strength.

Noah and his Family

The Lord said to Noah, 'Go into the ark, you and all your household, for I have seen that you alone are righteous before me in this generation.'

~ *Genesis 7:1* ~

Lord God, as children we loved the story of Noah's Ark:
    of the animals going in two by two,
    of the flood coming up and the rain coming down,
    of only eight being saved – the faithful Noah and his family.
Help us, as adults, to go on loving this story
but also to understand it –
    that, though you can be scunnered with humanity, your mercy avails;
    that, though you can destroy, you can also save.
As we confess that we do not always find favour in your eyes,
    set the Cross between our souls and our sins;
    make us righteous in your sight.
Remind us that by Baptism we are saved through water,
    and that by your love in Christ we are called into your company,
    the ark royal that is the Church Catholic.
Stir the Church when she is too comfortably becalmed;
    steady her when storm and flood might overwhelm her;
    maintain her on true course in the present as in the past;
    and drive her by the power of the Spirit onward to your future.
O Lord God, today we remember
    all who go to sea in ships:
those serving in the Navy and on merchant ships ...
    those fishing from our shores ...
    protect them from rock and tempest, fire and foe;
    be with all in peril on the sea.
    Support, we ask, all who strive for safety at sea ... all engaged in
        rescue ... all who minister to mariners.
Lord God, remember us,
    keep us true to our Baptism and safely on board the ark of salvation ...
    learning our role in the company of Christ,
    faithfully playing our part,
    caring for your creatures great and small,
    sending forth doves of peace into our troubled world. AMEN.

The Anawim*

My soul waits for the Lord more than those who watch for the morning.

~ *Psalm 130:6a* ~

They were called the Anawim.
Were they not the humble ones, the forgotten and powerless ones?

Yet in their openness and poverty of spirit, in their simplicity and faith,
they were the great ones in your eyes, Lord,
the powerful ones, the key players in your story.

I remember those who, like Mary and Joseph, Simeon and Anna,
    kept alight the lamp of faith when others had given way to cynicism or
      had settled into quiet despair.

They were there as your sentinels, alert and responsive to your Word,
keenly scanning the dark horizon for signs of your Kingdom's dawning.

Lord, I pray for your Anawim across the world,
    the humble faithful who refuse to abandon hope,
    for those who have glimpsed a reddening in the sky
and who are active in waiting for your coming.

Readings

Luke 2:25–38   *Simeon and Anna*

Prayer Activity

Read the story of Simeon and Anna. Picture the scene in the Temple. Visualise the facial expressions of Mary, Joseph, Simeon and Anna, the infant Jesus. What emotions do they show? Wonder? Fear and foreboding? Confusion? Hope? Longing? Think of people known to you (or featured in the news) whose situations reflect these emotions. Pray for them.

---

* plural form of an Old Testament word, translated in various ways as 'poor', 'afflicted', 'humble' or 'meek'. The Anawim were the faithful remnant, the powerless ones, whose only resource was God. The main characters in the first two chapters of Luke's Gospel could all be characterised as 'Anawim'.

Demons

Now the spirit of the Lord departed from Saul, and an evil spirit from the Lord tormented him.

~ *1 Samuel 16:14* ~

Lord, I want to model my life on you, love you, follow in your ways.
Help me when I feel as if there is a demon inside me –
like those times I find it impossible to control my thoughts or feelings,
or when I seem unable to stop myself from saying hurtful things and I
   wonder why I feel so powerless.
When my anger, distress or confusion breaks into the open and I, and others,
   see a side of myself I prefer to pretend is not there,
sometimes I experience this as if an enemy has got inside me, a demon.
Other times it is as if my emotions are controlling me.
Or are these the same thing?

I ask for your wisdom, your firmness and gentleness to prompt and teach me
to navigate the storms of my inner world
by listening to my emotions,
allowing your Spirit to teach me in the midst of them.

And I pray for people who live with particularly difficult emotional states,
asking for relief and release for them and, above all, hope.
I pray for people who help them, for your grace and blessing for them.
I ask for your help to discern with you how I need to take evil seriously,
to follow you with all my heart and mind and strength and to learn to fear
   nothing.

In Jesus' name. AMEN.

Prayer Activity

Think of a time when you had to wrestle with your emotions. What helped you to resolve the situation? Recognise how much help came from beyond your own resources.

Hannah

'Do not regard your servant as a worthless woman, for I have been speaking out of my great anxiety and vexation all this time.'

~ *1 Samuel 1:16* ~

Lord, be with me in my longing,
my yearning for you to remove the obstacles in my life,
to bring growth to my barren places within,
my desperateness to find my fulfilment,
to begin to realise my potential.

Lord, what is the missing link? What am I failing to do?
Is there something wrong with me?

Lord, bring me through the storm of my emotional turmoil.
Give me the courage to face and to watch
the swirl of my feelings, the confusion,
the distress that is in my mind and felt deep in my body.
Teach me, Lord, to be still in the midst of my questions.

Hear my cries – even if other people call me mad, or bad.
Hear my cries – for life, for birth, for release,
for possibility and new beginnings.
Lead me, help me find the people, the places, the connections
that will allow your life to flow in me and through me.
I dedicate this new birth to your Kingdom,
in this time, in this period of history –
that justice may come for me, for others. AMEN.

Prayer Activity

'Healed are those who weep for their frustrated desire; they shall see the face of fulfilment in a new form' (Matt 5:4, translated from the Aramaic). Reflect on how this could be for you today.

Martha

But Martha was distracted by her many tasks ...

~ Luke 10:40 ~

O God, we often look on the appearance but you look on the heart.
Forgive us for our superficial judgments, our casual dismissal of some
    people.
Give us the seeing eye and the understanding mind.

Help us this day to think of Martha – not as the moaning servant but
        one who receives Jesus into her house;
        one who, recognising his authority, appeals to Jesus;
        one who, at the death of Lazarus, goes out to meet him;
        one who asserts that Jesus is the divine physician;
        and one to whom Jesus declares that he is the resurrection and the life.
O God, help us to learn from her fuller story and to affirm as she did
        that Jesus is the Christ, the Son of God.

Lord Jesus Christ, who stands at the door, may I receive you into my home
    ...
Lord of the pots and pans, the plane and lathe, calm me when trauchled ...
Lord, good physician, soothe my spirit, allay my anxieties, restore and
    renew me in my worship and work ...
Lord, conqueror of death, with me in my living and striving,
with me in my dying, raise me with all who serve.   AMEN.

Prayer Activity

Traditionally many of us say grace before a meal. Try to write your own. Find
ways to include in it an acknowledgment of the difficult parts of your day as
well as thanks for the moments of delight.

The 5,000

'We have nothing here but five loaves and two fish.'

~ *Matthew 14:17* ~

God, whose hands held the fish, and tore the bread,
feed the hunger in me
for peace,
for justice,
for grace.

God, whose hands blessed the fish,
and broke the bread,
feed the hunger of the world
for balance,
for fairness,
for truthfulness.

God, in whose hands fish fed a multitude,
and bread delivered a banquet,
I come to you,
along with the world,
hungry for forgiveness,
and a new imperative,
where sharing becomes a sacred act,
where feeding the hungry shapes a sacrament, and where banqueting with
    the world
is the substance of heaven.

Prayer Activity

Find a photograph or an object that speaks to you about generosity. It may be
an image of your friends or family, it may be a present someone gave you.
Simply take some time to let these images or objects remind you about the
generosity you've experienced in life in many different ways.

Paul

So Paul stood up and with a gesture began to speak: 'You Israelites,
and others who fear God, listen.'

~ Acts 13:16 ~

Word of God,
we live in a world of words:
helpful words and hurtful words.
Sometimes language is used to build up and to encourage;
sometimes to break down and to destroy.
Help us to listen to your Word that encourages eternal values
and brings to light those things of endless worth.

We give thanks for those who,
down through the ages, have worked with words:
poets and philosophers, politicians and preachers, women and men of all
    faiths and of none,
who have sought to bring beauty and colour and texture, light and life and
    learning,
to a world that cries out for justice
and to a people who search for meaning.

God of words and of worlds:
help us to be the best that we can be,
to speak the words that really matter and care,
to be the people that you would have us be,
and to be your Word incarnate, here and now.

Prayer Activity

Take a piece of paper and a pencil. Write down as many words as you can
think of that describe what God might be for you (for example: peace, love,
goodness, Jesus, laughter, passion, patience, etc.). Once you have completed
this activity, look at the words you have found. Pray over these words and
give thanks to God for all that God means in your life and in the lives of
others.

Lost

*He was trying to see who Jesus was, but on account of the crowd
he could not, because he was short in stature. So he ran ahead and
climbed a sycamore tree.*

~ *Luke 19:3–4* ~

Feeling low in every sense, insecure in being and crushed by a crowd giving
no recognition or care – God, we can imagine so well how Zacchaeus felt
that day.

Confronted with his own deceit and bad track record, oppressed by the fear
that this was how it was always going to be,
Zacchaeus sensed your presence as an opportunity to rise above.

So let us have that kind of moment today, God.
Let us climb out of the depths to see who you are,
And in our shame and worry may we find that half-way house,
That secure branch to grab hold of,
That safe place to sit,
until you lovingly call to us, to finally let you in.

And help us too, God, to be rooted in your strength for others:
To be people they lean on
Places they shelter
Life they connect to.
That they too will see Jesus – in us.   AMEN.

Prayer Activity

Hold a piece of wood in your hand. Look at its grain, its colour, its shape.
Now imagine that small piece as part of the large tree it came from – where
did it grow? What did it look like? What happened around it? Offer a prayer
now for the Christian community you are part of – and reflect on the tree as
a symbol of the church.

Blessing

> The possibilities of forgiveness,
> The strength of life,
> The root of love
> Be shown in you this day
> For Christ's sake.

View

This is the land of which I swore to Abraham, to Isaac, and to Jacob,
'I will give it to your descendants'; I have let you see it with your eyes
but you shall not cross over there.

~ Deuteronomy 34:4 ~

God,
what are we to do when we see the horizon, but know we'll never arrive at
   it;
when we are called to hold and care for a promise
only a future generation will see fulfilled;
when we are asked to pass on the story for someone not yet born
not knowing if they will ever come to hear it?

Grant encouragement to your daily workers.
Gift the faith to recognise you are always found in the journeying,
that the learning is done in the travelling, that signs and wonders unfold in
   every turn,
and the vision of your realm is made real only on the pathway.

May we go always in promise,
with confidence that every journey in life is heading somewhere beautiful,
overflowing with milk and honey,
that we will one day call home.

So hear this prayer for those who journey without knowing where,
for life travellers weary of the journey,
for those with no purpose in their step and no trust in arriving,
that they all may find at the last,
your promise that is theirs,
and the love that will welcome them
home.

Prayer Activity

If you can, find an old photograph of your parents or grandparents. Reflect
on what they taught you, or a phrase they always used to use, or a journey
you went on with them. Think of their world, and how different it was to your
own. What things have grown in you because of their care for you? Give
thanks for those things and pray for those things we are entrusted with, for
children you know today, who will be adults soon.

Water of Life

With joy you will draw water from the wells of salvation.

~ Isaiah 12:3 ~

God of the ocean depths and awesome space of the sea,
God of the overwhelming wave and ice-sculpted landscape,
God of the flood that can damage, wash away and drown,
God of the down-pour – life growing and aiding, life enhancing and
   blessing ...
Today we give thanks for the power of water.

Help us today to see another kind of power in water
Shown in Jesus – the water of life.
Help us to realise that power in life and death, in sickness and in health –
Rivers to cross, pools to swim in, gardens to sprinkle, ponds to fish
Cleansing showers and soothing baths,
Diluted solutions and medicines swallowed,
Cold wet cloths on fevered heads,
Fresh, washed clothes and food prepared and cooked,
Drinks that quench thirst and celebrate news,
Tears welling up, fonts gathered round.

God, in it all, we find you and are refreshed.

Readings

Psalm 36:5–8	*God's goodness and graciousness*
Revelation 7:13–17	*A vision of eternity*
John 4:1–15	*The woman at the well*

Prayer Activity

Some churches have 'soaking services' where people are encouraged to soak
in the Spirit of God, to feel God's presence wash over them and surround
them and comfort them. Today, feel God's presence flow over you every time
you use water.

Blessing

Water, water of life
Wash me – pour afresh on me.
Fill me – bring me life anew.
I quench my thirst in you.

The Scriptures

Thy word is a lamp to my feet and a light to my path.

~ Psalm 119:105 ~

O Lord God, we thank you for the Scriptures –
    its thrilling stories of high adventure,
    its poetry that touches and lifts the heart,
    its disturbing and challenging prophecy,
    its letters of encouragement and exhortation,
    its strange and wonderful visions,
and above all its telling of Jesus: the Word made flesh.
We bless you that in the Scriptures
all human life is there, and your life is there for us
    to comfort and chastise and console us,
    to direct us to Christ and the everlasting way.

O God, who inspired people to record
your royal law, your lively oracles,
help us not only to read our Bible
but to discern its imperishable truth,
to hear your word in its words and to be enriched in every way.

O God, we remember
    all who translate the Good Book,
    all who publish the Scriptures,
    all who disseminate the Bible,
    all who study and interpret it,
    all who proclaim your Word in it.
We pray for ourselves
as we try to live by its precepts
and trust and follow the Word that is Christ. AMEN.

Chuza's Wife and Jesus

... and Joanna, the wife of Herod's steward Chuza ... and many others, who provided for them out of their resources.

~ Luke 8:3 ~

God, we know it's the lesser known ones that often make the bigger
  difference,
who have to stand out further and take the biggest risk,
like Joanna, the wife of rich Chuza,
funding a ministry with quiet conspiracy and greater danger;
a woman's passion that leads her to resource,
not the great things that bring applause and sponsorship deals,
kudos and a name for themselves,
but the daily things,
like food,
like water,
and like wine and bread.

May the world bless those who, at great risk,
provide the everyday needs for us:
those who work without security, to grow our tea and coffee;
those who work without protection, to grow our flowers and fruit;
those who work without freedom, to grow our rice and grain.

Bless those children of Joanna,
who know the risk of the everyday,
that furnishes our needs and lifestyles,
and whose voices ...

Prayer Activity

Make yourself a cup of tea. Think about the story of that tea, who brought
it to your table, who produced it, cared for it, blended it, grew the leaves,
harvested it, and who themselves may never have tasted it.

Blessing

Today, may we hear in whispers your whole story, in silence your cry for
  love,
and in the people we see, nameless and unknown to us, your saints among
  us.

Syro-Phoenician Woman and Jesus

... it is not fair to take the children's food and throw it to the dogs.

~ Mark 7:27 ~

Was there silence while you took breath?
Was there hushed stillness as you turned to see?
Was there an epiphany in the time it took you to recover from the retort?
  That woman was going where angels feared to tread and she trod on your
  toes!

And thank you, God, that she did,
for who wouldn't face the greatest hurdle
if they thought it would bring good to a loved one:
her daughter, my child, their partner.

Thank you, God, for the risk-takers,
who teach us the length love is willing to go,
and the barriers love will not stop at,
and the line love is willing to cross.
May we be such risk-takers for you.

But your cross was beyond any risk we can imagine.
Thank you, God, that you are the ultimate risk-taker:
without a limit to the love you offer us,
without a barrier at which love will stop,
without a line beyond which love will not cross
for us your daughters and sons,
your children,
your partners.

In such risk-taking for us,
it is we who find the silence that takes our breath away.

Prayer Activity

Fold a piece of paper in half and open it out again. What things would you
like to do but cannot? What lines would you like to cross but at which you
find yourself hesitating? Think of those who have crossed lines for love's
sake. Pray for them, and for strength for yourself that one day you may follow
them.

Sarah and Hagar

Abram said to Sarai, 'Behold, your maid is in your power; do to her as you please,' Then Sarai dealt harshly with her, and she fled from her.

~ *Genesis 16:6* ~

Power, for us, is such a tricky business.
We ascribe it slickly to you – *God of power and might* –
And instantly you challenge us, revealed in the flux of worldly power
As the powerless, crucified God.
But power, and who has it, still shapes our relationships – our lives.
We expertly read its flows, its peaks and troughs.
A shake of filings on a sheet of paper reveals the field of a magnet.
A sprinkling of people in a story
Reveals to us the field and play of power.
We are not innocent, or naive, where power is concerned.

It is Sarah's house; she writes the rules, sets the emotional thermostat.
That is power! The power to make life hell – albeit from sheer insecurity.
Hers is the present, and hers the long past with Abraham.

But pregnant Hagar is tomorrow,
And Hagar has the power of the weak,
And knowledge of the secret, hurting spot.
She knows where to press …

Abraham, the man, pathetic in his formal power.
He cannot placate or console Sarah. He cannot protect Hagar.
He simply abdicates.

The flux of life, the ebb and flow of power, shape our relationships.
We need faith, to be able to entrust to you
Those we love but cannot protect.
We need love enough to love
Those who can absorb all the love we give, and still need more.
We need strength, to be able to stand, gently, against power.
We need courage, to absorb hurt, and break the cycle …

Ahab and Jezebel

He said to her, 'Because I spoke to Naboth the Jezreelite and said to him, "Give me your vineyard for money; or, if you prefer, I will give you another vineyard for it"; but he answered, "I will not give you my vineyard."' His wife Jezebel said to him, 'Do you now govern Israel? Get up, eat some food, and be cheerful; I will give you the vineyard of Naboth the Jezreelite.'

~ *1 Kings 21:6–7* ~

I want, Lord. Don't we all?
And what I want is what I don't have.
Having does not kill the butterfly *Desire*.
It flits from what I have just got, to light on what I don't have. Yet.
Desire is, I know, insatiable. It empowers me,
Just as it empowers, charges, drives, this world of conspicuous
    consumption.
For I am a consumer, and the consumer is king.

My desire is not outrageous or brutal, Lord. Surely my desire kills no one.
It would be satisfied with very little more than I already have.
I could say 'Enough ...' *Any time I wanted to.*

But I hear the seductive whisper
'Why settle for less?' 'You're worth it!'
I lip-know, but do not heart-know, that these things
Are no measure of who and what I am.
Not before You. But they are, with me.
And still the voices whisper.
'Are you not a consumer?' 'Is the consumer not king?'

'*Is it my fault if the world works this way?*'
Sometimes I can manage to say it and believe it.
If consumer society empowers the consumer,
And I happen to be a consumer ...

Power is exercised in my name, Lord God, and I am complicit,
Because I am silent, and because I continue to consume.
My desire would consume the world.
Teach me how to decline, with proper revulsion.
Teach me what is *enough* ...

Jesus and Simon of Cyrene

As they went out they came upon a man from Cyrene named Simon;
they compelled this man to carry his cross.

~ Matthew 27:32 ~

Jesus, at your most broken and vulnerable a stranger came
and took up your cross, holding the weight, easing the burden and pain.

So we too pray for that presence in our lives, when the knocks of life seem
hard to bear and the accompaniment of someone near just might make the
difference.

We pray:
For those in debt who panic about where the money for the next bill will
come from.
For those who are unemployed or facing redundancy who need to hear an
affirming 'Yes! You are chosen'.
For those who are ill in mind, or body or spirit who need to feel a tender
healing presence
For those who are lonely who ache for human companionship
For the elderly waiting ...
For those who are experiencing a breakdown in relationships who need to
believe again in the potential to love

Come close to all, Lord, who need help with the burdens of life
Come carry the load
Come ease the pain
Come and be a presence alongside us.

Prayer Activity

Write down some of the burdens that you are carrying. Burn the paper over a
candle or throw it away. Give your burdens over to God and be free.

Blessing

Lord Jesus
When we carry a heavy load
May you accompany us in our sorrow
And give us the strength to carry on walking the way of your kingdom.

Hosea and Gomer

*'Go, take to yourself a wife of whoredom and have children of whoredom,
for the land commits great whoredom by forsaking the Lord.'*

~ Hosea 1:2 ~

How much it must have hurt Hosea to live in an unfaithful marriage,
to know his love was not returned, to live in a relationship that hurt,
yet not be able to give it up.
How much must it have hurt Hosea?
You don't ask folk to live in abusive relationships,
but this story is not about Hosea.
It is about you, O God.
You and us.

Sometimes our love cannot transform the other
and we can only walk away and allow it to repair us.
But Hosea's story is the reflection of your story and you don't walk away.
Here is a love that never gives up, cannot give up,
for you
are God and not a human being.

How can we speak of your love,
that alone can live through our abuse,
that remains strong despite the partings,
that hankers after us when we are gone,
and waits steadfastly for us?

With such a love we have no words to speak of it,
so may we simply trust we live within it.

Prayer Activity

Find a stone or an image of a rock or mountain. Consider how long it has
been there, what world crises and events have passed and yet it stands there.
Reflect on God's steadfast love: its constancy, permanence and eternalness.
Enjoy that truth.

Blessing

> Live the day in love:
> speak of it;
> walk through it;
> trust in it;
> and know you live in God.

Justice and Peace
and Forgiveness

Forgive us

Forgive us the wrong we have done, as we have forgiven those who have wronged us.

~ *Matthew 6:12* ~

Prayer for Reflection

Sometimes, Lord,
I blurt out my sins
as if your prime interest
was in watching me grovel.

Worse still,
I convince myself at times
that reciting the wrongs I have done
is tantamount to being forgiven.

Here,
let me declare clearly before you
what I wish to be rid of ...

Here,
give me the faith
to believe that I am forgiven;
and move me from my penitence
    to my potentials,
through which I can also praise you.

Prayer on Today's Theme

O Brother Jesus,
now, in your presence,
I picture those
whom I need to forgive ...

And I call on you to witness my intention
to bless and not to curse,
to greet and not to avoid,
to believe the best
    rather than remember the worst.

And, if there are any
whom I cannot forgive,
show me why
and what needs to be done.

God, kindle Thou in my heart within
a flame of love to my neighbour,
to my foe, to my friend, to my kindred all,
to the brave, to the knave, to the thrall,
O Son of the loveliest Mary,
from the lowliest thing that liveth,
to the Name that is highest of all.

~ Traditional Celtic ~

Compassion – Jesus Heals Blind Bartimaeus

'Rabbi!' The blind man answered, 'I want my sight back.'

~ Mark 10:51 ~

Lord,
I am Bartimaeus.
I too walk in the dark.
Too often, I am blind to the glory that meets me in creation,
that greets me in my neighbour, that leaps out from Scripture,
and that shines from the face of Christ.
Too often, I am blind to the opportunities that you lay in my path:
to reach out in compassion, to touch in healing, to speak in love.
Too often, I am blind to my true identity in Christ.
I am blind to who I am as your servant, and blind to all that I might become.
Jesus, Son of David, have mercy on me.
I want to see.   AMEN.

Readings

Genesis 28:10–17; Mark 10:46–52; John 8:12–18; 1 Corinthians 13:11–13

Silence

Prayer Activity

Look at a photo of a person you admire, or look at an icon. What do you see there? What message is God bringing you through them? What does their picture reflect in you?

Lord's Prayer

Blessing

> Be Thou my vision, O Lord of my heart;
> Naught be all else to me, save that Thou Art,
> Thou my best thought, by day or by night,
> Waking or sleeping, thy presence my light.

~ Translated from ancient Irish by Mary E. Byrne. Versed by Eleanor H. Hull ~

Compassion – a Widow's Grief

When the Lord saw her his heart went out to her ...

~ Luke 7:13 ~

Your heart was touched ...
She expected nothing but human sympathy.
You brought restoration, new life, new possibilities.
So simple –
'Young man arise.'

And he did!

I see the news,
with pictures of the latest sadness in the world,
my responses dulled by shocking familiarity,
wearied and overwhelmed at the scale of need.

But you saw the crowds
and were moved with compassion to act at the needs represented,
the worry and helplessness generated,
and sent disciples to share in your work of restoration.
Scary! Wonderful!
Make me tender and compassionate in your service.

Lord, is your heart touched as you see me today?
Do you see the deadness, and know the possibilities?
May I too receive your gracious, compassionate touch.   AMEN.

Readings

Ezekiel 36:26–7; Matthew 9:35–7; Luke 7:11–17

Silence

Prayer Activity

Place your hands in the traditional prayer position with your palms together
and bring them up to touch your heart area on your chest. Listen to what is
in your heart today and cry out to Jesus or whisper to him. This listening can
often be helped by opening your palms like the pages of a book and closing
them, and repeating this gesture, enabling you to open up what is within
there.

Forgiveness

*'How often should I forgive? As many as seven times?' Jesus said to
him, 'Not seven times, but, I tell you, seventy-seven times'.*

~ *Matthew 18:21–2* ~

God, how many times do I have to despair and be depressed by the news?
What a terrible world!
People are abusive, aggressive, cruel and uncaring.
People spoil their surroundings, misuse things given to them,
make my life problematic and never the way I'd like it to be.
Do you ever feel like that?
Do you ever weep at the things we do to each other?
Do you ever raise your hands in disbelief at things we say and don't say?
And do you ever feel ashamed of us, despairing and depressed?
God, how many times have we failed to do your will – seven times?
  Seventy-seven times?
How many times have we crucified you with our apathy and selfishness and
  deliberate sin?
God, I know how hopeless many situations seem.
I know how it feels to see no way forward or out of the mess.
I know the weight of past regret and constant doubting as to whether I am
  good enough for you and for the people in my life.
I know the sting of guilty tears and the discomfort of pride and greed.

Today, help us all to know you.
Help us all to find a way back to you
a way with a future of hope and promise,
a way with new beginnings, apologies accepted and burdens laid down.
Help us all to find your peace that truly passes all understanding and that
  leads to the possibility of life in all its fullness.

Forgiving (1)

Forgive us the wrong we have done, as we have forgiven those who have wronged us.

~ Matthew 6:12 ~

Prayer for Reflection

'I will never forgive him for that!'
'I'll never forget what she has done to me!'
And so I cherish my hurt,
and nurse my wrath to keep it warm.

Jesus said,
'Forgive us our debts, as we forgive our debtors'.
I know where that leaves you, Lord,
but where does it leave me?
If I ask you to forgive me,
I will have to forgive others first,
– and forgiving means forgetting too!

God says,
'I will forgive your wrongdoing,
and your sin I shall call to mind no more'.
It hurts God every time I do not accept his forgiveness.
Help me to rejoice that I am
     ransomed, healed, restored, forgiven;
time after time after time.

Prayer on Today's Theme

Lord,
help those who cannot forgive, nor forget,
    because they haven't been shown how to,
because they won't let go of the past,
because they would rather nourish grievances
    than make a new start.

Be with those who need to be forgiven:
help them to stop punishing themselves,
    to look their sins squarely in the face,
    to make their peace with those they have wronged.

Happy is the one whose offence is forgiven, whose sin is blotted out.

~ Psalm 32:1 ~

Prayer for Reflection

Lord Jesus Christ,
you are the Lamb of God
who takes away the sin of the world.
Will you take away my sin?

> ... not the small mistakes
> which hold no malice;
> not the things I quickly remember
> which I can quickly repair;
> not the questioning which
> helps my faith to grow.

Rather,
will you forgive and take away
the malevolence I carry in my heart
and broadcast with my tongue;
the bitterness or anger which scares some
and imprisons others;
the decisions to go for the easiest option
where that compromises my integrity
and may hurt others.

Take these things away, Lord Jesus,
and deep in my heart pronounce me forgiven
so that I may rise from my prayers
and live as a changed person.

Prayer on Today's Theme

Today, in your sight, O God,
I remember and pray for all
against whom, for whatever reason,
I bear a grudge ...

My resistance to them and avoidance of them
are the means by which I exert power.
In case I grow proud and fond of it,

let me release those I treat like captives.
Make me ready to shake their hand
rather than shake my fist,
knowing that in forgiving
I reflect
and am embraced by
Jesus Christ my Lord.

The Extra

If someone slaps you on the right cheek, turn and offer the other.

~ *Matthew 5:39* ~

Prayer for Reflection

O brother Jesus,
if I think long enough
I will remember them:
> those who let me hit them with blows,
> > and did nothing;
> those who let me hit them with words,
> > and said nothing;
> those whose decision not to retaliate,
> > changed my life
> > because it reflected yours.

Thank you, for all such saints.

Prayer on Today's Theme

Today I remember
all who are in the firing line,
because as politicians, managers
> or decision-makers,
their faces are slapped
by the press and the public.

And I remember
all who are in the firing line
because as police, social workers,
> prison officers or counsellors,
they have transferred to them
 the frustration others feel
with their past, their poverty
or their partner.

Shield them, Holy Spirit,
and let their refusal to be baited
be the measure of their deep integrity.

The Enemy

Love your enemies and pray for your persecutors.

~ Matthew 5:44 ~

Prayer for Reflection

Sometimes, Lord,
I pretend
that I don't have enemies.

I consign such words
    to other countries,
    to the Bible,
    to history.
I am not like that.

And then I remember
    the faces of those
whom I avoid,
and the faces of those who avoid me.

And I pray for that rare kind of love,
love greater than liking,
to be between us.

Prayer on Today's Theme

Once it was the Norsemen,
then it was the English,
then the Germans,
    the Japanese,
    the Russians,
    the Argentinians,
    the Iraqis.
Who will it be next, Lord?

Or shall my prayer for the world's welfare
and my openness to other races
bring closer the day
when nation shall speak peace to nation?

The Merciful

Blessed are those who show mercy; mercy shall be shown to them.

~ Matthew 5:7 ~

Prayer for Reflection

It is not natural, Lord,
    to do the Samaritan thing –
    binding wounds
    and paying the hotel bill
    of a total stranger.

It is not natural
    to run with open arms
    and kiss the creature
    who has squandered
    half a fortune.

It is not natural
    to crouch beside a whore
    and, in the face of her accusers,
    to say, 'You can begin again.'

Show me, who knows what is natural,
how to show the mercy which is needed.

Prayer on Today's Theme

Eternal God,
if charity begins at home,
let it begin in my home,
and in my use of time and money,
    in what I give, in how I care.

If charity begins at home,
let it begin in my home country,
in its willingness to cancel
the burden of debt imposed on the poor,
in its readiness to liberate our economy
from the need to sell weapons which can only kill,
in its keenness to listen to the voices
of the victimised in their pain and embarrassment.

Blind Judgement

Why look at the speck of sawdust in another's eye, with never a thought for the plank in your own?

~ Matthew 7:3 ~

Prayer for Reflection

Rising,
magnificent from the dead,
you, Lord Christ,
returned to those who had disowned you,
whose guilt was engrained in their faces.

And seeing their defects,
all too clearly,
you said, 'Peace be with you.'

Dare I,
who have much less cause to complain,
greet those whose faults I number
with poorer grace?

Prayer on Today's Theme

Today I pray
for those whose lives are pickled in jealousy,
trying to outdo what they admire in another,
and, if they cannot better it,
teasing a thread of fault into a fence of slander.

Have pity, Lord, on the bitter-hearted,
the envious,
the cantankerous.
Purge them of their poison and let them know that they are loved.

Justice

We are brought very low.

~ Psalm 79:8 ~

It's outrageous!
There's no respect anywhere, cynicism rules!
Your Church is discounted and faith derided!
Yet, Lord, when I point to what offends,
there are more fingers pointing back at me.

I fail you, Lord, in many ways,
but you never withhold mercy.
Thank you for that grace.
Enable me to leave judgement to you,
who know the secrets of all our hearts.

So I pray that you will continue merciful to this nation.
May justice, righteousness and integrity become hallmarks
of public service and private relationships.

Thank you that there will be a time out of time, when wrong will be righted,
when there will be no more evil, and death is swallowed up in victory.
Until then, may your kingdom come,
and your will be done,
in *my* life.   AMEN.

Prayer Activity

Yes, you can have a good moan at God about things which make no sense
to you. Name the situations in your life, in the lives of other people, which
remain unresolved; where you cannot work out what on earth God is doing.
Allow your emotions to surface and to be expressed safely in your prayer
time – just between you and God. It is often helpful to get those thoughts
and associated feelings out aloud in words or on paper written down to see.
Then wait. Follow the pattern of the psalm. Discover that there is more to
you than emotion only. Allow a re-formation of your prayer now, integrating
these emotions with other aspects of your being. Allow God to put you back
together.

Justice and Peace

'Blessed are the peacemakers, for they shall be called children of God.'

~ Matthew 5:9 ~

Prayer for Others

Today, Lord,
I will go out and about
and no one will stop me,
no one will ask my business,
no one will will haul me off to prison
> because my face doesn't fit
> or somebody has changed the rules overnight.

Yet I have brothers and sisters
who cannot go about their daily business
without always glancing over their shoulders
and watching their backs
and keeping guard over their tongues.

My life may not be peaceful in every part
but make me appreciative of the peace I know
and long for an end to the conflicts
that dog the lives of people in other places.

Prayer for Ourselves

In your great mercy, Lord,
forgive those who make war rather than seek peace,
who act towards others unfairly and with injustice.
In your loving kindness, Lord,
encourage those for whom peace does not come,
for whom injustice seems unending.
By your grace, Lord,
teach us to keep calling for justice
as long as there is anyone
whose life is in turmoil
because of what others do to them.

Peace and Certainty

Be still, and know that I am God.

~ Psalm 46:10 ~

Floods and earthquakes, war and accidents, backbiting and worry –
it's not easy being a person.
And if the mountains move
I'm afraid I would be afraid!
Lord God, I am so insignificant and frail, I pray that your peace
would rule in every area of my life from the core of my being in you.

I pray for the thousands I will never know,
whose lives are distressed by shocking circumstance.
Prince of Peace, give them peace of heart.

I pray for those I do know as family and friends,
whose lives are full of pain, disjointed.
Prince of Peace, give them peace of heart.

It's not complacency I'm looking for, but your peace,
and the assurance of your presence in my everyday being
to inform my actions and reactions, for your glory's sake.   AMEN.

Readings

Psalm 46; 2 Samuel 22:1–20; 1 Kings 19:9–13; John 14:25–31;
2 Timothy 1:8–12

Silence

Prayer Activity

Find the place inside your body where God dwells. (There is no 'right' place.
If it is not obvious to you, begin by focusing on your heart or breathing deeply
from your abdomen.) The Holy Spirit dwells within you. Go there and wait.
Practise feeling safe there, imagining all sorts of storms raging around. Feel
the trust inside you.

Lord's Prayer

Blessing

Deep peace of the running wave to you
Deep peace of the flowing air to you
Deep peace of the quiet earth to you
Deep peace of the shining stars to you
Deep peace of the Prince of Peace to you.

~ Gaelic Blessing ~

Love above Hatred

Hate stirs up trouble, but love overlooks all offences.

~ *Proverbs 10:12* ~

Prayer for Reflection

This is how you lived, Lord.

Your life was love from beginning to end:
love for the lame, the leper, the lost,
love for the ill-prepared who had insufficient wine for a wedding,
love for the mistaken who favoured money more than discipleship,
love for the misguided who identified you as their enemy,
love for the cowardly who denied you once, then again, and again,
love for the callous who bartered your clothes while you hung in agony.

Love all the way, and yours the footsteps I know I must follow.

Prayer on Today's Theme

To all whose lives are centred on hate,
    on encouraging war,
    on annoying innocent people,
    God, show the face of your anger.

To all who suffer through the hatred of others,
who sense their smallness,
who live with their persecutors,
God, show the face of your pity.

To us all, that we may spread your peace
throughout the earth,
God, show the face of your love.

Getting Your Own Back

Don't take it on yourself to repay a wrong. Trust the Lord and he will make it right.

~ *Proverbs 20:22* ~

Prayer for Reflection

All loving God,
my heart fails me
when I think of the grudges I bear
and my failure to forgive.

I, the one who prays with you,
'forgive us ... as we forgive ...',
find that hard to do.

And sometimes it is the smallest wrongs, not the largest,
which I mercilessly remember.

Help me to go on praying your prayer,
and to be determined, when my faith fails,
to rely on your love and strength
and thus to forgive.

Prayer on Today's Theme

Where fools are not suffered gladly because laughter is a threat;
where families are split because of wrong words at the right time;
where folk show on their faces revenge engrained in their pores,
be there, Lord.
Forgive them who do not know what they do
or why they do it;
and free them to forgive others.

Peace

The Lord puts an end to war: He breaks the bow and snaps the spear.

~ Psalm 46:9 ~

Prayer for Reflection

There was a time, Lord,
when an eye for an eye
and a tooth for a tooth,
though brutal,
limited the damage.

Now nations can maim or kill
those they do not see;
technology has made war so impersonal
    and people so cheap.

In the face of this,
I sense my inestimable weakness
and rely on your inestimable strength.

Prayer on Today's Theme

Woe to those
who lie awake at night plotting destruction.
Woe to those
who despise other races and nations
    just because they are different;
Woe to those
who encourage war in order to make profit.

Blessed be those
who work tirelessly for reconciliation.
Blessed be those
who see, beneath differences,
    the image of God stamped on all humanity.
Blessed be those
who turn weapons into welcome signs
    and the lust for power into a desire for peace.

Peacemakers

Blessed are the peacemakers; they shall be called God's children.

~ Matthew 5:9 ~

Prayer for Reflection

Peace –
your gift to us.
'Not the peace the world offers' –
your pledge to us.
'Peace be with you' –
your word to us.

And shall I stay still enough
to receive it;
or steep myself in busyness
and disbelieve it?

Prayer on Today's Theme

In the front line and back room
    where nations clash
    and weapons bristle,
    blessed be the peacemakers.

In the front room and back yard,
    where tempers rise
    and malice fills the air,
    blessed be the peacemakers.

Not avoiding conflict,
    but confronting it;
not waiting till blood is shed
    but pre-empting it;
not predisposed to bad news,
    but keen it should be good,
    blessed be the peacemakers.

Home Nursing

Anyone who nurses anger against another must be brought to justice.

~ Matthew 5:22 ~

Prayer for Reflection

If only you had repeated that it was wrong to kill,
and made an end of it,
I could cope with that, Lord.
I am not a murderous person.

But nursing anger comes
too easily.
And your words threaten me.

So, let me now declare before you
those whom I have most against:

Help me to find the narrow path,
      the right time,
      the needed words,
which show, like you,
that I am keen to forgive.

Prayer on Today's Theme

God bring justice
to those who have to deal with
     jibes, discrimination, and hate mail
on account of their skin colour,
     race or religion.

God bring justice
to those who have to deal with
     stony silence, dumb stares
     and furtive whispers
because they have dared to tell the truth.

God bring justice
to those who, within their own family,
feel spite and disapproval
which refuses to be reconciled.

Where anger rages,
God bring justice.

Generosity

Happy is the one who fears the Lord, who lavishes gifts on the needy.

~ Psalm 112:9 ~

Prayer for Reflection

Your hands, Lord, like your heart,
are always open,
ready to embrace, keen to bless.

The table you lay groans with good things;
the cup you fill overflows;
... and this not for the expected guests,
    but for the last and the least,
    for those to whom the world has shown
    no generosity.

Make my hands and my heart,
    my table and my wallet
    well worn, like yours,
    with love.

Prayer on Today's Theme

Lord Jesus,
for you, money was not a dirty commodity,
the stuff of private conversations,
the enemy of all that is spiritual.

You handled coins, paid taxes,
acknowledged the realities of trade and commerce,
and were unafraid to identify and condemn
the misuse, the false security, and the lure of money.

Through your Holy Spirit,
inform the consciences of all who govern our finances,
    fix trade prices,
    raise interest rates or cancel debt.
May money and morality never be kept poles apart
in national treasuries or private homes;
and though your head does not appear on our coinage,
may we use it as in your sight.

Kindly Folk

Blessed are the gentle; they shall possess the earth.

~ *Matthew 5:5* ~

Prayer for Reflection

I sometimes wonder, Lord
how you got away with it –
    watching women in the kitchen,
    and farmers in the field;
    conversing with criminals,
    eating meals with reprobates;
    crouching among children
    or beside the wretched of the earth;
as if it were the most natural thing
for God to express love from below.

If this is meekness,
if this is gentleness,
show me the path to it.

Prayer on Today's Theme

Today, I remember with you, God,
the people whose humility has
touched me.

I will not find their names
    in the newspapers.
I will find them in my childhood
    where kindly folk spoke to me as if,
    despite my smallness,
    no one else mattered.

I will find them in remembering
    those whose smile is never forced,
    those whose goodness never seeks applause;
    those whose prayers for me
        are offered without my asking.

I will remember them with you,
thanking you for them,
praying that they may receive
the quality of kindness
they naturally radiate.

Pray Today

'... that in sending volunteers abroad and receiving overseas guests at home,
our understanding of the essential international nature of the Church may be
broadened, and Christ celebrated as Lord of All.'

A Different Hunger

Blessed are those who hunger and thirst to see right prevail; they shall be satisfied.

~ Matthew 5:6 ~

Prayer for Reflection

Deep inside, Lord,
I know that all my dieting
will not satisfy the world's hunger;
nor will all my abstinence
satisfy the world's thirst.

And I know, deep inside,
that it would be easier
to expect those who are politically active
  or personally affected,
  or professionally employed
to do the agitating for justice
which I prefer to avoid.

Despite myself,
I pray for a new hunger
  and a new thirst,
not in the world, but in me
to see right prevail.

Prayer for Today

God of all people,
we have enough images of hungry folk
to last us a lifetime.
We have enough analysis
 to bring on paralysis.
We could discuss global problems
till kingdom come.

But what of global potential:
what of those who feed, educate
and enable the hungry?
what of those who today
will argue the plight of the poor
in the corridors of power?

Don't let this day pass, Lord,
without them knowing
your presence at their side,
my voice behind their voices,
our prayers behind their purpose.

We pray today for all who fund-raise; and we feel specially called to pray for
the world's hungry people that their cry may be heard in the high courts of
heaven and responded to by the parliaments of earth.

Pure in Heart

Blessed are those whose hearts are pure; they shall see God.

~ Matthew 5:8 ~

Prayer for Reflection

If I used kind words, Lord,
    only to impress;
or agreed with what I knew was wrong,
    for the sake of popularity;
if I have let my appreciation of someone else's abilities
    be swallowed up by jealously;
or showered compliments
    solely to gain personal advantage ...

then, Lord, wash me clean with your hands
for mine are dirty.
Create in me a pure heart
and put a right spirit within me.

Prayer on Today's Theme

In admiration and gratitude, Lord,
I remember the single-minded:
those who care for demanding or
    cantankerous folk,
    seeing their worth
    despite their wants;
those who confront lies and slander
    because they believe
    that truth sets us free;
those who look into the heart
    of the ugliest of humanity,
    and expect to see an angel.
Like Moses who met you on the mountain,
let their faces shine
and their lives forever attract others
to your purity
which they reflect.

Creed and Colour

He has abolished the law ... that he might create in himself one new humanity.

~ Ephesians 2:15 ~

Prayer for Ourselves

Yet another tale of intolerance,
yet again hatred caught on camera:
the brandishing of weapons,
the emptied village,
the mass grave.
But not always in a remote place –
sometimes almost next door:
the whisper of gossip,
the rhetoric of the bigot,
the jokes that are not quite jokes,
the innuendos and meaningful glances.

If today, Lord, I find myself
taking sides against difference,
help me to realise that you did not create clones
but a world rich in variety and love.

Prayer for Others

O God of peace and love,
where there is tyranny and bigotry,
let not the oppressed be overpowered;
where there is dissonance and dispute,
let not the quiet voices be shouted down;
where there is foolishness and obstinacy,
let not prejudice prevail.
Show us how to be open in mind and spirit,
that the day may come nearer
when the lion will indeed
        lie down with the lamb,
and when nothing will separate us
        from each other,
        or from you.

The Persecuted

Blessed are those who are persecuted in the cause of right; the kingdom of heaven is theirs.

~ *Matthew 5:10* ~

Prayer for Reflection

Lord,
when I open my mouth
before engaging my brain,
and take umbrage at the criticism
others rightly offer;

when I put all my eggs
in one basket,
and reel with disbelief
should another basket be preferred;

when I discover that the opinion
I have held dearly for years,
is no longer valid
and that for good reasons;

then, help me to swallow my pride,
rather than pretend that I am being persecuted.

Prayer on Today's Theme

Gagged and beaten in East Timor,
limbless in Angola,
removed from sight in Nicaragua,
silenced in the Philippines,
ostracised in Israel,
 ignored in Washington,
branded unpatriotic in London
... such is the fate of those who,
to let justice prevail,
stand up for what is right.

May they live to see this world take on the shape and qualities of heaven,
and inherit that redemption of humanity for which cause they now are
    persecuted.

Refugees

I know that the Lord will give to the needy their rights, and justice to the downtrodden.

~ Psalm 140:12 ~

Prayer for Reflection

God of Abraham and Sarah,
    of Moses and Miriam,
    of Joshua and Caleb,
    of Ruth and Naomi,
you are the summoner and saviour
of a travelling people.

No wonder that Peter and James
should have questioned
whether Jesus had lost his way
after so much walking.

But this is the way,
always to be moving on;
and He is the Way,
always en route to the next great discovery.

Keep me travelling along with you.

Prayer on Today's Theme

Lord Jesus, unlike you, who had to flee to Egypt,
and unlike the millions who wander the face of the earth
I know the term *refugees* but do not know the feeling.

For them I ask a measure of the safety I enjoy.
For them I ask that their names might be known on earth
as they are in heaven.
For them I ask a sighting of the justice you have promised.
Move all whose feet are still
to speak for those on the move
who wish they were wanted.

Homelessness

'Foxes have holes, and birds of the air have nests, but the Son of Man has nowhere to lay his head.'

~ *Matthew 8:20* ~

Prayer for Ourselves

Cardboard boxes, railway arches,
shop doorways.
Tonight will be no different for many.
Drugs or alcohol,
a failed marriage,
endless disputes at home,
a difficult relationship –
there are many reasons why they are there.
Others live in immigrant hostels,
longing for the land they have left,
fleeing hunger or cruelty.
Help me to find room for them in my heart
and make room for them in my country.

Prayer for Others

We pray for those with the power
to bring relief to those who wander,
seeking asylum and security:
the United Nations –
 struggling to keep in balance
 the interests of all its members;
national governments –
 looking for the middle way
 between welcoming everyone
 and closing their borders
 lest the economy suffers
 and unrest erodes their power to govern;
local authorities –
 tempted to direct their money and energy
 towards those who call the tune
 those who are already settled and secure.

Give us all courage
to risk a little more each time.

Poverty (1)

Let not the oppressed be shamed and turned away: may the poor and the downtrodden praise your name.

~ Psalm 74:21 ~

Prayer for Reflection

Eternal God,
I live in the face of the mystery
that you forsook the splendour of heaven which I crave,
for the life of this world of which I sometimes despair.

And, as if that were not enough,
you discerned the characteristics of your kingdom
not in the privileged lives of pampered people,
but in a poor widow, a trusting foreigner
and the spontaneity of children.

I do not ask you to make me poor,
I ask you to help me be humble enough
to see the luxuries of earth
set against the necessities of heaven.

Prayer on Today's Theme

Against the backcloth of gruelling poverty
in this nation and across the globe,
against the backcloth of rising debt
which the poor owe to the rich,
against the backcloth of every statistic
which charts poverty as a downward spiral,
I pray for conversion.

May the last become the first.
May the least privileged become the most favoured;
may the rich take the pain of the poor not their profit;
may the future of the most miserable of humanity
    be lit up with hope rather than draped with gloom.

May your kingdom come, O Lord,
in this nation,
in this world,
in this history.

Poverty (2)

The poor have hope again.

~ Job 5:16 ~

Prayer for Reflection

If the place in which I woke this morning
were not my comfortable room,
but a cardboard box on a city pavement,
would I look to the day with hope
and lay my plans in pleasant anticipation?

I find it easy to have hope
for I have plenty to hope for,
when my life is set in a pleasant garden.

But if today I pass through a wilderness,
teach me the hope of those
who have learned to hope even when hope is absent.

Prayer on Today's Theme

How generous is creation,
even to the point of wastefulness!
Water pours without being gathered,
only a proportion of seeds produce fruit,
flowers bloom unseen and unadmired,
only human beings are mean,
gathering for themselves at others' expense.

Help us all, Lord, to understand poverty
not as an undesirable state of affairs
which leaves some people short
but as something which dehumanises
not just those who suffer it
but those who inflict it.

Poverty (3)

I therefore command you, 'Open your hand to the poor and needy neighbour in your land'.

~ *Deuteronomy 15:11* ~

Prayer for Ourselves

Lord, I think about those
without food and without shelter,
whose eyes betray their feeling of alienation
from a world of abundance.

I look on those who have left behind their homes,
whose eyes have the blank gaze
of people without hope.

I meet some whose pockets are empty,
whose eyes blaze with a longing
to be like others, to pay their way,
to count for something.

Lord, you were comfortable with those who had little,
help me to be uncomfortable
    until those who lack have enough to live on.

Prayer for Others

Challenge us afresh, Lord,
when our quest for plenty makes others poor –
when we expect multi-national companies
    to deliver profit at all costs
    so that we can live in a stable economy;
when we look to government to deliver the goods
    so that we will be secure in our retirement;
when we demand that superstores
    and mail order firms
    keep prices down and quality high.

We pray for all who have to perform a balancing act
between the call of ethics
and the demands of customer and voter.
Give us the grace, Lord, to think before we buy,
to consider before we vote,
and always to be thankful for what you provide.

Simply Poor

If you oppress the poor, you insult God who made them; but kindness shown to the poor is an act of worship.

~ Proverbs 14:31 ~

Prayer for Reflection

If only it were 'the poor in spirit',
I would not need to see the close connection
between faith and economics,
> religion and justice,
> prayer and poverty.

If only it were 'the poor in spirit',
I could divorce aid from trade,
> evangelism from empowerment,
> mission from money.

But you, Lord,
and your word
will not let me.

Prayer on Today's Theme

Lord, in your mercy,
give us your eyes to see the beggar and the beggar's eyes to see us;
give us your ears to hear the disadvantaged and the disadvantaged's ears to
> listen to us;
give us your hands to help the disabled and the disabled's hands to help us.

Do this, in case we forget
that you alone are perfect and begin to imagine that we are.

Judgement

The ordinances of the Lord are true and righteous altogether. More to be desired are they than gold.

~ *Psalm 19:9–10* ~

Prayer for Ourselves

How quick I am to pass judgement on others, yet slow to judge myself;
I am afraid to acknowledge how far I fall short
    of the standards you set for your children.
Others may see me in black and white;
full of excuses, I prefer the shades of grey
    which give me better protection.
Teach me to desire your true judgement, O God.

Prayer for Others

From the comfort of our homes,
we look at a world torn apart
by sectarianism and racial strife;
starving children fill the television screen
while we sit down to a hearty meal.
Help us, Lord, not to be slow to judge a society
which tolerates prejudice, poverty and indifference.
Help us not to forget our part in creating a world of inequality.
Bring home to us, we pray, the words of Jesus:
'Just as you did not do it to one of the least of these,
you did not do it to me.'

Courts

*Do not judge, so that you may not be judged. For with the judgement
you make you will be judged, and the measure you give will be the
measure you get.*

~ *Matthew 7:1–2* ~

Lord Jesus Christ, you were tried by various people and courts in Jerusalem;
help me to see, to realise, that somehow I too was there and still am!
There among the Scribes and Pharisees: the unco guid;
there, like Caiaphas and Annas, conscious of my power;
there in the courtyard with Peter, afraid for my own skin;
there with Pilate, recognising truth but wanting to keep my position;
there beside Herod, interested only in some entertainment;
there in the crowd: my voice adding to the cry of 'Crucify!'

Lord, my Judge and Saviour,
forgive me for my vanity and for my misuse of any power I may possess;
forgive me for my poor discipleship, for which if on trial as you were I
    might be convicted;
forgive me for any moral cowardice – for often knowing the truth but not
    acting upon it;
forgive me for just going with the crowd.

Lord, we pray for the courts of our and every land –
that causes and cases be decided in equity and fairness.
You are the eternal judge.
Help me and all who call on you
        to face the heavenly tribunal with confidence,
        assured that your righteousness exceeds all sin.   AMEN.

Prayer Activity

If you were on trial for being a follower of Jesus, would you be convicted?
What is there in your life that would make you innocent or guilty? 'An
unexamined life is not worth living' – examine yourself, discover what you
are. And, with such knowledge, your own willpower and the grace of God,
aim for that conviction – of being a follower of Jesus.

Unused Fields

Unused fields could yield plenty of food for the poor, but unjust men keep them from being farmed.

~ *Proverbs 13:23* ~

Prayer for Reflection

How ironic, Lord,
that in this country
fields which could produce food for us
are kept fallow,
while abroad
fields which could produce food for the hungry
are made to grow crops for us.

This is a bold injustice,
of which I know little,
but from which I benefit in the things that I buy.

O Christ, who walked through fields,
    pulled the grain
    and told stories about farming,
expose our agriculture and our appetites
to your will for the world.

Prayer on Today's Theme

While one child in the hungry world
    has her life threatened by debt
    imposed by the well-fed world;
while one farmer in the poor world
    is paid a pittance for his labour
    by design of the rich world;

while the harvests of the earth
    are disproportionately divided
    with more food for the nourished
    than for the starving;

… then, Lord,
do not let us say grace
without the desire and intention
that all your children should be fed.

What Hurts God

Condemning the innocent, or letting the wicked go – both are hateful to the Lord.

~ *Proverbs 17:15* ~

Prayer for Reflection

You saw me, Lord,
when I went with the crowd,
agreed with the general consensus,
ganged up against the underdog,
condemned the innocent,
let the guilty go.

And this despite my frequent reading
of you and Barabbas,
and 'crucify him'
shouted by people like me.

When lies are traded
and the wrong folk take the blame,
as if it won't hurt anyone,
it always hurts you.

Prayer on Today's Theme

God help those who have been hurt:
    the verbally abused
    and the physically abused,
    and the psychologically abused,
    and the emotionally battered,
    and those who suffer from being ignored.
Change the hearts of the careless, strengthen the hearts of the carers, heal
the hearts of the hurt.

Goodbye to Sin

Confess your sins and give them up; then God will show mercy to you.

~ Proverbs 28:13 ~

Prayer for Reflection

Let it not be the things I always confess to make me feel good;
let it not be the things I feel I should confess to make you feel good;

rather let it be what is hard and hidden,
deep and unacknowledged,
not docile but festering,
let it be these sins which now I face squarely and confess honestly.

Let me give them to you, Lord, with shame and with relief.
Let me know the blessing of your peace as this month ends and another
    begins.

Prayer on Today's Theme

Where today
ministers and priests,
social workers and counsellors,
Samaritans and sensitive listeners
hear of the secret malevolence
which ruins the lives of others,
sit with them, Lord.

And through them
open paths to repentance and change
at whatever cost honesty and love demand.

The Excluded

For this reason Jesus is not ashamed to call them brothers and sisters.

~ Hebrews 2:11 ~

Prayer for Ourselves

I see them every day:
the old woman, ill-shod, struggling,
wearily carrying her bags around,
offending my nose if she comes too near;
or the young man in the shop doorway,
with his faithful tired-eyed dog
     and a can of beer by his side;
or the child in her wheelchair
     dribbling mouth and twisted limbs,
     eyes fixed on me.

Lord, help me to look more closely
     to see the loneliness of the old lady,
     the despair and desperation in the young man,
     the bright gleam of friendship
          issuing from the child's eyes.

These are my brothers and my sisters.
Help me to see them not with my eyes
but yours, Lord.

Prayer for Others

For those who campaign for better facilities and better laws,
we thank you, Lord.
For carers who give the best of their lives to give others a better life,
we thank you, Lord.
For those who go out of their way to help,
even when it is not their responsibility,
we thank you, Lord.

Keep before us all
the vivid picture of a Galilean
who opened his arms to children,
who went to tea with a tax collector,
who passed the time of day with a leper,
and on the cross embraced rejection
to enfold all creation in the arms of God.

Exile (1)

There will be hope for your posterity; your children shall return within their own borders.

~ Jeremiah 31:17 ~

Prayer for Reflection

So your Kingdom, Lord,
is not a distant, puzzling place
where we have to start all over again,
but like a great homecoming
which we will feel we have always known
because we have seen it in your life
and met it in your life in us.

Help me not to be so engulfed
    by the events of this day
that I forget that I am also
    a citizen of heaven.

Prayer on Today's Theme

I pray for all who wander the earth,
forced to leave their homes
through ethnic cleansing, famine, fear and war.
Help countries who have stability
    to learn hospitality,
and how to welcome the stranger
    without putting the refuge at risk.

I pray also for those who have fled
    the conflict of their homes,
and now live rough in our cities,
that, through those who befriend them
    and the policies and initiatives we support,
they may build on a hope that one day
    there will be a place for them.

Exile (2)

By the rivers of Babylon – there we sat down and there we wept when we remembered Zion. How could we sing the Lord's song in a foreign land?

~ *Psalm 137:1 and 4* ~

Lord, we haven't been to Babylon,
but each of us has our own exile to contend with.
The inevitable exile of growing into adult life.
The hard graft of human experience: relationships, health, money,
work, conflict, guilt, death; childhood forever past.
And what of this when measured by
the silence hanging over Auschwitz
(that terrifying symbol of all forced exile)
– no songs, no hope,
a one-way train to exile and death?
Lord, what are the choices for exiles? Looking back in remembrance?
Anger, revenge, genocide?
Even the slaughter of children?
Lord, deliver humankind from the evil
that is born of persecution, the hatred that festers in places of alienation.
Make hope our only choice, Lord.
We pray for those who have lost hope, whose souls are a prey to despair:
the homeless, refugees, asylum seekers, and so many others besides.
We sing for these by our prayers and deeds,
the new song of compassion and hope. AMEN.

Prayer Activity

Tears are so precious. They help us to express the truth of our sadness. When that is expressed, acknowledged, faced with honesty, it often allows tears to emerge. Grief deeply and truly experienced becomes the doorway to something new. What unresolved sadness is there in your life? Allow this to come to the surface. This sadness may be your own, or a sadness from a previous generation of your family, or it may be other people's sadness which is touching you at present. Ask God for the healing gift of letting the sadness flow in and through you. Wait ... and see how God is leading you within your grief and exile.

Exiles

*I will put my spirit within you, and you shall live, and I will place you
on your own soil; then you shall know that I, the Lord, have spoken
and will act.*

~ Ezekiel 37:14 ~

For those who grieve the separation of exile,
for those far from home who know they will not be back,
for those who have long since given up
expecting that you will speak and you will act,
my spirit calls out to you, God, in prayer.

Home is where the heart is – but where is your heart, God?
Surely with the wanderers in the wilderness – although they do not know it.
With the asylum-seeker and the terminal patient who want to be somewhere
    else,
somewhere better, somewhere promised?
God, surely your heart is within us –
beating for those whom globalisation has made into outsiders
stirring for those excluded from comfort, dignity and peace,
longing for those estranged and distant to be close again.

So let your heart pulse within us now,
carrying life to every dry and barren land,
inspiring people to get up, believe and hope once more.
Help us return to you, God, help us find the kingdom where we are
and move us to see and touch and hear where we belong – with you.

Prayer Activity

Think of a time when you have been away from home, perhaps on business
or holiday. What do you look forward to coming back to, what helps you feel
that you have really returned home? Reflect on this, and the next time you
experience this be aware of all it means, giving God your thanks.

Slaves in Egypt

'If only we had died by the hand of the Lord in the land of Egypt.'

~ *Exodus 16:3* ~

The restrictions, the checkpoints, the reprisals, the put-downs,
the relentless discomfort, the beyond tiredness, the lack of dignity
which affects our relationship
even with those in the same predicament,
not least wives, husbands, children,
when we ask ourselves –
Is there not something we could have done? Could do? With a bit of get-up-
   and-go?

Lord, we pray for whole peoples today who live under restrictions,
as minorities in their own land, or exiled in refugee camps,
or as conquered peoples with only their memories of a nation that was once
   great.
We pray for people who are victims of circumstance:
   asylum-seekers in our land tied to a gangmaster,
   nannies from abroad who are taken advantage of,
   sex workers lured under false pretences,
   sweat-shop labourers choosing slavery or starvation,
   when to speak out is to find oneself on the next flight.

Is there something, Lord, of the slave mentality in us –
like Moses' followers wishing themselves back again in the security of not
   having to take responsibility?
And are we not in thrall to the sinful impulses that drive us, security-tagged
   so that we cannot escape ourselves?
And was not this why Christ came,
throwing wide the gates and inviting us to risk life with him,
travelling together to the promised land?

Prayer Activity

Is there any negative thing in your life that you hope God will never remove
because you cannot do without it – a problem, attitude of mind, bad habit?
Imagine life without it. Ask God to help you find a way through the desert –
and take the first step today.

... an angel of the Lord appeared to Joseph in a dream and said, 'Get up, take the child and his mother, and flee to Egypt, and remain there until I tell you; for Herod is about to search for the child, to destroy him.'

~ *Matthew 2:13* ~

Sheltering God,
no boundary or barrier can limit you,
no nation or name can control you,
no people or place can own you.
In all places, at all times,
your nature is the same:
lovingly embracing all peoples and nurturing your life within us.

God of the refugee,
like Mary and Joseph
we all need places we can escape to:
sometimes distant places,
physically withdrawing us;
and sometimes inner spaces,
mentally protecting us.
In those moments of retreat,
O God, encourage us to be and to become.
Reassure us of your presence
and strengthen us in your love.
Send us into our lives refreshed
and ready to engage with all that you offer.

Prayer Activity

Reflect on your upbringing, your beginnings in life or the birth of your faith. What do you want to affirm and be glad about? What do you want to draw a line under and leave behind? Ask that God may become your true home.

Babylon

How could we sing the Lord's song in a foreign land?

~ Psalm 137:4 ~

Lord, sometimes I feel so small and so powerless:
I watch television, I read the newspapers,
and it seems that the world belongs to the mighty, to the powerful and to the
strong.
Sometimes, I feel a stranger, an exile, an alien, in Babylon and far from
home.

Yet, you speak to me of my true homeland:
your Kingdom, your new society, already here and in embryo,
in which to know my weakness is to be strong,
in which to be a servant is to be great,
and in which the smallest act of kindness sends tremors across the universe.

Prayer Activity

We are often thrown when a familiar way of praying loses its meaning for us,
or when we have changes in styles of worship, or the person leading worship
changes. Like the people of Israel in Babylon, we are called to find God in
new ways. They began to realise God was not restricted to one place, one
area of land. Where in your life is God challenging you, making you feel 'in
exile'? Ask for God's help to plumb the depths and find yet more life.

Egyptians and Babylonians

Now they told David, 'The Philistines are fighting against Keilah, and are robbing the threshing floors.'

~ *I Samuel 23:1* ~

There are times when I weigh up my life –
and among the many blessings lie times of darkness where I have been hurt,
or caught in some memory I cannot be rid of,
caused by a pain that oppresses me of an uncaring word or selfish act of
    someone else.
It seems to scar memory and crush all love.

And then I recall the times I too have unthinkingly oppressed others
with language that is careless, actions that are selfish, beliefs that are
    narrow.
And I consider all the things that drain life from people, rather than offer
    them a blessing.

God of this day,
in this world where there is too much taking, and not enough giving,
may I give a little more today.

Where oppression takes life,
may I give it back again with words of encouragement or acts of kindness,
    like yours. When prejudice binds up life,
may I free it again with grace-filled compassion and gentle acceptance, like
    yours.

God, in all the places my life takes me, help me redress the balance,
opening the door to freedom and giving shape to grace.

Prayer Activity

Take a look through the newspaper today, focus on one particular story, and reflect on it now and find some space at other times during the day. Ask questions about yourself such as 'How do I feel about this?'; 'What would it mean if this person was me or I was in the situation?' Write a few thoughts across the story symbolising the hope in which you pray for the situation.

David in Hiding

When Saul returned from following the Philistines, he was told, 'David is in the wilderness of Engedi.' Then Saul took three thousand chosen men out of all Israel, and went to look for David and his men in the direction of the Rocks of the Wild Goats.

~ *1 Samuel 24:1–2* ~

Lord,
hiding in the hills, amongst forest, in caves,
was David, your chosen one,
Your anointed King,
Called and set apart for the doing of your will.

Yet, his first palace was the wilderness,
And his first throne the hard ground.

To be chosen by you was to be hated by Saul;
To be appointed by you was to be hounded by your enemies.

In David I see foreshadowed another King
Who had nowhere to lay his head,
Who became the friend of the dispossessed
And the champion of the marginalised.

Today I remember all who live on the edge,
I remember those who are persecuted for their faith
Or for their passion for justice and peace,
And for whom loyalty to their vocation
Means tension and enmity with those around them.

Bible Readings

1 Samuel 18:6–9	*Saul's growing jealousy of David*
Matthew 2:1–4	*Herod and the birth of Christ*
Luke 4:16–19	*The manifesto of the Servant King*
Psalm 13	*A prayer in time of persecution*
Matthew 8:18–22	*Jesus and the call to discipleship*
1 Samuel 26:6–13	*David refuses to kill his enemy*

John the Baptist and Herod

And Herodias had a grudge against him, and wanted to kill him. But she could not, for Herod feared John, knowing that he was a righteous and holy man, and he protected him. When he heard him, he was greatly perplexed; and yet he liked to listen to him. But an opportunity came when Herod on his birthday gave a banquet for his courtiers and officers and for the leaders of men of Galilee.

~ Mark 6:19–21 ~

I often feel powerless, Lord. We all do. We say so all the time.
It feels like our usual condition in the world. Corks on a tide ...
Often it is our excuse, and seldom does it convince us.
But still we feel powerless. *Really* powerless ...

Yet even powerlessness can choose whom it empowers.
There is *always* a choice of masters.
John chose, and in imprisoned powerlessness
He spoke the painful, powerful truth.

Or we can be Herods, mesmerised by truth, even *painful* truth,
Longing for courage to vote it to power.
'The truth shall set you free ...' – but liberation is a terrifying thing.
So John in chains was free, and Herod, enthroned, a captive.

Like Herod, we listen, and do not commit. We empower, not truth, but our
    own captivity, Our very disempowerment!
Fascination, bluffed boundaries, compromise,
And we, too, are bound fast by blurted, hasty words.
Somehow – we missed the moment – our pledge has been extracted.

Show us the freedom we have, even in life's limitations,
To embrace the truth;
The power we have, even in our powerlessness,
To refuse to yield to power.
Show us the choice we have, when other choices have run out,
To choose the empowered powerlessness of the prophet
Over the finite power of the power-brokers.

Prayer Activity

Review the situations in your life in which you or someone else experience powerlessness. Which of them does Herod's situation cast most light on? Which John's?

Pharisees, Sadducees, Zealots

*The Pharisees and the Sadducees came, and to test Jesus they asked
him to show them a sign from heaven.*

~ Matthew 16:1 ~

Lord, there is something of the Pharisee in me:
sure that basically I am a good person
but not so sure about the others;
yet I need more of the Pharisees at their best:
    firmly focused on God,
    letting their religion shape their lives,
    fiercely dismissive of substitutes.

How difficult for Jesus to stand out against people with right on their side,
so that he could offer more than they thought possible.
How difficult to contradict the Sadducees, the establishment no-one
    questioned, embedded in church and state.
How difficult not to throw in his lot with the Zealots, passionate about
    freedom and liberty.
How daring to challenge the Scribes, experts in religion, law and morals.

Give those who espouse causes,
who construct programmes for the good of all,
who want the best for everyone,
the grace and courage to examine themselves,
to be able to question and continually reassess their goals and their motives,
and the quality of their love for others.

Prayer Activity

If you are like most, there will be some people you don't really approve of.
Pick one of them and list their good points. Give thanks for these, then pray
about the things in them you cannot like. Finally, ask God for honesty about
the reasons that cause you to disapprove.

Jesus and Judas

'Why was this perfume not sold for three hundred denarii and the money given to the poor?'

~ *John 12:5* ~

Sometimes I just can't keep up with you, Jesus.
One minute you talk about the poor,
the next you talk of banquets and feasting.
One minute you tell the rich young man to give up everything,
and the next you are producing more wine for the wedding.
One minute you said there will be poor with us always
and the next you are being bathed in expensive oil.

But then, maybe these moments call me to see beyond:
not seeking an immediate quick fix, but living into the future;
not solving a problem by throwing a solution at it, but choosing to live a
   more permanent way of justice.

Jesus, help me recognise the sacred moments
that call for a change in my living,
that call for a change in me.
May I now not imagine problem A will be solved with solution B,
or there is a formula to solve all the world's problems,
but that by living more justly,
I may be ready to celebrate goodness and hope when it happens,
knowing each is part of a lifetime's journey,
where I am called to give my whole life
to being an agent for change in the realm of love.

Prayer Activity

Being an agent of change begins with prayer. Tear out stories of injustice from the paper today and paste them into a scrap book or onto a sheet of paper and hold them with you throughout the day and the rest of the week.

Blessing

      Celebrate the wonder of God;
      celebrate the moments when heaven dances with earth;
      celebrate the doorways that set justice free;
      and live your life as that celebration, everyday.

Paul and Silas Freed

*About midnight Paul and Silas, at their prayers, were singing praises
to God, and the other prisoners were listening ...*

~ *Acts 16:25* ~

Today, Lord, I remember all who are imprisoned:
by prison walls,
by addiction,
by their own selfishness,
and by the greed of others.

I remember the Church of which I am part,
a church so often imprisoned by fear of change,
of commitment
and of the future.

Pour out your Spirit, Lord,
on us, your faltering disciples,
that our fears might
give way to faith,
our weakness
to your strength,
and our anxiety to your peace.   AMEN.

Readings

Psalm 27; Isaiah 43:1–5a; Acts 16:16–40

Prayer Activity

One way to reduce our tendency to fear is to associate a cleaning task with a
daily washing away of our fear. So – brushing teeth, washing hands can be
a reminder, a prayer to wash away any fear that is lingering with us and to
remember Jesus' often-repeated statement 'Fear not'.

Imprisonment

I hope for your deliverance, Lord.
~ Psalm 119:166 ~

Prayer for Reflection

Let me go free, Lord.
When I meet people I feel shut in,
    unable to converse
    in case they are not interested in what I say.
In the work I do,
    I long to break out and take risks
    and break new ground
    but I'm afraid that no-one will trust me any more
    if it doesn't come off.
When I am alone,
    I find myself thinking and imagining things
    that I could not possibly tell anyone else,
    trapped by my own thoughts.
Deliver me, Lord, from my secret fears
    and my fearful secrets
that I may look you in the face again
and face the world with confidence.

Prayer on Today's Theme

We remember all those who are oppressed,
those who suffer under cruel governments,
those who are abused
    and cannot escape for fear of their abusers,
those who are trapped by dragging debts
    which they can never hope to repay.

Prisoners

'I was in prison and you visited me.'

~ Matthew 25:36 ~

Prayer for Ourselves

I often feel like a prisoner, Lord.
The children dog my every step,
aged relatives make me feel my day is not my own,
guilt from a past action still pins me down,
fear of rejection prevents me from making new friends.
Even the routine of the day feels like a straitjacket.
Visit me in my prison, Lord;
bring me news of the freedom that you have already won for me,
and give me the courage to step over the bounds.

Prayer for Others

God our Father,
you love everyone you have created.
Everyone is made in your image.
Surround with your love today
all who have difficulties that cause them to feel shut in:
     those whose actions mean they fear going home,
     those whose fear will not allow them to leave their own home;
all who live their lives under physical restraint:
     those who have broken the law,
     those who are under house arrest
     because they are a threat to the powers that be.
May they turn to you, find you close,
and discover a freedom they had not known was there.

Joseph (Son of Jacob)

And Joseph's master took him and put him into the prison, the place where the king's prisoners were confined; he remained there in prison.

~ *Genesis 39:20* ~

Lord, I can imagine, but dimly,
what it would be like to be incarcerated ...
away from the light,
away from friendly and familiar faces,
in some stinking rat-hole.

I can only imagine the demons of the mind that would emerge with glee
from the dark corners of the subconscious to torture and torment.
I can only imagine the hours of questioning, the endless spirals of self-
    analysis,
the labyrinth of regrets and recrimination.

Yet – would the storm not abate,
would there not be a still small voice
after the earthquake and the fire?
Would there not be a Word
to bring a spiritual dawn:

'Where can I go from your Spirit?
Or where can I flee from your presence?'
Today, I remember all prisoners of conscience.

Prayer Activity

Imagine you are imprisoned. Which biblical texts would strengthen you?
What things that seem important to you now would lose their significance?
How differently would you view life if you were given your freedom?

Liberation – the Man with the Withered Hand

'Stretch out your arm.'

~ Matthew 12:13 ~

Lord God,
the desire to conform and the fear of social embarrassment
causes barriers between people.
The ties we have to tradition and the uncertainty we feel about change
close us off from your possibilities.
The priorities we make and the high opinions we hold about the wrong
    things
keep us to ourselves and make us not for others.
God, let us be aware of the things which limit us today:
restrictions placed on us by our circumstances,
assumptions we make and those that are made about us.
Our emotional inhibitions and physical weaknesses.
Father, through your freeing Spirit,
push us beyond these limits today sometimes gently, sometimes firmly,
but at all times so that we may see your rich gifts
and purposes beyond our expectations.
In all our experiences this day,
stretch us to reach our potential,
to touch the reachable and to grow in faith
in the free space you create for us.   AMEN.

Prayer Activity

What part of your life makes you feel withered and rejected? Let go of
other people's judgement of you; loosen yourself from your own inner
condemnation, the withering which will continue unless you say STOP or
NO. Let Jesus speak to you of his love for you and of your potential.

The Healing of the Samaritan

'He was a Samaritan.'

~ Luke 17:16 ~

Lord Jesus,
thank you that you did not sort us
into 'locals' and 'incomers'.
Friend and foe,
before you extended love and healing.
In your kingdom all are welcome:
there's no discrimination,
your grace freely extended
to each in our need.
Father, forgive us that in church, in nation,
and in private, we categorise and exclude.

Lord, your generosity shames us,
you blessed all who came to you,
not asking for anything in return.

We pray for your church
to be a place where all are welcomed,
included and valued.
We pray for those in society who work
towards social inclusion,
for those who have been marginalised.
We pray for a world where safe havens and exclusion zones
exist as testimony to human failures.
Lord, in your mercy, hear our prayer.

Prayer Activity

Sing a song of thanks, whichever song comes into your head. Be glad about
something that has happened. In what way did that reflect the experience of
inclusion or of welcome or of value being given to yourself or others?

Abraham

No longer shall your name be Abram, but your name shall be Abraham; for I have made you the ancestor of a multitude of nations.

~ *Genesis 17:5* ~

Eternal God,
God above all gods,
Name beyond all names
and Author of life,
you have blessed the world
with generations of people
who have kept faith with you.
And with Abraham –
Arab and Jew,
Christian and Muslim –
we celebrate our common heritage
and commit ourselves to live, as Abraham,
within your life-giving presence.

Breathe your life within us, O God,
and encourage us to recognise
the worth and value of each other's ways
and, whenever our differences bring difficulties,
teach us to discern your holy breath
even in that which is wholly other;
and so, like Abraham,
rename us as your own.

Prayer Activity

Sit quietly for a few moments. Listen to your breathing. Think of God as 'Holy Breath' and cherish how close God is to you. Now acknowledge that God is also as close as that to others.

Freedom

The hope that the universe itself is to be freed from the shackles of mortality and is to enter upon the glorious liberty of the children of God.

~ *Romans 8:20–1* ~

Prayer for Reflection

'Things which would make me free' –
    not having to fit in with a family,
    not having to go to work every morning,
    a perfect body,
    living in the Mediterranean,
    being famous,
    not having to live alone!

But is this *your* freedom, Lord?
Did you not remain gloriously free
    in the midst of interruptions,
    misunderstandings,
    accusations,
    cross-examinations,
    having no regular home at all?
Even when death came, you remained free.

May I live today
like someone who can taste the real freedom
that one day will come for everything that exists.

Prayer on Today's Theme

A thought
for those who manufacture shackles,
handcuffs, electric prods,
and other instruments of torture ...

A thought
for those who silence opposition
by force and intimidation ...

A thought
for those who keep silent
in the face of these infringements
of human freedom ...

... people like me.

Redemption

O Lord, my rock and my redeemer.

~ Psalm 19:14 ~

Prayer for Ourselves

How often, Lord,
when events overtake me
and I don't know where I am,
you have been my rock.
How often, Lord,
when people have questioned my judgement
 and I have felt my self-confidence draining away,
you have given me a firm place to stand.
How often, Lord,
when I have felt overwhelmed
by the difficulties life brings each day,
you have rescued me
and given me something to live for.
Truly you are my rock and my redeemer.

Prayer for Others

Lord, teach me to pray
for the world you have created and redeemed,
for men and women caught in the web of addiction, pain and anger,
remembering those
   trapped in the dark, who fear the light,
   who long for freedom yet dread responsibility,
   who pray for redemption but baulk at the cost.
May they know your love and friendship, firm as a rock;
and may they be assured of the presence of Christ,
who long ago gave himself on the cross
and rescued them from harm and danger.

Jerusalem

Pray for the peace of Jerusalem: 'May they prosper who love you.
Peace be within your walls, and security within your gates.'

~ *Psalm 122:6–7* ~

Lord God,
not only in the city on the hill that could not be hidden did you make your
    home –
Jerusalem,
a mighty city, with mighty walls, and gilded palaces
of kings and queens arrayed in splendour –
but in our humble hearts and homes.
> *May peace come.*

Not only in the place of conflict, then and now –
Jerusalem,
where warring factions strive for mastery,
and what passes for religious fervour
is little more than ill-concealed bigotry and naked aggression –
but in our troubled lives, where hurt and grief and bitterness come too.
> *May peace come.*

Not only to the place where pilgrim souls directed faithful steps –
Jerusalem,
a temple shimmering in polished gold,
a place of power and majesty and awe,
of prophet, priest and holy law and sacrifice –
but to our daily lives, where faith is fashioned,
Lived out and real to us.
> *May peace come.*

Into our lives and hearts and souls,
the workaday Jerusalems,
where power and struggle and pilgrimage
reside for us.
> *May peace come.* AMEN.

Prayer Activity

Think of the current situation in the Middle East and pray for the particular
aspects in the news now. Pray for peace, and have a sense of letting peace
flow from you to that part of the world and to the current concerns. If you
find thoughts interrupting, let go, and stay with your focus of sending peace.
May peace come.

Miscellaneous

Salt

You are salt to the world.

~ Matthew 5:13 ~

Prayer for Reflection

Why did you say salt, Lord?

It is so cheap,
    so unsophisticated,
    so affected by dampness,
    so simple in its activity.

Why not gold,
    or diamond,
    or plutonium?

Is it because we can live without the one,
but can't do without the other?

Who would have preferred salt to silver?
Only you!

Prayer on Today's Theme

Today, Lord,
I remember those who are the salt
of the earth: the woman whose baking
    feeds more families than her own;
    the old man whose warm face
    fascinates my children;
    the teenager who knows just when
    to do a daft thing and defuse tension;
    those who are wise enough
    to see my troubles in a bigger context;
    and all those whose eyes
    tell me I am important.

Don't let them ever lose
    their savour,
or lose touch
    with their saviour
    and mine.

Light

You are light for all the world.
~ Matthew 5:14 ~

Prayer for Reflection

How often have I looked at the church
as the place where I should get
my batteries charged,
and been disappointed,
and blamed you know who, Lord.

It is as if I had never heard
that you believe in solar power,
and expect us to find our energy
by direct contact with the Sun.

So, when I pause to pray,
let me expect that this moment,
where I am and as I am,
is the time to be made new.
Your presence is enough
to make me radiant.

Prayer on Today's Theme

Where the darkness is very deep,
where decisions about morality
    are plagued by double standards;
where decisions in politics
    are sullied by double dealing;
where decisions regarding money
    are governed by self interest;
 where one child of God
    is in the grip of an evil fixation,

there let those who know the light of Christ,
    appear as heaven's candles,
    not avoiding the darkness,
    but showing the way through it.

Tree of Jesse/Tree of Life

*A shoot shall come out from the stump of Jesse, and a branch shall
grow out of his roots.*

~ *Isaiah 11:1* ~

Rootedness
Trees linking me with the earth beneath my feet
Opening to the depths – history

Standing
Trees conveying my need to be located in space and time
A point of reference – location

Transcendence
Trees expressing my need for expansiveness
Feelings of beyond – ecstasy

Generation upon generation seeing one tree
Wisdom, sacred space, giver of food
where kings were crowned
Justice dispensed

We see our families in trees
Family trees

I am of the tree of Jesse
I am of the tree of life

Wow

My prayer is to live with rootedness that brings life
To stand in a way that upholds truth
To open my life to grow way beyond my hopes and dreams

Prayer Activity

The oldest tree in Europe is said to be the yew tree at Fortingall in Perthshire;
and there is also the legend that Pontius Pilate was brought up in that area,
where his father was posted in the Roman army. Tree of life and tree of death
– which holds most meaning for you at this moment?

First Impressions

Put all your trust in the Lord, and do not rely on your own understanding.

~ Proverbs 3:5 ~

Prayer for Reflection

Often I have thought,
    'She has brought that upon herself ...'
    'I wouldn't have done that in his shoes'.
And so I have entirely missed the plank in my own eye
in my all-absorbing concern
with the speck in my neighbour's.

I have been impressed by
    the smart appearance,
    the melodious voice,
    the smooth manners,
while turning my back on the shabby suit
and the unhappy eyes.

Fill me with sympathy, O God,
with the poor, the undesirable, and the unloved.
Help me to remember that you see
not just the outward appearance,
but into the very heart of us all.

Prayer on Today's Theme

Lord, be with all who interview people for jobs, or in the media.
Help them not to be taken in by appearances, but to seek the real person
    underneath.
Help all who must make snap decisions:
may they always be listening for your voice.
Be with all who are obsessed with keeping up appearances:
help them to find joy
    not so much in creating an impression
    as in cultivating the soul,
and help them to make better use
of their time and resources,
    in the service of your kingdom.

Joy – The Nativity

'But Mary treasured up all these things and pondered over them.'

~ Luke 2:19 ~

Lord,
I love the Nativity story.
It's all so cosily familiar,
like an old sweater
or a well-worn pair of slippers.

It brings memories
of childhood's magic:
the smell of fir
and the aroma of tangerines.

Perhaps, however,
its very familiarity
has hidden the sheer wonder
of your coming among us,
of your joy exploding into
the lives of very ordinary people.

You remind us, Lord,
that ordinary folk are not bypassed by you,
and that, no matter how powerless we feel,
we have a part in your ongoing story.   AMEN.

Readings

Jeremiah 31:10–14; Matthew 22:1–10; Luke 2:1–20; 1 John 1:1–4

Silence

Prayer Activity

Imagine yourself as a baby. Reflect on both the joy and the difficulty of your birth for your parents. Are you carrying pains and fears from that time which restrict your potential – all you were born to be? Speak to Jesus as honestly and as openly as you can. What new birth is coming into being in you?

Bethlehem

In the time of King Herod, after Jesus was born in Bethlehem of Judea ...

~ *Matthew 2:1* ~

Gracious God,
every year this place begins our Christmas story –
Bethlehem, place of beginning, place of birth.
But this was not the beginning – you had loved us before that.

Every year we think about how it was on the day, at the time:
    the hustle of the crowds with 'No room at the inn',
    the sounds of angels to shepherds on a cold hillside,
    the smells of the stable where the lowly birth took place.
We come back to these time-honoured thoughts and reflections, so easily,
    every year and think, Bethlehem – star, stable, manger, little donkey –
    Nativity Play.
God, although we have to admit that it would have been a draughty and
    unpleasant place to be that day, how easily we ignore the bigger picture.
We don't give much attention to all the careful detail and attention you gave
    to making it the 'right' place and the right time for the Word to be made
    flesh.
Thank you, God, that you put up with our often 'Disney' view of Christmas.
Thank you, God, for choosing the line of David with its dubious genealogy.
Thank you, God, for bringing your son into the world in a place where he
    was in danger right from the start, under Herod's rule.
Thank you, God, for taking risks, for taking time to communicate yourself
    to us and for taking each of us into your family.

Prayer Activity

God in a stable – God inside me. Where do you sense need for God, a new birth of love and hope? Ask for new life from God where you experience physical pain, difficult thoughts or hard feelings. Remember your body is a temple of God's Holy Spirit. Stay with this truth, contemplating it for several minutes.

Blessing

    Know the love of God this day,
    for it has gone before you and
    will go ahead. In the small things and
    in all things, God will be with us. AMEN.

Rome

In those days a decree went out from Emperor Augustus that all the world should be registered.

~ Luke 2:1 ~

Almighty God,
violence, control, oppression still figure large on the world stage.
We pray for the leaders of nations who are called to shape policy,
whose lives may readily become disjointed from the realities of those they
    represent,
as power and pressure and fear take hold.
Show your mercy, Lord.
We pray for the world, where violence, control and oppression do get
    results,
at shocking cost to individuals and communities,
where plausible tyrannies stunt lives and control minds. Show your mercy,
    O Lord.
Lord God, through history the powers of this world have been set against
    your authority.
We ask for discernment that we will not collude with wrong, but live with
    integrity before you.
Show your mercy, Lord.
The tensions are within me too, between power and humility,
ambition and being, constraints and freedom,
so I need your help in the balance.
If I start to control and oppress others, at work, in the Church,
even within the family,
remind me that your truth sets me free, not to control but to serve,
and that freeing truth is to all alike.
So may I love and serve within your kingdom on earth,
until that time when you take your power and reign.   AMEN.

Prayer Activity

Listen to the news or read today's paper. Take time to listen for the voice
of the Lord, too, asking him to highlight the serious issues of at least one
national and one international situation and hold this before him in prayer.

Nativity Visitors

Human God,
when we think about your birth, we have to remind ourselves that you,
 become flesh,
were in our world, in a manger, in a stable.
You were outside the comforts of hotel or inn, outside in the cold and the
 dirt,
outwith the 'normal' family set-up –
painfully born into human experience so that we may make our way
 painfully back to God.

And when that news sank in, Human God,
the world was amazed at love come down –
you, actually here with us!
You walked where we walk, saw what we see, felt what we feel.
Those shepherds rejoiced in that – one of us, God with us!

But the good news to the poor didn't stop there, for soon the rich, wise men
 knelt down, amazed, too.

Today, as we remember the story of your birth, Human God, whoever we
 are, whatever we are and wherever we are in life, we give you our thanks
 for sharing our humanity.
Let us hear the angels sing, see that you are holy and learn to kneel down.

Readings

Isaiah 9:2–7 *Those in darkness see light*
Luke 2:8–20 *The shepherds and the angels*
Matthew 2:1–12 *Visitors from the east*

Prayer Activity

In many church traditions, kneeling is a position used for prayer. If you can, try this position today; how does your perspective/sense of being change as you do this? If you do not wish to kneel, think of times when you have seen others kneel, and reflect on the significance of this with God.

John the Baptist

John the baptiser appeared in the wilderness, proclaiming a baptism of repentance for the forgiveness of sins.

~ *Mark 1:4* ~

Almighty God, in a world gone mad with sound,
where the still, small voice has long ago been drowned out,
raise up people with something to say and the power to say it:
the men and women who will not be cowed by pomp or position
or society's disapproval or incomprehension,
but who will still speak out and say what needs to be said
until, at last, they are heard.

For prophets who persist
    we give you thanks.
For prophets who say the unsayable
    we give you thanks.
For prophets who challenge our complacency
    we give you thanks.
For prophets who keep bringing God into our godless world
    we give you thanks.

Where heart and mind and soul and conscience
have gone deaf to need and injustice and cruelty and wrong,
may prophets from God speak out and speak up
until the time when justice rolls down like waters. AMEN.

Prayer Activity

Prophecy is not always about foretelling the future, but is often about providing a critical lens through which we can see what is going on in our world today. Who are the men and women with 'prophetic' voices today? What are they saying? How do they make you feel? What do they make you do? In the light of today's news, what 'prophetic' word needs to be heard in the world, in the Church and in your life?

Writing, Poetry, Art

When I look at your heavens, the work of your fingers, the moon and the stars that you have established ...

~ Psalm 8:3 ~

Living God,
you are the Creator,
indeed you are the primal artist.
For human art in its glorious diversity,
in all its multi-faceted wonder,
is at best a reflection of your beauty,
an echo of the music of your singing,
an accent of the Word by which you brought worlds into being.

You, Lord, are the potter, the craftsman, the Makar,*
and from the crude raw material
of this my life,
from the crude raw material
of this your Church,
you would shape something of eternal beauty.

Today I pray for your Church:
that the community of faith
might truly be a welcoming place for artists,
that in word, in music and song, in dance,
in form of clay or stone, wood or paint,
your glory might truly be reflected,
your Gospel celebrated.

Readings

Exodus 39:1–7	*Beauty in the finest details*
Psalm 8	*Reflections on being human*
Psalm 19	*Symmetry and pattern in creation*
John 1:1–5	*Thoughts on design and the Designer*
Romans 1:18–23	*No excuse for idolatry*
Revelation 4:1–11	*A vision of worship*

---

* Makar = poet (Lowland Scots).

Dance

... then the Lord God formed man from the dust of the ground, and breathed into his nostrils the breath of life; and the man became a living being.

~ *Genesis 2:7* ~

In the beginning was the Word ...
sound, vibration, movement, the essence of Life.
Without movement of breath,
without movement of heartbeat,
we would not be alive.

Thank you, Lord, that my breath and heartbeat dance together
although I do not understand and can but slightly control their rhythm and
    interaction.
Help me to trust in the dances of life within me.

May my breath make love to your Spirit within me;
may my passion reel with your Passion;
may I 'Strip the Willow' in reality or imagination;
and may I know you have given me this joy.

May each of us value the forms of dance that have enlivened us.
Whether we physically dance or not,
help us recognise the Dance of life.
Help us look for patterns in our relationships –
    people with whom we tango, others with whom we waltz.

Help us recognise you in movement and feelings
that evoke love and joy, fullness of well-being.
Enable us to be people who find you in our bodies.
May we experience our bodies as living text for us,
our Living Word dancing us into vibrant existence
from the dance of our breath and heartbeat.

Readings

Genesis 2:4–7	*Breath of Life*
Job 12:7–13	*Learning of God in nature*
2 Samuel 6	*David dances before the Lord*
1 Kings 1:38–40	*Processional dance for King Solomon*
John 16:19–24	*Dance of life*

Music

What music makes my heart sing?
What rhythm and melody sets my heart on fire
with love and desire for life?

What music brings me relief,
lets my pain flow and grow into new form?

What music opens me up inside,
leading me on pathways familiar and unfamiliar,
rhythm bringing security, melody inspiring spontaneity?

What music enables friendship for me
– with people – with the Spirit,
creating a community, an orchestra of companionship that arises from I
    know not where?
Yet I recognise when it is there … and here.

May music be prayer for me,
gateway to joy for me,
doorway to reassurance for me,
touching place of love for me,
release of tension and suffering for me,
harbinger of balance and healing for me.

Lord, help me to use the gift of music
to allow your life to sing within me,
to enable me to live my life in harmony with you,
vibrating to the music of your Love.

Prayer Activity

Make your own music. Here is a way to do that. Take a word or text that is
meaningful for you at present. Repeat it to yourself, chanting it first on one
note only. Continue. Then let a melody arise out of that.

Sleep

*I will both lie down and sleep in peace; for you alone, O Lord, make
me lie down in safety.*

~ Psalm 4:8 ~

O Lord God, who neither slumbers nor sleeps,
we thank you for sleep –
> for a good night's rest,
> for a blessed forty winks,
> for sweet dreams.

O God, we thank you for Jesus
> who knew weariness and tiredness,
> who could sleep in the storm –
> for his heart was stayed on you,
> who can raise us from the sleep of death.

Forgive us for
> taking sleep for granted,
> not giving time to sleep,
> sleeping when we should be awake,
> and for any sleep of faith.

Be with those who cannot sleep:
> because of illness and pain,
> because of worry and anxiety,
> because of a bad conscience.

Grant them healing, balm,
and the serenity that is there in Christ for all.   AMEN.

Readings

Genesis 28:10–17	*Jacob's dream at Bethel*
Judges 16:18–22	*Samson's sleep*
Mark 4:35–41	*Jesus asleep in the storm*
Mark 14:32–42	*The disciples sleep in Gethsemane*
1 Thessalonians 4:13–18	*Concerning those who are asleep*
1 Thessalonians 5:1–11	*Whether we wake or sleep*

Prayer Activity

Sit in a comfortable chair – perhaps before a good fire and after a pleasant
drink. With no pressing engagements, no phone liable to ring – relax, and
with Christ's balm, enjoy, enjoy …

Crowds around Jesus

When he saw the crowds, he had compassion for them, because they were harassed and helpless, like sheep without a shepherd.

~ Matthew 9:36 ~

Lord Jesus, you knew all about crowds:
> you moved among them, you taught and healed them, you fed them even;
> they were often captivated by you:
> amazed at what you did, in awe of your authority, impressed by your words.

As we in our day sense you,
> may any fascination turn into faith, any wonder turn into worship.

As we hear you speak may we, like many long ago, hear you gladly,
> and may we acclaim you as the Palm Sunday crowd acclaimed you.
> Son of David, help us to go with the crowd, such a crowd as shouted 'Hosanna!'

Lord Jesus, you knew all about crowds:
> that other crowd who came with swords and clubs to arrest you,
> that other crowd who replied to Pilate's question as to what he might do,
> that crowd which shrieked 'Crucify! ... His blood be on us!'

Save us from going with such crowds:
> those who in blood-lust seek supposed retribution,
> those who shout in nationalistic malice or sing some chauvinistic sinister song
> those who watching some exciting game express bitter bigotry in chant or chorus.

We pray for situations where men and women meet in large numbers:

political demonstrations ... football matches ... pop festivals ... evangelistic meetings ...

may there be enthusiasm with sense, excitement without danger, enjoyment unalloyed.

Lord Jesus, we pray for crowds and for ourselves when we might be in them.

Let not panic take a grip, with folk creating their own disaster.

So may they and we come to that crowd that no one can number

who see you face to face in the Father's House.   AMEN.

The Psalmists

I love you, O Lord, my strength.
~ *Psalm 18:1* ~

Their voices rise from the pages of Scripture, the greatest choir of all
  history,
putting praise in the mouths of all who followed, bringing even creation to
  utterance,
providing the sounds that surrounded a Saviour, as he grew, ministered, died
  and rose:
'God is gone up with a shout,
the Lord with the sound of a trumpet.'

Lord, show me how to look at the world, so that your praise will be on my
  lips also.
Help me like the psalmists to see you in all things, in the good, the bad and
  the ugly;
help me like them to be honest before you, able to ask questions, to
  complain,
to plead, but also to trust you completely, as my Rock, my refuge, my
  defence, my comforter.

Hear my prayer for those among God's people who make music, and enable
  others to make music,
but those who praise too in stone and wood, in movement, and lives of
  service,
in vows of silence instead of verses of song;
and those also who castigate God –
who lament for the suffering in the world
and demand that it cease.

Readings

Colossians 3:12–17   *Sing from the heart*
    Mark 14:26–31   *The Passover psalm*

Prayer Activity

Everyone has a song – not a favourite that someone else has written, but the
song that is yours alone, that expresses your personality, faith, outlook on the
world. What is the main theme of your song? What would the melody that
should go with it sound like – joyous, melancholy, repetitive? If you like,
hum it.

The Woman at the Well and Jesus

A Samaritan woman came to draw water, and Jesus said to her, 'Give me a drink.'

~ *John 4:7* ~

Loving Jesus, in our misunderstanding, meet us.
Loving Jesus, in our secret lives, meet us.
Loving Jesus, in our solitary living, meet us.

Meet us with the full force of heaven,
gently,
with a grace-filled moment and a living word, that speaks into all living
  deserts:
the dryness of our relationships,
the barrenness of our community,
the solitariness of our culture
to every woman enslaved,
to every asylum seeker turned away,
to every child abandoned.

Water these deserts,
not just with water,
but with living water,
that each may never thirst again,
that this world may never thirst again.

Loving Jesus, in our thirst for connection, within a community
  disconnected,
may we pass the cup abundantly and with reckless generosity.

Prayer Activity

Place a cup of water before you. Reflect on it, how it gives life and how it can
equally harm with disease and flood. Give thanks for its life-giving properties
and pray for those affected by the harm it can bring. Drink the water and hear
Jesus' words to us: 'I am the water of life.'

Blessing

> May God fill every cup you drink with life and eternity
> in equal handfuls.

Elijah and Jezebel

Then Jezebel sent a messenger to Elijah, saying, 'So may the gods do to me and more also, if I do not make your life like the life of one of them by this time tomorrow.'

~ *1 Kings 19:2* ~

You were too easy to see in the whoosh of flame;
On that mountain of vindication and *power* ...
Elijah had to unfind you, after that, in order to find you again.
Yet Jezebel trumped Carmel with just a death-threat.
Naked, corrupt, unbounded power. And totally credible.
Broken by power, Elijah fled. To a different mountain.

`What are you doing here, Elijah?' On Horeb ...
Out it all pours. 'I was faithful, I made a stand, it was all going so well!
And now they seek my life, to take it away.'
And what's unsaid. 'I need power to countervail power. I need God.'

Earthquake, lightning, storm-wind; minatory, dazzling, power aplenty.
But God isn't there. Power just isn't where God is. So where is God?

And then – *the sound of nothing at all* ...

Same question – 'What are you doing here, Elijah?'
The answer – completely different. *Yet word for word the same.*
Yet everything really is different.
Jezebel, and her power, and her pomps, are still there,
But Elijah goes back. Suddenly, he can face it.
Now he knows where God will be. There ... *Just* ... *there.*

I open my eyes from prayer – did I miss something, Lord?
How, when nothing has changed, has everything changed?
How, when I turn from the assurances of power,
Having failed to find you there,
Do I find you in the stillness of my own acknowledged powerlessness?

Prayer Activity

Listen to the silence – and acknowledge that it isn't actually silent.
Acknowledge, one by one, the sounds it contains. Think about the difference
between **silence** and **peace**. Offer the silence – such as it is – of real life in the
real world to God. Ask him for peace such as the world cannot give.

'I am there among them'

Prayer for Reflection

What can one person do?
... I sometimes ask, Lord,
as if worship and mission
    and spreading the Gospel
    and renewing the church
    and feeding the hungry
    and clothing the naked
    and protecting the environment
    and making peace
were all solo activities.

Help me,
who here prays to you on my own,
to live for you
in the company of the very different others
who are your friends,
and among whom you have promised to meet me.

Prayer on Today's Theme

Where two or three are gathered
... in a small church in a lonely glen;
... in a large church in a lonely city;
... in a corner of a country
    where Christians are threatened;
... in deserts or jungles or outbacks
    where meeting places are few;
... outside a hospital ward
    waiting for the theatre door to open;
... around a bed
    at the time for last farewells;
where two or three are gathered
in your name,
may they treasure the time
and know your presence.

The Church – a Gift

Now you are the body of Christ and individually members of it.

~ I Corinthians 12:27 ~

Lord – your church a gift?
Sometimes I look round and cannot believe I'm here!
Can this really be what you meant?
My fellow Christians are so different from me.
They are full of awkward edges.
They don't always seem to have got it quite right.
Must I love them all and carry their burdens?

And what of the wider church?
Sometimes tradition seems to overtake compassion,
bigotry and intolerance take the place of acceptance,
divisions give the lie to the message of reconciliation.

Yet you have called us to be a *sign*
of the true community that God plans for the world;
and as the word of God is preached, believed and obeyed,
we are shaped into an *instrument* for bringing it to pass;
and as we share in communion at the table of Jesus Christ
we become a *foretaste* of the reconciled life in God's kingdom.

Grant that as Christ's body we may see diversity as a gift,
and so challenge a world where differences are taken as cue for conflict.
Grant that our awkward shapes may fit together to build strong walls of a
    temple to your glory.
Grant that we may live in our traditions and customs in such away
that we are continually open to the renewing of your Holy Spirit.

Prayer Activity

Call to mind your local church. What is your immediate image of it? Rows of
people in pews? A solid stone building? Re-imagine your church using some
of the images above. Choose one of them, e.g. vine, bride, body, wedding
party, and think of the way your church would link together, move, react, pray
if that were the only possible picture of how things should be.

Joy – the Church Grows

And day by day the Lord added new converts to their number.

~ Acts 2:47 ~

Lord Jesus Christ,
we pray for growth in the Church –
banishing apathy,
bringing individuals new blessing,
making society whole.
May your kingdom come.

Lord Jesus Christ, we pray for
a deepening of faith
a strengthening of relationships,
And grace to perceive your life in others.

May the signs and wonders of your kingdom
bring life and growth
to our Church
and our world. Amen.

Readings

Isaiah 55:1–9; Acts 2:44–7; I Corinthians 3:5–9

Prayer Activity

Put on some music and dance, or imagine dancing. Let your body pray by moving and reveal to you that it is the dwelling-place of God and the Holy Spirit. Let yourself be drawn into the dance.

'I am the Vine; you are the Branches'

~ *John 15:5* ~

Prayer for Reflection

Unless
I remain
united
to you,
I can bear no fruit.

Unless
I allow myself
to be pruned
by you,
I cannot be more fruitful.

You said it, Lord,
so I must take it seriously.

Prayer on Today's Theme

Lord, keep us together
        as your church,
especially when we become
        obsessed with our differences,
        or put fund-raising before faith.

Keep us together
        when we disagree about favourite hymns;
        when some want to protest for peace
        and others want to hold a praise evening.

Keep us together;
and let our tensions be creative
only and because we are all rooted in you.

The Local Church

*How dearly loved is your dwelling place! I pine and faint with longing
for the courts of the Lord's Temple.*

~ Psalm 84:1–2 ~

Prayer for Reflection

Thank you Lord
for the Church –
the church in which I was baptised
the church in which I was reared
the church in which I was confirmed
the church in which I am a member.

Forgive me
    if I have been quick to criticise in it
    the faults which are also in me.
Forgive me
    if I have expected of it
    more than I have ever given to it.
Forgive me
    if I have continually seen that church as an 'it'
    and not as a community of your people.

Prayer on Today's Theme

Today, Lord,
I remember my local church ...
      my minister ...
      my elder ...
and ask you to bless them.

Today I remember those I always sit beside
    and any who are strangers,
and ask you to make us one.

Today I remember the needs of my local church
    and its great potentials,
and ask for their fulfilment.

Today I remember how much I give to my local church and ask you if it is
    enough.

Mission

Send out your light and your truth to be my guide; let them lead me to your holy hill, to your dwelling place.

~ Psalm 43:3 ~

Prayer for Reflection

If I met you, Jesus Christ,
I might not think that you were on
a mission.

Your talk would be of common
and curious things: salt, dough,
                      lost lambs, lost coins,
                      paying taxes, hosting a meal,
                      wise virgins,
                      and foolish house-builders.

I would not know you were on a mission,
I would think you were making sense of life,
lighting up the ordinary, identifying the truth.

When next you look with compassion on the world
and need mission done in your way,
Lord, send me.

Prayer on Today's Theme

God of all nations,
whose Church blossoms in lands
once considered barren,
and whose name is holy in every tongue,
set alight with your love
us in the once Christian West
whose zeal can hardly smoulder.

Where we have sent missionaries,
      make us keen to receive them;
where we have taught the world,
      make us keen to learn from it:
where we have presented our Lord in our image,
      let us receive him as seen by other eyes.

We ask this because world mission is not ours,
it is Christ's;
and we are part of the world in need of awakening.

Builders of the Temple

Unless the Lord builds the house, those who build it labour in vain.

~ Psalm 127:1 ~

Lord, we thank you for those sacred places
    where your Word is declared, your Sacraments administered,
    when we sensed that you were there, when a fellowship was enjoyed,
    where and when we really worshipped you,
    where and when your grace was given.
We thank you for the many whose giving and doing built the churches of
    our land;
for the many whose praising, preaching and praying hallowed their walls;
for the many who in times past built our towns and cities:
architects and engineers, masons and bricklayers, and many more.

Recalling those who, with Nehemiah, restored the Temple of Jerusalem,
raise up in our day builders like Nehemiah's
to repair and to create new sacred spaces.
Strengthen us to be the Church without walls,
breaking through barriers for the good of the Gospel.
Make us living stones in that great enterprise.
Lord, as we commend to you all who strive for a Jerusalem on earth:
statesmen and sociologists, economists and planners of all kinds;
watch over the watchmen: those in the police and emergency services;
and strengthen the hands of those who would do a good work for your
    Kingdom.   AMEN.

Prayer Activity

Remember the children's question, 'Are you a stumbling block or a stepping
stone?' Or, 'Are you a real brick?' Think how you may help others and the
Other; how you might play a better part in the fabric of society and in building
up the Church – and don't be afraid of being used!

– 'I am with you always, to the End of Time' –

~ *Matthew 28:20* ~

Prayer for Reflection

Ah, Jesus,
if I met you on a train
and heard just a snippet of your conversation,
I would ask countless questions until we parted company.

I would be so excited
to meet and make such a unique friend;
every second would be precious.

Just because you have promised
to be with me to the end of time,
don't let me take you for granted,
or fail to show the enthusiasm
which would be so evident
if we met only for a few hours
on a train.

Prayer on Today's Theme

Today, Lord,
I pray for those at the end ...
    at the end of their tether, wondering what next;
    at the end of a relationship, wondering what next;
    at the end of their employment, wondering what next;
    at the end of their life, with the same wondering.

Whatever happens next,
may those threatened by the future find in you faith enough for today;
and know that it conies from the one who is already in tomorrow.

We pray today for those who are committed to sharing the scriptures and the
deepening the devotional life of people at home and abroad, that the seed may
fall on fertile soil and yield a good harvest for their Lord.

Index of Biblical Characters

References are to page numbers

General Index

References are to page numbers

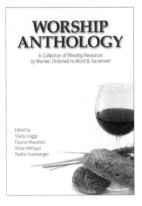

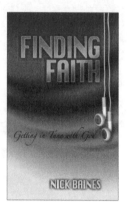

Finding Faith

Getting in Tune with God

Nick Baines

978-0-7152-0868-7 · £11.99 · Paperback

We live in a fast-paced, noisy world that seems to get more and more complex and uncertain with every passing year. It's hard to hear your inner voice and to stop and reflect on what life is all about. Where do we find our anchor?

Nick Baines has always found that popular music has offered a rare haven in which it is possible to step back and look at what life is. Throughout his own long journey into faith, there has always been a great song that has helped, encouraged or provided space for reflection at the key moments. In this book, Nick draws on these songs and explores what being a Christian really means. How does it fit with the world in which we live?

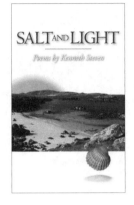

Salt and Light

Poems by Kenneth Steven

978-0-7152-0842-7 · £8.99 · paperback

Kenneth Steven's latest collection of beautiful and evocative poetry is inspired by the Celtic Christian world and the islands of the Hebrides. Some poems recreate those early Celtic days in Ireland and western Scotland; others are concerned with the finding of God's presence in our lives amid the ordinary and the everyday.

SAINT ANDREW PRESS

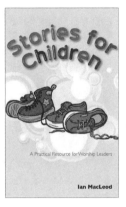

Stories for Children

A Practical Resource for Worship Leaders

Ian MacLeod

978-0-7152-0848-9 · £7.99 · paperback

Have you ever wondered what you're going to say to the kids in church this Sunday?

For all who give the Children's Address or who need a useful resource for junior church and school assembly, this is an invaluable book that can be used again and again.

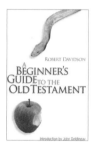
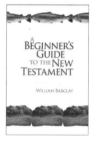